Becoming Ordinary

**A Youth Born of the Holocaust,
What I Kept, What I Let Go...**

A MEMOIR

MICHAEL FOX

This memoir is based on the author's recollections; some names have been changed to protect the privacy of individuals mentioned.

Published by:
Small Print Press
NEW YORK, NY

ISBNs: 978-0-578-32517-0 (paperback)
978-0-578-32935-2 (epub)

Edited by Carol Killman Rosenberg • www.carolkillmanrosenberg.com
Cover and interior by Gary A. Rosenberg • www.thebookcouple.com

Front cover photo: Michael at Camp Hemshekh (1961), a half year after leaving yeshiva. (Taken by my dear friend, Jakob Litman.)

Back cover photo: Recent photo of Michael taken by former Camp Hemshekh participant George Rothe, who is now a retired attorney and grandfather, as well as camp archivist.

Printed in the United States of America

This work is dedicated
in loving memory
to my parents,
Chaim Leib and Lea,
whose worlds I inhabited,
and to my brothers, my mentors,
Mayer and Jay,
for whom I have
enduring longing.

Menachem

Chaim Leib Fox

Like wild wolves the winds
From the mountaintops blow.
My wife in birth-throes writhing,
It's time – the child lies low
Hushed and trembling as if to Isaac's binding
To the hospital we go

Summer night in Kazakhstan
Village huddled, sweet, asleep
The River Ili quick beside us
Rippling, splashing from the deep
Two Jews lock step in silence –
Outcasts with no time to weep

Above the peaks low clouds unfurl
Somber, gray, they spread
Like faces from my far-off land
Their call rings out unsaid:
Bring forth new life, they clamor –
To replace six million dead.

Night takes its bow, river banks grow bright
Flames the horizon sear.
The wind, the savage, shrieks.
My people's cries I hear
Through fire, through ash,
Close behind, so near.

With mile-long steps, on wind and wave
Rushes in the morn.
Each drop of day, a golden ray
From the heavens torn.
With dawn, to an orphaned folk
You, my son, are born

I did not ask you first
On my own I saddled you
My people's lot now yours to bear:
To wander forth, unwanted –
A homeless, beggar – Jew

You sleep, you cannot hear my fury –
Your father's blood it sweeps.
You cannot see his tears, the rain –
The world is crying
For you, my child, it weeps.

You sleep, pale smile upon your face –
Your first respite, I coo,
From fate ordained, unsparing:
Mean streets to roam, forlorn –
Less than a dog, a Jew.

You sleep, I rock your meager cradle
As if it were of gold
But the gold-fleeced kid is dead
And gone is grandma and her song,
And I have no words for horror yet untold

You sleep the sleep of life
I wake among the dying.
From my homeland, borne by winds
Their souls set sail and come to rest
Upon the crib where you, new-born, are lying

Far is it better that you sleep?
Better yet were it all a dream?
But the wind is real, and my mother's cry I hear
Her last sigh, her last plea
To God, for a sign, for a beam

The wind is real, and in every rustle I hear
Messiah's first steps – It won't be long.
In his shade you gently sway
Don't cry my son, my little great Jew
My living song.

(VILLAGE OF ILI, JUNE 1945)

Translated from the Yiddish by Rena Berkowicz Borow

For Lonya, My Mother

Michael Fox

I do not know how to sing for my mother
Who sits at the kitchen table stock-still
A piece of rye bread suspended from her fingers
A movie flashing from out of her eyes

Scenes of her Konin, the days of her childhood
Where she blossomed in physical form and in spirit
Her tomorrows she clutched, with dread, desperation
To make her way elsewhere was her only choice
As she left unknowing
She would never return
There would be no one left
What had she done

The woman child that I knew as her child
Recited in humor the rhyme that defined her
Green canary, the dark cellar has turned you to gold
Would she could soar like a golden eagle
But she's tethered to the invisible Konin stone

Now only the movie flashes before her
In a darkened room her father sits stooped
His eyes are blurred by the Talmud no longer
Pricks his fingers on needles, the pain has long gone
Hums a psalm to the rhythm of the seam he is threading
As he sews the urgings in other men's clothes

Her mother in her sickbed did not die soon enough
She lies withered before her, her eyes hollow but sure
With feeble words whispered she rends Lonya's soul
You must leave now, we have nothing left for you here

A threadbare dress should not be your tomorrows
Or a crust of bread three ways to share

If only she had stayed and lain next to her mother
And held her as the beasts came to beat down the door
And had stood near her father and pressed his garments
To be his last raiment, his iron in her hand
If only she'd been dragged in the street
Butchered beside them
And honored them thus with her dying breath

A life she's since made, she's not sure how to judge it
Could there be any judgment when there's no justice at all
In moments she triumphs over evil's destruction
Her laughter resounds in peals of pure joy
When she dances along with the ghosts of her childhood
The shards of her friends from those days long ago
And her children she tends to with hands always trembling
Along with the shadows that hover behind them

The movie keeps running, the good and the horror
Lie next to each other in unbearable calm
And she hangs suspended like the bread in her hand
A crust to be shared with how many mouths

Hear mother, I'm singing, a song of tomorrow
I've blossomed in spirit and physical form
You'll be my child as I carry you onward
I am your raiment, your own silken dress
I am the iron you hold without shirking
As I hold you in the gaze
Of my hollow eyes

Lonya was my mother Lea's Polish name.

Two Brothers

Michael Fox

There were two brothers once
Both strangers in this land
They'd seen too many things in too few years
Their eyes were black as coal
But light shone out of them
Their vision crowded out their tears

There were two brothers once
Quiet and rageful men
Few knew the measure of their muffled cry
They raised their fists and shrugged
And pitied those that asked
The why and wherefore of the sky

There were two brothers once
Gentle as they were strong
All that they had they gave away with ease
They watched the seasons change
And that was good enough
Gone like the whisper of a breeze

◆ ◆ ◆ ◆ ◆ ◆

Contents

Acknowledgments xiii

Prologue xv

◆   ◆   ◆

Chapter 1. Mayer 1

Chapter 2. Jay 21

Chapter 3. My Future Foretold 49

Chapter 4. My Pittsburgh 62

Chapter 5. Lubavitch Winter 69

Chapter 6. Fate and Choice 81

Chapter 7. Deceit 100

Chapter 8. Parents, Entrances, and Exits 122

Chapter 9. Paradoxes and Contradictions 146

Chapter 10. Jesus and Exegesis 154

Chapter 11. Lubavitch Summer 165

Chapter 12. Light and Heat 196

Chapter 13. My Friend 202

Chapter 14. Forgery 217

Chapter 15. At the Beach 224

Chapter 16. Cataclysms 227

Chapter 17. Catharsis 230

Chapter 18. Secrets and Lies 234

Chapter 19. A Chance at Freedom 238

Chapter 20. Becoming Ordinary 246

◆   ◆   ◆

Epilogue 249

Author's Note 251

About the Author 253

◆ ◆ ◆ ◆ ◆ ◆

Acknowledgments

I owe a tremendous debt of gratitude to two people I hold so dear who lovingly read every piece of this manuscript as it emerged and who urged me on to keep writing. Thank you, dear Gabriel Ross and dearest Rena Berkowicz Borow.

I would not be the person I am or be able to share this early part of my life experience without the love and support of dear friends. My friends from Hemshekh to this day have given me succor and the deepest sense of belonging: Elliott Palevsky, my friend, confessor, and brother. Also, my dear Donna Palevsky, Ruth Goldberg Ross, Steven Meed, Rita Goldwasser Meed, Anna Fiszman Gonshor, Aron Gonshor, and Raizel Fiszman Candib. Also dear are Larry Amsel and Diane Dreher Amsel, Sherry King, Jeremy Tannenbaum, Ellen Asbyl Tannenbaum, Arthur and Margareta Gilman, Michael Schwartz, Judy Mortman Schwartz, and Joan and Richard Keiser. All these people are my community and family.

Among the gifted people who nurtured and supported my artistic talents that I cannot fail to mention are Ruth Rubin, Miriam Hoffman, Avi Hoffman, Ben Yomen, Zalmen Mlotek, Chana Mlotek, Joanne Borts, Mike Baran, Stanley Brechner, David Mandelbaum, Moshe Yasur, and Shane Baker.

I would also like to acknowledge Yoel Babad and Pinchas Kempler, who, especially, among other loving members of the Hasidic communities of Brooklyn, accepted me as a colleague and, more important, as a close friend, just the way I am. I cannot fail to mention two Hasidic teachers who helped me see the beauty that is possible in a life of true faith, Moishe Lazar and Mordechai Nitzlich.

My children and their partners in life, Josh, Kali, Alex, Chihiro, Oriana, and Janak, as well as my grandchildren, Cosmo, Elara, Kainoa, Zora, Kerensa, and Tegen, supply enormous richness to my life.

I owe a tremendous debt of gratitude to Carol Killman Rosenberg, my editor, for her sharp literary eye and her warmth, support, and encouragement, and to Gary Rosenberg for his artistic sense in the layout of this book.

Prologue

We had seen life through the window of a fast-moving train. Everything being transitory, we had clung to each other to feel at home. The past dominated our present. It was a bank that paid out significance and context; the innocence of the here and now was the currency we lacked. What would be the rate of exchange if I traded in the past? But how could I trade in the past? That's all I really had, and I had to hold on to it. And at what cost, when sadness was certainly a better keeper of memories than happiness?

That's what it meant to be fourteen in this open and wonderful country, wasn't it? Here, you could shed your skin and be anything you wanted. You could trade in what had happened to you, like a used car for a new one, and drive away.

What is a Jew? A Jew is someone who argues with God whether he believes in Him or not.

CHAPTER 1

◆ ◆ ◆ ◆ ◆ ◆

Mayer

"You can't remember that," my brother said. "You were too young. Someone must have told you."

But how could someone have told me? The images are too clear. I came out of the low clay house, with its thick spattered lime walls and its damp, cool earthen floor. I stepped from the sepia shade, through the doorway, and into the blinding, silent midday sun. To my right, in the open space before the road, is the stolid wood stove made of brick and clay with its steel-rod grate and the chipped and sooty enamel kettle. I teeter past it and turn left onto the rutted dirt road.

On my left is a high picket fence in need of paint. On my right are parched wooden steps that lead up to three elevated outhouse stalls, with their sweet and fetid human smells. I walk on, and to my right are several rowboats, wet and rotted, dark and textured, resembling pine bark. The road gives way to an expanse of tufts of dry grass and then to gray, sandy mud that seeps between my toes. In front of me is a large, dark puddle that smells like a mixture of the mud, the grass, and the cool, bittersweet water. I feel close to the ground. I can encompass these things.

"It wasn't a puddle," my brother said. "It was a lake, and people splashed and swam in it in their prickly, shapeless, woolen bathing suits. But you were a year old when we left Kazakhstan thirteen years ago, and you can't remember that."

At this time, my brother Mayer was eighteen years old. It was late in the evening, and the room was dark, illuminated only by the light of the gooseneck lamp. A cigarette dangled from Mayer's mouth and his thin, muscular body lay sprawled on the high-riser in the room he

1

shared with Jay. The cigarette smoke curled behind his glasses and stung his good eye into a squint. He held one of his ubiquitous science fiction books propped in his hand. It was one of those volumes with a blue and red spine that had two books in one, back-to-back and upside down from each other. He read at least a volume a day, and the evidence of a year's indulgence was neatly stacked in rows on the maple bookcase and not so neatly stacked in columns on the desktop and the floor. I chided him that he should stop reading such fantasy and come back to reality. He had registered for both freshman terms at Hunter College but had spent them in his room, reading this drivel.

"You'd be surprised, Michael, how much reality there is in fantasy. You can learn more about what something is by looking at what it isn't. I know more about people from reading about what they're not."

"So, if you go away, will that bring you closer to home?" I asked.

"It's best that I go," he said dully.

"You won't be moving ahead with your life, you know. You're just taking time out, and three years is a long time."

He smiled then and began reading again. In the silence that followed, I pictured him alone among strangers, small and ignored—a projection of my own fears, to be sure. But, more than that, I was afraid his leaving would change the family forever. Something would be missing. We would be like a man with a phantom limb. Or we would resemble a man with one eye missing. Our perspective would shift.

Mayer's absence would not create a precedent. He had been in and out of the house a number of times, once for a whole year. And Yankel, whom we now called Jay, had spent two years in Brunoy, at the Vladeck home and sanatorium in one stint. But I had succeeded in filling in the blanks caused by their absences, which were, after all, long ago. I had woven a family myth: we were all, ultimately, together. But this time it would be different. Mayer wanted to leave, and I doubted he would be coming back.

I could not admit to myself that I was also happy to have him go. The vicarious thrill of knowing he would be "in the world" was close to consciousness. But, more important, I was eager for the peace his going would bring.

We all ate our supper together, the five of us—my parents, my brothers, and me. Huddled around the small kitchen table, elbows and knees jostling too close for comfort, friction was inevitable. Mostly it was Mayer who exploded in tears and rage. It seemed to start innocently enough. One time, Mayer asked my mother a simple question.

"You remember, in Poland, when you put Jay and me in the orphanage, and I took him with me and ran away? We got pretty far. I wasn't even six, and Jay was four, and I found the way to the train station. We nearly made it home," he bragged.

My mother became sad, distressed. She couldn't let it go. "No, you weren't in a home then. It was another time. We had no place to live. We had no choice."

"No, it was then," Mayer insisted, tensing up. "I remember, I wasn't even six, and I ran away and nearly made it home!"

"Ah, please. You don't remember," fumed my anguished, guilt-ridden mother, not wanting to be reminded. "Anyway, the time you 'ran away,' they found you a short distance from the front gate."

"That's not true! I nearly made it home. I remember! *You* don't want to remember!" Mayer jumped up from the table, his face contorted, arteries throbbing in his forehead, his open mouth wailing like a siren. "YOU WANT TO ERASE MY MEMORY! YOU WANT TO ERASE MY LIFE!"

My father looked up from his meal then, his mouth and fingers shiny with grease. "Stop the yelling!" he protested to Mayer. "What's the purpose of needling your mother? Can't we eat in peace?"

Mayer flashed his rage at him. "What would you know? You were hardly ever around!" He shoved the table, knocked over a chair, marched off to his room, crying, screaming, and slamming doors.

At night, I was often afraid that Mayer would stab us all in our sleep. The truth was, he was a very gentle soul. He wanted to forgive our parents, but they never gave him an opening. And so, he couldn't fully love them. His tantrums and fights with them served as the most intimate contacts he had with them throughout his childhood and youth.

Mayer's rage was never directed at me. My older brother was very protective of me. I remember in Paris when he chased away a gang of boys in the schoolyard who were menacing me. In their navy capes and berets, they had resembled crows as they encircled me, shouting, *"Sal Juif! (Dirty Jew!)"*

What would life be like without Mayer there? The fear outweighed the promise. Perhaps his leaving struck a painful chord, a wordless reminder of the times when I was very small and he or Jay, or both, would just disappear for a long time. I knew where they had been taken, some children's home or other, far away, and I was powerless to change it. Now, Mayer's leaving was another affront to my self-importance: I could not hold him here, although I kept trying. I sat in the shadow as he read in the light of the gooseneck lamp.

"Now, could you just leave me alone," Mayer said with an air of finality, still looking at his book.

But I couldn't move. I sat on the stool by the desk, looking at him, not knowing what more to say. Behind me was the window, girded by a fire escape. Beyond that, sloping down from the plateau of Broadway, was Riverside Drive, and falling away precipitously beyond that was the tattered ribbon of brush, trees, and dusty ball fields gashed mercilessly by the Westside Highway and the railroad tracks, a sorry excuse for a park that bordered the view that made living in this apartment at the edge of Harlem almost bearable.

The river never looked the same twice, changing with the light, the current, the season, the time of day. It always caught me by surprise, and I could never ignore it. As I looked out now, the Hudson was a vast, majestic expanse of purple-black flashing glints of light that heaved steadily from right to left, moving from the just-visible George Washington Bridge to the north to the huge Lipton Tea sign that hugged the other shore to the south. Specks of light moved slowly, silently along the water, the only evidence that ships were about.

"Now, could you just leave me alone," Mayer had said yet again. I thought I could easily leave him alone, but it sounded like a challenge and an accusation every time he said it. This time he had said it calmly, dismissively. But I had also heard him many times desperately pleading to be left alone.

I remember one emotional explosion at Vladeck Heim, the

children's home and sanatorium in Brunoy, in the countryside outside of Paris, where we had been sent. He was nine years old. His large shaven head and deep, dark eyes accented his thin, wiry body and made him look almost as skeletal as the camp survivors, whose pictures we had all seen. That morning, Mayer had pleaded with *Chaver* (Mr.) Zaltsman not to cut off his hair.

◆ ◆ ◆

"Merder! Farbrecher! (Murderer! Criminal!)" Mayer shrieked full force at the director, his throat strained, his face crimson and hot.

"You have ringworm," Mr. Zaltsman had said. "We have to keep your head clean."

"But the others hardly want to be with me now! If you shave my head, they'll really run away!"

"And why do they stay away from you?" asked the director.

"You know why! Because of my eye! It scares them!"

"Nonsense. It's hardly noticeable. You just don't let anyone near. It's your scowl that scares them," said *Chaver* Zaltsman.

The afternoon was dank and cold with late-winter rain. The children were gathered in the large dining room, which doubled as a playroom when they could not go outside. Some played chess or checkers. Others chased each other between chairs and through the sets of doors. A few girls played house under a table with makeshift dolls. I stood in the center of the large, noisy, and hectic room, not joining in with anyone. I could not give myself over to play. I watched. I constantly watched. Mayer sat near a group of boys, waiting his turn to play chess, a game in which he excelled and for which he was even sought after.

The director entered the far end of the dining room, his arms lowered, a hair clipper in one hand. He walked slowly in Mayer's direction. Two young men with hesitant step walked with him. Mayer was absorbed in the game two boys were playing. He was staring intently at the chessboard on which the army of one sheikh had just eluded a trap set by the other. The young men quietly approached him. One grabbed Mayer's thin arms; the other clutched his head down.

Mayer screamed as he struggled, *"Arrettez! Arretez! (Stop! Stop!)"*

The chess pieces flew, and the boys scattered as Mayer twisted and flailed his legs to no avail. *Chaver* Zaltsman stepped behind the young caretakers and began clipping. The sharp metallic sound mixed with Mayer's wails, as the clipper cut furrow after furrow from Mayer's neck to his forehead, revealing the red welts on the pale landscape of his scalp.

"Lesse moi tranquil! Lesse moi tranquil! (Leave me alone! Leave me alone!)" he pleaded, as the thick black hair fell from behind his ears. The other children had gathered around the spectacle, eyes wide with bewilderment, as the final locks fell. *"Lomich leybn. Lomich leybn, (Let me live. Let me live,)"* he begged, defeated, as the two young men eased their grip.

Finished with his work, *Chaver* Zaltsman turned and retreated through one of the doors, leaving Mayer and his fallen tufts of hair to the young men. Mayer whimpered softly, as he searched the faces of the children around him. They averted their eyes and moved off in twos and threes, whispering to each other, suddenly preoccupied, attempting to spare him shame. Then, as if from a dark cave, a deep moan welled up from inside Mayer's heaving frame and escaped his lungs as a shuddering wail, as he lunged toward the door in pursuit of Zaltsman. The two men bolted after him and caught up to him just as the boy jumped up and clawed Zaltsman's shoulders, reeling him around. They seized Mayer's bony arms and yanked him away from the director, who looked stung by the effrontery.

"Murderer! Criminal!" he shrieked as the two young men pulled him away.

Zaltsman stared at Mayer with a knowing superiority before he turned back toward his office, the clipper still in his hand.

The young men dragged Mayer back to the dining room. They pressed him down into a chair. One brought him a glass of water. Mayer pushed it aside. "You just want the water to calm me down. I don't want to calm down!" But the rage that had been so palpable moments before now quickly drained out of him and vanished and, like a suddenly misplaced pair of glasses, he could not find it. He was defeated.

I stood near his chair as Mayer sat, shoulders slumped, rubbing his eyes with the palms of his hands. His head looked cold and bare and vulnerable. If only Yankel had been here, he could have helped him. Yankel was almost eight, younger than Mayer. He was considered sickly, but he was so strong, stronger than Mayer, stronger than many of the older boys. But Yankel was in the infirmary again. I was four and a half, and I was ashamed that I could do nothing. I took Mayer's hand in mine. He jerked it away and lifted it, about to strike me. Then he held back. With scared and injured eyes that said I had betrayed him, he looked at me and whispered, "*Lesse moi tranquil. Lomich leybn. (Leave me alone. Let me live)."*

◆ ◆ ◆

But this day I did not leave. I sat on the stool, staring at Mayer, waiting for him to react, but he kept on reading by the light of the gooseneck lamp. This had been a difficult Sunday, usually my favorite day of the week.

It was the beginning of spring, and the sunset that brought the Sabbath still fell so early on Fridays that our fifth day of mandatory secular instruction, what we called "English" at my yeshiva, continued to be held on Sunday mornings. Monday through Thursday, the secular classes began in the fading light of midafternoon. Heralded by the end of afternoon prayers, they droned on well past the darkness that allowed for the evening devotions whose final "Amen" released me for the subway trip home.

In contrast, there was always a surprising lightness and playfulness to the material when it was presented on Sunday morning, like the sunlight that came through the windows: "So, *chevreh*, guys, what would you say are the benefits of a bicameral legislature? Can you conjugate the verb *etre*? What did Dickens mean when he wrote, 'It was the best of times, it was the worst of times'? Can you calculate the angle of incidence and the angle of refraction of the light going through the lens?" I could only imagine how good it would feel to come to school to this kind of learning every morning, like they did in public school, instead of facing the arcane Talmud. The best part of Sunday was that it would be light for a long time when school was out, and I could do what I wanted with the rest of the day, a once-a-week luxury.

When I returned from school that spring Sunday, expecting to find my mother quietly sitting, musing to herself in the kitchen, I heard the voice of a stranger, an intruder, instead. The recruiting officer was at the house on a courtesy call to my parents. He sat at the dining room table with Mayer and my parents. His crisp uniform and shiny brass buttons conveyed authority, and my parents treated him with the respect due a powerful government official; their experience in Poland and Russia had taught them that. My mother had spread her best damask table-cloth on the mahogany table in the dining room. She had laid out the finest cold cuts and sponge cakes and served them on the good china, hoping to curry favorable treatment for her eldest son, who was now leaving home.

The sergeant politely accepted a cup of coffee and assured my mother that Mayer was now one of the Army's own and would be well cared for while he served his country. She listened intently, searching the soldier's face for hints about Mayer's future. Her English had improved considerably now that she worked as a salesclerk in the bakery, and she understood most of what the man said. My father only nodded when the man spoke, communicating that he understood, although in truth he grasped only the broad outlines. While he was to spend most of the next thirty years in America, my father never could learn the language.

What was most clearly understood, as Mayer and the officer sat on one side of the table and my mother and father sat on the other, was that a line had been drawn, a division effected. As I sat at one end of the table, I could feel it growing wider and wider as the officer described basic training and the specialty training that would follow. Mayer had chosen a new life, quitting the old. He had chosen between us and the outside. He had decided to enter the larger world and leave the insular family. It struck me as peculiar, curious, and ironic, that despite all the other separations and chaotic twists in our early lives, we were still so closely bound together. Or was that only the way I had experienced it?

Had the fine thread that had woven us together in my mind not held Mayer in the same way? Had all the moves, orphanages, fights, and other events set him apart long ago?

My mother's worried eyes darted from Mayer to the recruiting officer, then to my father, and then to me. *Can anyone stop this?* they asked. I looked at my father, but his face was impassive. Jay was at the supermarket, working. He was always working. Did he know this was going on? What could he do, anyway? Would he try to stop this?

"Have you been in the Army long?" I asked the recruiter.

"About twelve years, now," he answered amiably. "Yes, the Army takes care of its own. I've made a career of it. It takes care of all my medical needs, pays for my apartment, even does my laundry."

Then I spoke the unmentionable words my mother hadn't dared utter. "I thought you took only people who were completely physically fit?"

Mayer shot me an anguished look.

"You know he can't see out of his right eye." I had played the trump card.

Maybe the Army didn't know. It was possible. Mayer had fooled American government officials before. When we were displaced persons in Paris, my parents tried to emigrate, afraid of another war in Europe, this time between America and Russia. We were routinely rejected from, Australia, Argentina, and Canada because of Mayer's blind eye. It was not obvious. It looked a little askance, and the pupil was jagged, but it was otherwise unnoticeable, except in Mayer's mind and to the doctors who examined him. Mayer, who would later hold a responsible position at the Federal Reserve Bank, was devastated every time a doctor said he could not let into his country a flawed individual who might become a burden to the state. He felt guilty about our predicament.

When we applied to enter the United States, it was different. We were examined in a clinic by a team of nurses in the assembly-line fashion this country was famous for. One nurse took your pulse, another listened to you breathe, while still another checked your vision with a Snellen chart. The vision nurse asked Mayer to cover his right eye with his hand and read the chart. No problem with his good left eye. Then she asked him to cover his left eye. I watched as Mayer read the chart perfectly with his blind right eye.

"*Comment t'a fai ca? (How did you do that?)*" I asked, as we walked out of the clinic.

He giggled and demonstrated his technique, spreading the fingers of the hand that covered his good eye. "Just like seeing stars through the roof of a sukkah," he laughed in relief.

The sergeant moved uncomfortably in his chair. "It's true that your brother would not have been drafted," he said. "But he enlisted, and he has chosen to specialize in the Signal Corps. Except for the basic training everyone goes through, he won't be trained for combat. The preliminary tests we've given him show he has a good aptitude for electronics, so his limited vision in one eye does not disqualify him physically for the field he's selected." The recruiter looked at me sternly as he put one hand on Mayer's shoulder. "Besides, maybe in the Army he can get the medical help to remove the cataracts he's told me about. The Army takes care of its own."

◆ ◆ ◆

Mayer closed the book in front of him, and, as he looked up at me, I challenged him, "So, did Ray Bradbury reveal yet another universal truth, or was it merely galactic?"

Mayer gave me a thin smile. "You think you're smart, don't you?" he said slowly. He removed his glasses, and his eyes looked squinty and tired. "I'm disappointed in you," he said, rubbing his eyes. "That yeshiva has taught you to have a narrow view."

"I'd rather see things as they are than as they are not," I retorted.

Mayer looked up at me, his left eye fixed on my face and his right eye wandering off. "Be careful that your two eyes don't give you a false sense of confidence that what you see is the truth," he said softly. "At least I know that, with only one good eye, I have no perspective. Everything looks like a flat picture. I always have to be conscious about what's distant and what's close, what's real and what's only an image."

"You're mad at me for what I said to the recruiter, aren't you?" I responded to his oblique criticism.

"I don't go dragging out your flaws, do I, Michael? And I don't butt into your decisions."

"It's your decision, Mayer, but we'll all have to live with it."

He smirked. "It'll be easier than living with me."

"You're screwing up your future," I pleaded. "You should stay here and go to school."

"I can't do it. I don't belong here right now. I've known for a while that I have to leave." He fumbled for his pack of Du Mauriers. His thick eyebrows furrowed, and his face hardened into the look that meant he was losing patience. He said with finality, "Now you have to leave."

"You're making a mistake," I said as I rose to go.

"You're a real expert on mistakes," he said quietly, as I reached the door.

"What do you mean by that?" I asked, walking back into the room.

"'What's real, what's not.' It makes good philosophy. But everyone has to keep the secret to protect little Michael," he said deliberately.

I waited in the silence that followed.

"It was your fault that I lost my eye," Mayer whispered.

My mother sat at the kitchen table, and she said, "No, it wasn't your fault. You were two years old when it happened. How could it be your fault? What did Mayer have to tell you a thing like that for?! It was the *strush's* son, the super's son who shot him. An anti-Semite. He wanted to get himself a Jew."

"I've heard this many times, Mom. I remember the super's boy and what happened. What was my part in this?" I responded.

"I told you—nothing. He was a boy? He was a teenager. He knew right from wrong. The police didn't even detain him. An accident, they said. But it was no accident." My mother averted her stricken glance as she spoke, avoiding my eyes, and I knew Mayer had told the truth.

Mayer had told me that I had been pestering my mother to go to *pchetchkola*. I wouldn't listen that the nursery school was closed because it was Saturday. No one noticed that I was gone until I was out of the house. She sent Mayer and Jay to catch up to me and bring me back. Mayer was seven and Jay was five—old enough, in those days, to negotiate the local streets.

"Reboynu Shel Oylem, cho' nisht genig gelitn?" my mother cried, her hands covering her face, her body slumped over the kitchen table. "Master of the Universe, haven't I suffered enough? Now you're turning one brother against the other."

In the dining room, Jay was doing his high school drafting homework at the table. His dark locks of hair were silhouetted against the white paper. He had that look of slow, satisfied concentration he got when he did something he enjoyed. His full, sensuous lips puckered, almost kissing the air, as he examined the pencil he had just sharpened to a perfect point. But the glance he gave me when I entered the room told me he had also been listening. "So, you finally found out. I'll say this for you, you knew the direction to the school. You had gotten yourself down the stairs and about a block away when we caught up to you," he said. "It was raining, too. We would never have gone out if it weren't for you."

"So why don't I remember that?" I asked.

"You were two years old," he answered.

"But I remember a lot about that day," I said.

"People remember what they want to, even you," Jay responded, with a wry embarrassment in his large brown eyes. Jay always looked as if he kept secrets behind his doe eyes, and now I knew what one of them had been.

"Why didn't anybody mention this in all these years? Why didn't I ever hear anybody talking about it? We rehash everything else."

"It was just understood that we would spare the baby of the family, Michael. I wouldn't have told you now, except that Mayer did. I guess it was always up to him."

"So, you must all think it was my fault, even though I was two years old."

"If you hadn't gone out . . ." Jay's voice trailed off.

Jay found me at fault, as he had when he was five. By the time he was three, he had spent time in an orphanage. Before the age of eight, he had spent three years in orphanages and sanatoriums, and he had declared his independence. Jay had accepted the hardships and the vulnerabilities he had faced so early as his own responsibility. He considered any error in judgment that resulted in calamity as a failure of his will. So, he saw my actions and their consequences as my responsibility, no matter how young I was.

Jay was thin but strong. "Wiry" and "clever" he called himself, able to fight or wriggle himself out of anything. "You know, sometimes I say to myself I should have seen it coming. If I had gotten Mayer to go upstairs without talking to that guy . . ." Jay's eyes took on a distant look.

I walked away in bewilderment and confusion. They had all kept this secret from me. My actions were the vital link that had led to Mayer's injury, and the wound was still fresh. How often had they looked at me and undone that step in their minds? Was it a conspiracy of protection or blame that had led them to keep this from me?

For as long as I could remember, my brothers had protected me. And they had willingly filled the void in those areas of a child's wants of which my parents had little awareness or concern. As soon as they had started working, Mayer and Jay began to buy me little things, to take me to the movies.

From the time Jay was fourteen and Mayer sixteen, they worked at the Thrifty Supermarket as delivery boys. They got fifteen cents an order, plus tips. They kept their earnings, the small bills they had converted from the dimes and quarters they got as tips, rolled up in juice glasses in the kitchen cabinet. It was their money, but it was in the public domain, so to speak. They often gave it to my mother to buy those necessities my father didn't understand, like clothing. They rarely spent any of it on themselves, outside of the small indulgences of cigarettes and the movies. Almost every Saturday night, after the supermarket closed, often as late as eleven o'clock, we saw the last showing of the double feature at the RKO Hamilton or the Dorset. They splurged on loge tickets so they could smoke. They had taken up the habit, they said, because it kept them warm while pushing the over-loaded carts to Riverside Drive against the biting snow and icy winds in winter.

For my twelfth birthday, they had pooled what was to us a considerable amount of money for an extravagance, to buy me a bicycle. As we stood in Mr. Simms's shop on Amsterdam Avenue and they longingly looked over the sleek, green Schwinn three-speed they had just selected for me, I knew that by indulging me they were fulfilling a wish for themselves: to be given a gift just for being. They had turned their longing to be cared for as children into a caring for me.

Bicycles held a special significance for us. We all remembered Mayer's bicycle, and for us, a bicycle was the ultimate gift a boy could receive. Jay had never had one. I had had one before. When I was in Vladeck Heim the first time, when I was almost five, after a few months, my father visited and brought me a small two-wheeler. I remember him pushing it along the wet gravel of the courtyard in front of the main building. It was a dark, cloudy March afternoon. I walked up to him slowly, not expecting the bike to be for me. He was unshaven and he wore a wrinkled shirt under his rumpled jacket. His lips smiled, but his eyes looked sad as he rolled the bike toward me. *"Nah, dus is far dir,(here, this is for you,)"* he said

I took the handlebars and just looked at him. He was a kind of mirage, but the bicycle was real. This was our greeting. We stood separated by the bicycle that was intended as compensation to a four-year-old for having been sent away. As I later tried to learn to ride it by coasting down the incline outside the infirmary where Jay was often housed, I sometimes thought of that other bicycle, the one that Mayer had been given to make up for losing his eye. Bicycles had always cost a lot.

I now wondered what Mayer had been thinking when he looked at the Schwinn he was about to give me on my twelfth birthday. Did he have any memories about his own bicycle and my part in his getting it? Had he been silent all this time because he was a loving big brother? Why had his hair-trigger anger that had erupted so often against my parents never been unleashed on me? Had he forgiven me? Or was he holding back his rage? Could it be that I had feared being murdered in my sleep because I sensed the latter? Had I kept this from myself in the same way that I had joined the conspiracy of silence by keeping a crucial memory from myself?

I stood in the hallway between the dining room and the bedroom, trying to will the memory back. The images I conjured of Mayer and Yankel catching up to me in the street were like an old newsreel. But it was a street in Paris I saw, and the fancy suit I wore was obviously from a photograph of myself from that time. I rejected these false images. I would not let my mind play tricks. Instead, I went over and over what I remembered for certain, hoping that this would spark genuine recollection to gain perspective and to find a place for myself. . . .

The apartment house in Lodz where we live when I am two is built around a large courtyard. In the center is an empty circular fountain. There are several dark archways that run the width of the building from the street to the courtyard. A doorway inside each archway frames a nondescript stairwell that leads up to the apartments in each section of the building

It is a sunny afternoon, and the children fly down the stairs and stream into the courtyard to play. A cacophony of sounds accompanies the activity. Little girls cluster in the basin of the dry fountain. Some older children push hoops or scooters around its perimeter, while some others shout up to their mothers who sit at open windows. It is Friday, and both the Catholic and the Jewish children come down with their once-a-week toy, the swim bladders from the carps their mothers have just dressed for the evening meal. Some run with them streaming behind them, tied to strings, as makeshift balloons. Others sprinkle salt on them to watch them twitch and see their bubbly pink translucence turn to bright crimson. Eventually, before these primitive lungs wilt away, the children smash them underfoot to hear their loud pop. I watch as children whirl about me. Then Mayer takes my hand and leads me through our archway and up the stairs.

It is the next day. It is quiet. The afternoon light is soft, and the gentle clutter of the room is as enveloping as my crib. I look through the metal rails of the crib and see my father reading a newspaper. He sits facing away from me, the paper folded in his hands. I stare at his angled profile, the tufts of wavy hair on his head, his high, lined forehead, and the thick eyebrows that shield his eyes from sight. I feel the intense stillness.

It is later that day. We are in the archway, Mayer, Yankel, and I. It is gray and cold, and no one is about. In a moment, we will be climbing the stairs. A tall boy comes out of the gloom and greets us. He stands between us and the stairwell. He has something to show Mayer. It is a compression pistol. He speaks softly. We back up toward the wall, Yankel and I huddled next to Mayer. The tall boy points the gun at Mayer's face. There is an explosion. Mayer screams and yelps. He struggles up the stairs, with Yankel and then me following behind him. I hear his cries and shrieks and the scuffle of shoes, as thick drops of bright-red blood spatter on the worn wooden stairs. I see him lying on the *koyber*, the large rattan trunk that served as his bed, his thin body writhing as he cries and a policeman and an ambulance driver arrive to take him away to the hospital.

◆ ◆ ◆

I could not bring back the other memory of my leaving the house for the nursery school. I stood in the hallway. My face and arms felt like setting plaster. I was numb with the knowledge that an event I could not remember informed my life, that an action I must have taken had irrevocably altered Mayer's. I felt as though I had been sucked into a vacuum, and I was not really there. I could not feel myself. My body was without definition. I faced a gaping hole in who I was, and I was ashamed.

When I walked back into the bedroom, Mayer had turned on the overhead light. The yellow glare exposed the drabness of the room. Furnished with odds and ends, it already looked abandoned. Mayer was packing his toiletries, cigarettes, and a few books into the small canvas duffel he was to take with him to basic training the next morning. The Army would provide the rest.

I sat down on the stool by the desk and just stared at him as he worked. Mayer stood, leafing through a book, deciding whether to take it or leave it behind. He caught notice of my staring. He looked back at me in silence. After a long moment he smiled faintly, realizing that I could not say I'm sorry.

"Sometimes we have to forgive ourselves for what we're not," he said. "I should have been a better brother. It always bothered me that I stayed mad at you. You're a good kid."

I lay in the dark, on the narrow pullout bed crammed into the corner of the dining room, jammed between the swinging door to the kitchen and the radiator beneath the window. This was the last night I would be sleeping on the lumpy mattress whose springs groaned and complained beneath me as I tossed in the dark, trying to find a comfortable position for us both. I stared out at the silhouettes of the table and chairs whose space I shared. They had become familiar friends in the night.

In the daytime, everyone knew them for their function, but they were not taken for granted. The chairs were admired for their delicate shapes and the table for its rich mahogany grain; it warmed our hearts that we had arrived at a level that we could possess them. They were also the stage for my mother's dramatic entrances as she brought in her splendid gefilte fish or a golden roast when my parents entertained their friends. My father painted signs on the oval table, and it supported his beat-up Yiddish typewriter as he pounded out his poems with one finger. Jay and I would spend hours squirming in the chairs while playing Scrabble at the table, the unabridged *Funk & Wagnalls* dictionary sitting on its surface serving as arbiter of the oddities we invented in the final throes of the games. And the sateen-covered chairs and the lace-covered table, adorned with dainty china cups and saucers, had been silent witnesses as Mayer and the recruiter had sealed his departure.

But at night, only I knew these pieces of wood pared down to their shadows, as they stood in stolid and constant vigil. Maybe it was true what the Hasidim said, that every object has a soul. In the darkness they spoke to me and said, "Patience, Michael. Feel the passage of time, like us. It is enough. Why want more?"

I turned away from them, trying to find the sleep that was evading me. I wrestled with my bed and with my thoughts. "I'm tired of being an observer."

The next morning, we all got up at five to say goodbye to Mayer, who looked calm and determined. We stood huddled together in the narrow apartment hallway as my father raised his hands to hold Mayer's bowed head to whisper a blessing. He kissed his forehead, and Mayer smiled and nodded graciously.

Mayer and Jay patted each other's backs in manly fashion. They did not allow each other any more public affection than that.

"Don't do anything I wouldn't do," Jay said with a forced laugh.

"Don't worry, I will," Mayer responded.

Mayer turned to me and looked me hard in the eye. "Be good to yourself," he said as he shook my hand. I tried to force a smile, but my eyes felt even more squinty and puffy than usual.

My mother then grabbed Mayer with an enveloping hug. She could not hold back her tears as she told him, "*Zay forzikhtig.* Be careful. Don't take any risks you don't have to."

"I won't be allowed to call for the first two weeks of basic training, but I'll write and I'll call as soon as I can," he answered softly.

With that, Mayer picked up his duffel bag and opened the door. "*Mitn rekhtn fis, (Step out with your right foot,)*" my father said as Mayer crossed the threshold with an exaggerated right step.

Accompanied by my parents, who would walk with him to the subway station, Mayer vanished into the elevator. Jay closed the door, and we looked at each other. Now it was just us.

"I'm going back to bed. I don't have to be up for another two hours," Jay said, his eyes brimming.

"Me too," I answered, knowing he needed to go back to his room to be by himself.

In the next room, Jay would be mourning his loss. Mayer had been his main anchor. They had been closer to each other than to anyone else in all the wanderings that had not been of their own choosing. They had supported each other in all the choices they could make. Now Mayer had picked a direction and gone off on his own and abandoned Jay. Jay would have to fend for himself, without his "Hey, Mayer, what do you think?"

I lay down in my bed, but it kept jabbing me and would not let me go back to sleep. The words I wished I had said to Mayer popped up in my mind like bread from a toaster: "I want the same thing you do." That happened to me all the time, discovering what I should have said or done only after the fact. "I want the same thing you do" kept repeating itself and wouldn't let me go.

I woke with a start to the sound of a resonant gong and a baritone voice. It said, "This is WQXR, the radio station of the *New York Times*, bringing you the news every hour on the hour."

My father sat in one of the dining room chairs, his head cocked toward the radio, which was propped on the windowsill at the foot of my bed.

"*Kenst mikh nisht lozn shlufn nokh a pur minit? (Can't you let me sleep a little longer?)* I don't have to get up until seven thirty."

He ignored me. He stared off as he listened, his mouth pursed and his round left cheek distended from its own weight as he leaned in to hear. He raised the volume, as if that would help him understand the English better.

I withdrew into my thoughts. What was it that I wanted? I certainly couldn't articulate it. But I could sense what it would feel like—a certain lightness, an anticipation in my body, the excitement of an answered urge. I was fourteen and my body called.

"You want to be like an animal?" I could hear the rabbis argue in my brain. "The needs of the body have their place, but each one of us has a soul. We are given thought so that we might control our animal nature for the sake of that higher part of ourselves."

Oh, to answer an urge with the awareness of only the moment, without the intrusions of the past that had gotten me here. That's what it meant to be fourteen in this open and wonderful country, wasn't it? Here, you could shed your old skin and be anything you wanted. You could trade in what had happened to you, like a used car for a new one, and drive away. Still, if I traded in my life for a new one, would I drive away from my past? I did not want that. My past was my badge of honor, my coat of many colors, my soliloquy in the family drama.

Memories were the currency of my house and, poor as we were, we had amassed a fortune in them. Each time my parents argued, my mother would dredge up every slight and betrayal that my father had inflicted on her over the years. "*Gedenkst*—remember, you told me this and that and then you did such and so . . ." She made her one-way pleadings as my father hid behind a blank expression and clutched his folded newspaper on his way out of the room. My brothers would challenge each other over details of their mutual experience.

"No, Le Barbu did not get his limp as the result of a war injury. He had a motorcycle accident," Jay said, revealing inside information to Mayer.

"Coeur De Lion built Chateau Gaillard. It was not built in the sixth century as you suggest," Mayer said with confidence, correcting Jay's speculations.

We had been so many places, my brothers and I. In my own experience, I remembered the hut in Ili, the small room in Tuszyn Las, the apartment in Lodz, the farm in Duszniki Zdroj, the communal living on Rue Guy Patin, the two rooms on Clignancourt, the long dormitories of the children's home in Brunoy, the fields of wheat in Les Andelys, in and out of schools at odd intervals, the all-too-short idyllic life in Pittsburgh, and now the harshness of Harlem. We had seen life through the window of a fast-moving train. Everything being transitory, we had clung to each other to feel at home.

The past dominated our present. It was a bank that paid out significance and context; the innocence of the here and now was the currency we lacked. What would be the rate of exchange if I traded in the past? But how could I trade in the past? That's all I really had, and I had to hold on to it. And at what cost, when sadness was certainly a better keeper of memories than happiness?

CHAPTER 2

◆ ◆ ◆ ◆ ◆ ◆

Jay

Jay stood in front of the mirror, posing in his undershirt and tight chino pants. He flexed the well-defined muscles of his chest and arms, evaluating his physique.

"You see what these are, Michael? These are called pectorals. These are the laterals. Some people show off their biceps, but feel how hard my triceps are. There are some advantages to physical labor." He stepped back to get a fuller view of himself. "When I look in the mirror," he said, "I see in layers. I'm not talking just about anatomy. There's more to what I actually see. I look at my face, and I could be Sal Mineo, cool and confident. I can hang out with any crowd." He scrutinized his face more closely and added, "I also see the colors of my face, the hidden blues and a little flash of red in the corner of each eye.

"And I know that other people can't see that. And that lets me know that other people just see a blur, just get an overall impression. They don't see the patches that make up another person. My vision is twenty-ten. I can see at twenty feet what other people see at ten. So, what can they tell me that I haven't already seen? But I keep silent about what I see."

Jay often talked to me about what he saw, especially when he stood in front of the mirror or when he drew. A few days earlier, I had walked in on him sitting on the high-riser in the room I now shared with him. His drafting board was placed across his lap, a piece of drawing paper taped to it. I sat next to him as he worked, infected by his sense of calm. With a few fine strokes of his pencil, there emerged on the paper a young girl's eyes, then her small nose, then her soft mouth and chin. A few more lines created the curls of her hair. I could tell he was pleased with his drawing by the way he seemed to taste it with his eyes and mouth.

"The secret to drawing children," Jay said, "is that the eyes are right in the middle of their heads. And everything has a roundness. As people get older, their eyes get narrower, and their faces grow longer, so it looks like the eyes move up a little on their heads, but not much. Just enough to make the difference."

I looked at the proportions of the drawing and wondered how Jay knew that. "Can you draw people you know?" I asked him.

"That's harder. But I could, if I had enough time to practice. It's not just getting the details right. You can put in all the features but still miss the real person. That's why when you look at your own photograph you sometimes say, 'That's not me!' To get a true likeness, you have to overemphasize some parts." Jay opened his eyes wide and began to speak more deliberately, nodding his head for emphasis, as he often did when he was in his teaching mode with me. "To portray reality, you have to exaggerate. It's like 'The child is father to the man.' It's a paradox."

"How do you know these things, Jay?" I asked.

"It's simple," he said. "You just have to know how to look."

Still looking at the mirror, Jay now put on a clean white shirt and tucked it into his pants. He rolled up the sleeves to expose his muscular forearms and said, "You see how this shirt puffs out in front of my stomach as if it's too big? The fronts of shirts are made large like this because American kids are soft. They have large bellies to get them ready for drinking beer." He adjusted the front of his shirt. "If their stomachs are soft, their minds are usually soft too," he added.

It had been two months since Mayer had left for the Army, and Jay hardly ever mentioned him, although he worried about Mayer among those big, soft Americans. Their relationship had always been one of extremes lived at the same time. Jay was less than two years younger than Mayer. To be sure, there were many times when Jay snapped at Mayer's heels, and just as many times, Mayer had swatted him down. And each struggled to break out into his own, to define his own personal territory, with an eye toward the reaction of the other.

Their bond was sealed when Jay was four and Mayer barely six. They had fled together at Mayer's behest from the children's asylum in Poland, where my parents had placed them while they looked for housing. One night, Mayer whispered to Jay, "Yankel, maybe they've left us for good this time. Maybe they've forgotten where we are. We can't stay here. Let's go find them." And Jay had reluctantly followed. When they had reached the gate of the institution, Jay pulled at Mayer's coat, pleading that they should go back. But Mayer had not even turned around. He just kept walking into the night.

"Mayer, *kim tserik! Ch'vil nisht shatarbn! (Come back! I don't want to die!)*" Jay had pleaded.

"*Vus hobn mir du? (What do we have here?)*" Mayer had answered.

And despite his hesitation, Jay cast his lot with Mayer and went on. When they were captured, Jay had fought harder than Mayer, kicking and biting to get free. Back in the children's home, they had both stood silent as one, refusing to speak. When the adults had separated them to weaken their resolve and to reassert authority over them, still neither spoke. And through the years, when their differences resulted in huge blows over who knows what, they still let no one intrude. They held their tongues about what had set them off.

It was Saturday morning, and Jay was getting ready for a fourteen-hour day of pushing a grocery cart up and down the streets of northwest Harlem. Speed was important for a successful day. He loaded as many orders as he could into the cart at one time that had to be delivered in generally the same direction. Then he had to deliver each one quickly so as not to leave the others unattended too long in the vestibule of some building. He often climbed five flights of stairs, two stairs at a clip, with several heavy bags of groceries in his arms. He wrote each address on a small brown paper bag he kept folded in his pocket, with a line separating each address. At the end of a Saturday, he often had more than a hundred addresses on the bag. Sam, the owner of the supermarket, sometimes looked in disbelief at the number of orders, but each was verified.

Mayer and Jay were the delivery boys for the store. Mayer never clocked as many orders as Jay, usually around sixty and as many as eighty, which was more than enough for him. It would have been enough for Jay too, but he had to make sure that he and Mayer were all the store needed. Two years before, Sam had hired some other neighborhood boys who were always asking him for work to make deliveries, giving them only ten cents an order instead of the fifteen cents Jay and Mayer got. This meant war. Jay saw the threat and insisted to Mayer that they boycott work the following Saturday, and this time it was Mayer who acceded to Jay's decision. The next Saturday, the store was inundated with undelivered groceries and swamped with phone calls about missing bags, broken eggs, or melted ice cream, as the rivals could not keep pace with the load. Sam returned to employing only Mayer and Jay.

Now that Jay was working Saturdays by himself, he had to work faster to make up for Mayer's absence. One of the store clerks filled in the balance of Mayer's quota. On Friday afternoons, I earned a few dollars by working the early shift before the Sabbath, when Jay took over. I must have been a curious sight, a yeshiva boy with a yarmulke pushing a laden shopping cart along the streets of Harlem, sometimes following behind a large black woman or hauling bundles clumsily up the steps of tenements. But the black housewives did not seem to notice the incongruity when I rang their bells and placed the plentitude of food on their kitchen tables and accepted their tips. Perhaps incongruity was the norm for them, I speculated. I delivered to a saxophone player who was said to be in Arthur Godfrey's band. He lived in a dilapidated walk-up, but his small apartment was artfully decorated in deep colors that hid the cracks in the walls, and it was bathed in soft light. I could not believe that a celebrity had to live in such a shabby building.

Nor did I believe that great musicians like Lionel Hampton and Dizzy Gillespie really played in the local bars, like Carl's Corner, as was advertised on banners across their facades. When I first noticed such announcements when I was about eleven, I thought they must be impersonators. World-famous musicians would not be performing in such small places. I did not understand the economics of art and color. I was desperate to see them in person as I had on television, but, of course, I could not enter a bar then, much less so at night. Although in Paris the cafés had been open, casual places, bars here seemed danger-ous, forbidding, and mysterious. Now, in my yarmulke, I often deliv-ered huge sacks of potatoes and lettuce to those dark, pungent-smelling caves, where time seemed to stop the moment you crossed the thresh-old. And I was not self-conscious about my yarmulke or my job. With my own variation, I was emulating my brothers, retracing their experi-ence, accepting it as a rite of passage.

When the sky grew dark on Friday nights, Jay would meet me at the supermarket. Taking the cart I had just loaded, he invariably said, "It's almost Shabbos. You better get home."

At home, my mother lit the two Sabbath candles that stood in the dented silver candlesticks she had brought from Poland. She gathered the holy light to her eyes and held it close there with her hands as she whispered the prayer that brought on the Sabbath stillness as her mid-dle son pushed his metal cart in street traffic, its wheels clattering in ceaseless racket.

◆ ◆ ◆

We followed our Saturday breakfast routine. I poured the bowls of cereal while Jay put up some coffee for himself. He watched me tamp down my cornflakes into the milk with my spoon before I ate them.

"Ugh! How can you eat soggy cereal?" he asked with a shudder.

He scooped his own lightly moistened flakes and crunched them in his mouth. When he finished his cereal, Jay scrambled some eggs for us. He ate his eggs slowly, deliberately, turning over each forkful in his mouth. He then took a bite of his generously buttered roll, which he had first toasted by piercing it with a fork and holding it just so over the flame of a burner. I could hear his teeth chomp as he proceeded to chew his coffee before swallowing each mouthful with a gulp. He sighed as he watched me wolf down my eggs and rip into my own soft, wilted roll.

"That's not a roll. That's a lung," he said with contempt.

Two months before, Mayer had been part of this breakfast ritual, except that Mayer used to make his own *shpigl eyer*, sunny-side-up eggs. After sliding them onto his plate from the sizzling butter of the frying pan, he methodically tapped out a layer of salt to evenly coat the glistening yolks. Then, with a soup spoon, he scooped out each yolk from its white borders without breaking it. He swallowed each down whole with a look of immense satisfaction. An elaborate procedure for a moment's joy.

When Mayer had been there, Jay used to talk to him instead of to me. They would find something to disagree about: the consequences of some law of physics (the distortion of time on the moon is not the same as it is on earth; or a factual detail about an event they had lived through together but with parallax views (four hundred francs was a lot of money then). And suddenly one of them would remember a funny incident. It would take just one phrase to telegraph it: "Cold cherry soup!"

Mayer's face would turn beet red. His eyes tightly shut and his shoulders hunched over and convulsed, his laugh would come out of him in an uncontrollable torrent, like steam forced from an overheated kettle. Jay tipped his chair back with sudden force. Tears escaped the corners of his upturned eyes as he clapped his hands and let loose with sobbing peals of laughter. They laughed not so much from the humor of the story as from the shared memory of it. They parried loudly as they placed their dishes in the sink, put on their jackets, and walked out the door, without so much as a look back at me on their way to work.

Jay took another bite of his roll. The flaky crust cracked under his teeth, like fissures from a tiny earthquake. "Michael, do you know why the crust turns brown and black when you hold it over a flame? It's because the carbon burns. All organic substances contain carbon."

He was not satisfied with my perfunctory "uh-huh." Mayer would have found something to debate. So, with mischievous eyes, Jay added, "You know all living things are made of carbon, oxygen, hydrogen, and nitrogen. The chemical initials spell COHN. Like the name of the priests in ancient Israel. Do you think this was a secret message from God, confirming the chosenness of the Jews, yeshiva boy?"

I took the bait. "Your logic is as mysterious as the Holy One's, *boruch hu, (blessed be He)*" I smiled back. "In Hebrew, the name Cohn has only three letters."

"Maybe the Bible was first written in English. For God, all is possible," Jay retorted.

"And maybe the name was spelled K-a-h-n, like your friend David spells his last name. Where would your theory be then?" I laughed.

"Maybe it was Moses's problem," Jay suggested disingenuously. "Maybe God didn't realize when he whispered the Bible into Moses's ear for him to transcribe that not only did Moses have a lisp, but he was a lousy speller too."

"Every letter in the Bible has a meaning!" I informed him, incredulous.

Jay stared into his coffee cup. "Can you imagine all those rabbis in the Talmud interpreting every letter of the Bible, and it turns out Moses was a lousy speller?" Jay shook his head. "It boggles the mind."

"But maybe God is from the planet Krypton, where the main ingredients of life are kryptonite, argon, hydrogen, and nitrogen. KAHN. That's the secret message!" I shouted, gesticulating wildly. "God is from Krypton, like Superman!"

Then Jay laughed happily.

❖ ❖ ❖

Jay savored little tidbits of knowledge as if they were morsels of exquisite pastry. Each fact, each sensation, the less obvious the better, was a curiosity to be examined, a secret treasure that he sometimes shared as a gift or a conspiratorial bond.

One morning in Chateau Rose, in Les Andelys, the children's sanatorium in Normandy that we were in when I was about six and he was nine, I came upon Jay in a thicket of woods. In one hand he held a small jar. He dipped his index finger into the jar, and when he pulled it out, it was covered in a shiny, golden, translucent substance. He examined the light as it played on his finger. Then he put his finger in his mouth and pulled it out slowly, holding it as long as possible in the tension of his thick, full lips.

His eyes misted and his eyes half closed as he reverentially said to me, "*Tu sais que c'est ca? C'est du miele.*" He offered me the jar of honey. "*Tu veu l'essaier?*"

I dipped my finger into the jar and pulled out some of the silky, viscous fluid. I imitated Jay's method, half closing my eyes as I slowly pulled my finger out of my mouth. Jay's eyes and dimpled cheeks smiled as he caught me in sudden pleasure.

We began walking along a footpath that led out of the thicket and onto a quiet dirt road, taking turns at the jar of honey. On the other side of the road, we stopped to examine a clump of maple shoots to see if they were yet ready to be made into the arrows, bows, and swords we would need when we would later be Robin Hood, D'Artagnan, or Cochise. The fresh young trees glowed with a pale-green color, their unfurling leaves shot through with crimson veins. We breathed in the moist, acrid, woody smell.

"Do you know why we strip the bark from the arrows but not from the bows?" Jay asked me. Then he answered, "Because when you strip the bark, the wood keeps the shape you give it. You want arrows and swords straight, so you strip the bark and straighten the stalks if you have to, and when they dry, they will keep that shape. But a bow has to keep its spring. When you draw the string, it tries to get back into its natural position. The thicker the bow, the harder you have to pull and the farther and truer your arrow will fly. But it's the bark that keeps the tension in the wood. So, the secret is that you leave the bark on, even though it makes the bow look plain."

We walked into the wheat field that bordered the road and followed along the wheel ruts made by the wagon that usually crossed the field. We were surrounded by sheaves of wheat that were turning golden at this stage of the summer. The jar of honey was just about empty. Jay turned it deftly in his hand and pressed his finger along the inside, squeezing out the last of it.

"Where did you get the honey?" I asked.

"Bernard and I broke into the pantry last night. He said he wanted to practice his old skills, now that his bandages are off. It was great. The staff was sitting and jabbering in the dining hall while we were in the shadows by the kitchen door. Bernard picked the lock while I kept lookout. We had just gotten in and closed the door quietly behind us when we heard the voice of Le Barbu as he walked by the door. As we left, Bernard ever so quietly closed the lock so no one would ever know we scavenged the place."

"What else did you take?" I asked.

"Another jar of honey for Bernard, some sausage for his kitten, and a whetstone to sharpen our knives."

Jay had met Bernard early that summer, when they first shared the converted carriage house that served them and six other boys as a dormitory. Bernard was fourteen, five years older than Jay. Everyone knew Bernard's story. He was one of the few real orphans in the place. The rumor was that he had come here when Chateau Rose was still an orphanage. Now that it was a loosely run sanatorium and summer camp, he was still here.

Not long after the summer season had started, Bernard had watched an acrobatic boy propel himself higher and higher on the huge swing that stood at the side of the large court in back of the main house. Bernard had stood at the top of the hill behind the swing, watching the boy pumping himself higher and higher in the air. Bernard studied the moment of each arc. Then he suddenly bolted down the hill, gathering speed, his pace perfectly synchronized to meet the swing with the middle of his forehead.

When Jay had entered his dorm later that day, he stopped cold. Bernard sat slouching on his cot, which was cluttered with his few possessions, an island amid the bare mattresses and bedframes that surrounded him. Jay looked at Bernard's bandaged head with wide eyes.

"What's the matter, haven't you seen a corpse before?" Bernard taunted.

Without a word, Jay heaved his own bed next to Bernard's.

Jay and I made way for the ruddy-faced farmer who trudged past us without expression, his nag and wagon ambling behind him along the road in the wheat field. Neither he nor the horse broke stride as we jumped on the back of the wagon, hitching a ride. It was always a surprise to feel how smooth the ride was in the wagon. From our elevated vantage, the field was a light amber sea. We gathered up some stray tear-shaped kernels of wheat that lay scattered on the railings and amid the straw on the floorboards of the cart. We cracked them open one by one in our mouths and spit out the chaff. The small, hard grains made little explosions of protest as they succumbed to the pressure of our teeth.

"What's wrong with Bernard?" I asked Jay.

"Nothing," he answered. "Bernard is one of the last ones. Where do you think he was when he was as little as you are? The older kids like him, here and in Brunoy, survived by their wits. They were scavengers and con men, and who knows what else. *Et ils ont reussis contre les Boches. (And they succeeded against the Nazi bastards.)*"

When we reached the edge of the field, we jumped off, yelled *"Merci!"* to the horse and the farmer and returned silently along the path we had just traveled. Back in the woods, Jay said, "We need hiking sticks." He studied a stand of young, strong trees. He placed his hand around the trunk of a very straight one to see if its girth suited his grip. Then he had me select one the same way. He took out his pocketknife and sliced into his tree at the base. The sharp blade cut deep and sure, as if he were sharpening a pencil, until the stem was severed. He then sliced off the branches just as easily.

"You cut the branches outside the joints, not from inside them. You get a cleaner cut. If you cut from inside the joint, you risk splitting the trunk," he instructed. He then measured the rod against his height and cut off the stem at head level. "A tall staff makes you steadier. But, if it's too tall, it is difficult to maneuver," he advised.

I had taken out my pocketknife and was laboring to cut the base of my sapling when Jay was finished with his cutting. "A sharp knife works better," he said. Pushing me aside with his elbow, he completed my trimming. "A sharp knife is also safer. You have more control over the blade with less force. You'll have to sharpen your knife with my new whetstone," he said with a smile.

When we returned to the grounds, Jay asked me to bring his hiking stick back to his dorm. "Give the whetstone to Bernard if you see him, or put it under his pillow," he said. "We're sharing it, and he might want it." He looked at my expression and added, "You don't like Bernard, do you?"

"He's strange," I answered.

"He's seen too much," Jay admonished, as he turned toward the main house.

Bernard was sitting on the edge of his cot when I entered. A new bandage, spotted with crusted blood, covered the crown of his head. A fresh red gash ran from his left temple to his nose. Bernard looked at me through his steel-gray eyes as I stood frozen in the doorway. "Come in or go out. Don't be Sunday deciding to be Monday," he said.

I entered the room and closed the door behind me. The kitten in his lap started to climb up Bernard's shirt to get to his wounded face.

"He smells the blood," Bernard said and grinned.

"What happened?" I heard myself say.

"Oh, I was riding this bicycle with no brakes down the road outside the main gate. I got it going real fast. I thought I could smash it into the war monument in town. But the stupid bald tires skidded on some sand, and this is all that happened." He laughed with embarrassment at his failure. "I didn't even crack my skull this time."

The door suddenly smashed open, crashing loudly against the wall. His face a mask of terror, his eyes drilling into Bernard's, Jay lunged at him and screamed, "How could you do this!"

Later that morning, I followed Jay up the plank stairs to the loft above his dormitory. It was a large, open space with rough-hewn floorboards and rafters. There were several rickety chairs and an old wooden table in the center, which gave the place a clandestine air. As the late-morning light revealed the curlicues of dust that swirled silently in the attic, Jay and I sat, carving designs around our hiking sticks by slicing stripes, spirals, and checkerboards out of the soft bark. My hand slipped, and off went a section of spirals I had painstakingly worked on.

"I'll sharpen your knife," Jay said, taking out the whetstone from his pocket. I watched in silence as he spit on the stone and rubbed the edge of the blade in circular motions against the grit of the stone. Lulled by the motion of his body as he honed the blade of my knife, he withdrew into the quiet.

Finally, as if continuing an interrupted conversation, his voice emerged. "Sometimes I can't believe that my two years in Brunoy are actually over. Mayer was there for about a year, but the rest of the time, he wasn't there."

Then he stared at me for an instant too long, the slight tremor of his face betraying the flash of jealousy he could not suppress. While I had spent some time in Brunoy, it didn't amount to much compared to him. I had stayed with my parents when he and Mayer were sent away.

"You can't know what it was like for me. Especially in the infirmary." He turned away so that I would not see his eyes brimming over. He began whistling to regain his composure. It was a dolorous tune, but with light hopeful trills and bright inflections. It soothed and calmed him and took him far away again as he kept working on the blade that was already sharpened to a razor's edge.

He returned the knife to me, and I proceeded to remove the evidence of my mistake. The sharp blade easily stripped off the bark, exposing a swath of pale wood in place of my botched spiral. I usually had many bare rings on the sticks I decorated.

I tried to imagine Jay in the infirmary. I had been there myself for about a week the one time I had been sick. Vladeck Heim in Brunoy was a large, walled estate. Although tinged with neglect and the rough use it now endured, the chateau, its stately rooms, its formal gardens and courts bordered by towering chestnut and walnut trees, and its dreamy lagoon served as consolation to a child away from family. Even La Petite Maison, The Small House, the annex for the older children like Jay and Mayer, which was down a short road from the big house, must once have been the manor of a well-to-do squire. It was surrounded by fields that were punctuated by solitary, massive shade trees and wire fences. Its small outbuildings, which were excellent hiding places for young boys, were treasure troves of rusting tools and musty clay pots.

These idyllic settings throbbed with the activities of over a hundred children who coursed their paths, poked straw into their rabbit hutches, and pilfered radishes from their kitchen gardens. The shady arbors, open fields, and mossy grottos were the sites for childish adventures, intrigues, and romances.

Going from this setting to the infirmary was a shock. The infirmary was housed in a squat, nondescript building beyond the front courtyard and up a small incline from the big house. Inside, the beds were arranged two to a cubicle. The cubicles, which came off a long, narrow hallway, were made of metal partitions painted a sickly cream color, with glass panels in the walls on either side that allowed a full view of the entire row of cells. The infirmary was usually off-limits if you were not sick because of the fear of infection from the patients housed there. Nonetheless, sometimes children would come to the windows to wave to their friends inside.

When you were a patient, there was nothing to do except look at the bare walls and watch the periodic medical procedures. The temperature readings done rectally to the inmates of the other cubicles served as a diversion, except when it was your turn to be the object of interest. The most curious procedure was the cupping, a method used to reduce fever. The nurse swirled a bit of alcohol in each of the dozen thick glass cups and ignited them, one at a time. The alcohol burned up in a flash. The nurse placed the cups in neat rows on the bare backs of her charges. The children flinched with the shock of each cup, both from the sudden heat and the suction on their backs. The cups would clatter when the children moved, despite their efforts to lie still. When the cups were removed, with a whoosh of air rushing in, they left a pattern of red circles that resembled small bologna slices on the backs of the patients.

Time droned on palpably in the infirmary. After being there just a few days when I was sick, I tried to will my body to get better. When

I was let out after a week, each sensation was accentuated, from the cool scent of the air to the bright rasping sound of the gravel under my shoes as I walked again.

Jay had spent two years in Brunoy. He was six when he was first sent to Vladeck Heim, and he had spent a good part of his time there in the infirmary. He often ran an elevated temperature, and he had tested positive for tuberculosis, although his X-rays were negative. Jay was said to be frail and sickly, but I never noticed. How could they call someone so strong and agile sickly? Whenever his face flushed or he seemed fatigued, he was hauled to the infirmary. What did he do with his time there? I imagined him all alone, lying on his metal cot, the cups on his back, whistling his forlorn tunes.

But I did not have to imagine how Jay reacted when he was told he would have to be quarantined. I remember being in the dining room of The Small House, where I had been transferred just days earlier. I was seated with some of the younger boys at lunch. We watched some of the older boys at another table, studying their swagger and bluster. Jay and Mayer were among them. A number of the boys were howling about the strange violet color and wretched taste of the cold cherry soup.

"This isn't soup," one said. "It's witches brew."

"It's witches piss, you mean," retorted another.

Mayer laughed with his whole body, but Jay did not join in the banter. His large brown eyes were fixed on the soup, enchanted by its color. He dipped his spoon in his bowl. Then he took it out and stared in fascination at the hues that the film of soup made on it. He slowly turned the spoon one way then the other, trying to get the soup to cover the entire scoop evenly.

A group leader noticed that Jay was too quiet and seemed not himself with the other boys. He walked over to his table and placed a hand on Jay's flushed forehead. He then said something quietly to him.

Jay bounded up and screamed, "I'm never going there again!"

With this, Jay bolted from the room, chased by several adults and followed by a hoard of children, excited by the commotion. By the time they reached the outside of the house, Jay was gone. The group leaders and some of the older boys searched for him in the cellar and the outbuildings, down the road, and as far as the edge of the woods, but there was no trace of him. Mayer and I sat on the steps at the side of the house, surreptitiously looking up at Jay in one of his favorite spots, resting on the top branch of the giant fir tree that graced the yard by the house. No one had thought of looking for him there. The first climbable branch was more than two meters high, obviously beyond the reach of an eight-year-old, as it had been for every other youth who had attempted to climb the tree.

Jay sat securely nestled in the notch of the tree branch. He gazed out at the breadth of the fields and the people running from place to place without direction, looking for him. *"Comme des fourmis, (Like ants,)"* he later described them. And he also described to me the breeze that rocked him gently in his perch long after the adults had given up the search and had yelled at the other boys, herding them off to rest hour.

Jay knew he could not stay indefinitely in his hiding place. He climbed slowly down, his hands and legs hot with fever. He found Mayer on his cot, playing chess with a neighbor. *"A bientot,(See you soon,)"* Jay said.

Mayer just stared at him sadly but could say nothing.

I met Jay at the door of my dorm room. Jay's eyes were holding back tears.

"What do you see up there?" I asked to divert him.

"I look for the road to Paris. But I've been away so long, I don't know where our parents live," he said wistfully.

"So then, what do you see?" I asked him softly.

"It's so peaceful," Jay said. "I see the play of colors on the leaves of different trees, and the swatches of colors of the landscape, especially the shades of green and yellow. I see houses both near and far away, and I wonder who decided to put them in their odd placement on the land. And I like to look at the different shapes of the roofs and whether the chimneys are smoking or not. I wonder who lives behind the darkened windows. It is all so beautiful. The images will have to last me for a while."

"Could you teach me how to climb up the tree when you get out?" I whispered to him.

Jay seemed to think about it for a while before he answered. "Climbing up is easy. It's the coming down that's hard."

Then he went downstairs to give himself up to a surprised group leader.

◆ ◆ ◆

And now here we sat at the kitchen table, just eight weeks since Mayer had left.

Jay chewed another mouthful of coffee and gulped it down. "You know, Michael," he said, "we can all be reduced to the same four elements, but just try to put us together from those elements. That's a different story."

Jay looked at me long and hard. I could tell he was assessing me. Maybe I would do. On the day Mayer had left, I had moved out of the dining room, where I had slept on my convertible bed, and into the room he had shared with Jay. Jay could have taken Mayer's half of the high-riser, which was bigger. He chose to let me sleep on it, although his bed was narrower and shorter, and his feet stuck out over the end of it. Mayer's bed was only borrowed. It would have to be returned when Mayer came back. That was the message.

But I knew this was now my bed. Mayer would be gone for three years, and I did not wait to establish my claim. I claimed the bed and the room. I had never had a room that was mine, shared or otherwise. True, in Paris and Pittsburgh I had sometimes slept in the same room with them, but it was their space. They shared it, as they shared their history. Now, at fourteen, I fully intended to find out what it was like to have a real share. It wasn't as if I had no territorial rights in the room.

My clothes were kept in one drawer of the dresser, and my Sabbath suit hung in the closet. I also had an old nightstand that belonged to me exclusively. It was one of those ornate, timeworn little cabinets, made with broad-grained, symmetrical veneer, and it rested on carved feet that were shod with little wooden wheels. It had a small door that opened with a click, and inside the compartment I kept my stamp collection, which I had originally inherited from Mayer. Inside were also some frayed papers and a few composition notebooks in which I wrote occasional stories or poems. In the narrow drawer, amid the dust and lint that somehow accumulates in such places, were a few pencils and pens, some baseball and flag cards, a dog-eared homework pad, and one of those pink circular ink erasers with a green plastic brush on the end. Except for a few books in the bookcase and my schoolbag, which stayed in the corner of the dining room, and my bicycle parked in the hallway by the front door, this was the extent of my possessions. I always felt that I was living on the edge of things. Not anymore.

"I claim this bed," I whispered to myself when I first laid on it. "I claim it" was the legalistic formula Jay and I used to establish ownership of anything since I was ten. It came from the Talmud. I had been studying *Bava Metziah* in the fifth grade. Two men find a *tallis*, the story goes. Who gets to own it? If one man says he claims it because he saw it first, it doesn't count. It's the one who actually picks it up who owns it.

"Possession is nine points of the law," my rabbi had said. Despite that, when Jay and I both saw an object that seemed lost or abandoned, we each tried to yell out, "I claim it!" as we both ran to be the first to grab it. What was an abandoned object? The same Talmud, *Bava Metziah*, had discussed the matter:

If a man finds coins in the road, how does he know whether they are abandoned or that someone still has ownership? The answer is, if the coins are scattered on the road, they are considered *hefker*, abandoned, because they were likely to have been unintentionally dropped. The original owner, upon discovering them missing, presumably considers them lost and abandons hope of recovering them. This is so even when two coins are found stacked one on top of the other. This is because they could have fallen that way randomly. If, however, three coins are found stacked on top of each other, it is definite that someone stacked them because coins would not have fallen that way by chance. It is clear in this case that the owner placed them there for a purpose and expects to come back for them and has not given up ownership. Thus, the Talmud posits a probabilistic method of determining if something is lost and may be kept by the finder.

Jay and I were very good scavengers. We could tell if something was ownerless when we found it in the street or when it was brought into the house by our parents. It was surprising how many things we found to be ownerless. With regard to Mayer's bed and room, Jay and I had obviously different views on the subject. I suppose it had to do with our different reactions to Mayer's leaving. When I was young and Mayer left to go to a children's home, I just accepted it. I still had parents. When he was small and Mayer left him, Jay was alone in an institution, waiting for his older brother to be returned to him.

It was good not to sleep in the dining room, where I had felt as cramped and contorted as the fold-out bed I had to put up with every night. When I had lain on that lumpy mattress, trying to find a space for myself between its jutting coil springs, sharing the dark with the table and chairs, I had imagined Jay and Mayer leaning on their elbows, in their parallel beds, whispering secrets in the stillness. Now, stretched out on the high-riser, I often woke, startled by my sudden awareness of Jay's labored breathing or even his moaning in his fitful sleep in the bed next to mine. And there were secrets that Jay now shared with me.

Sometimes as we lay in our beds, heads on pillows, staring up in the darkness, before sleep overtook us, Jay's disembodied voice would begin a narrative with questions. One night I heard his voice say:

"Michael, are you asleep?"

"No," my voice responded.

"Do you remember your dreams when you wake up?" Jay's voice asked.

"Sometimes."

"Do you have dreams that keep coming back?" the voice continued.

"Every once in a while, when I just drift off to sleep, I suddenly feel like I'm falling, and my legs jerk to keep me from hitting the ground, and that wakes me up," I answered, now fully awake. "That's not really a dream, though. Otherwise, no." I turned to look at Jay's silhouetted face against the ambient light from the window. "Do you?" I asked, ready to hear him out.

"I have dreams that come back just to remind me that they're still here," said the shadow of Jay's mouth. "One dream in particular comes back a lot." Jay's voice was a tremor. "In this dream, it is night, and I'm walking in a field. At first, it's pitch black, but as I get used to the darkness, I can make out that there are large stones and scrawny trees in the field. But soon I realize that these aren't stones and trees. These are pale, spindly corpses. Some are huddled on the ground, and some are standing, swaying. And, as I pass them, they start grabbing at my legs and arms. One cradles my head in its icy arms. I feel terror, but I don't scream.

"I start to run, but I am caught. I use all my force, and I break free, but I am bleeding from the places where they touched me. I run, but I am moving so slowly. 'Yankel,' they call me. 'Don't go. You belong with us.' I turn and I scream at them, 'No!' but I make no sound. They grab me again. 'Stay with us,' they plead. But I rip myself away. I am crying, but no tears come out. I am torn. Part of me wants to stay with them, I realize. And that panics me the most. They reach out to me again. I cover my eyes so they can't touch me. I know that this is the only way I can walk out of the field. Then I wake up, exhausted and wide awake, a huge weight in my chest."

"What do you make of it?" I asked, breaking the ensuing silence.

Jay's voice answered, quavering, "All I know is this. If people only knew what I feel sometimes, they couldn't stand it. If they only felt just once what I feel, the whole world would fall apart."

I was silent, not knowing what to say. I heard a stifled sob coming from the other bed.

"Good night," Jay's voice said into the darkness.

◆ ◆ ◆

"I think I'll have another cup of coffee before I go," Jay announced as he got up to flip the knob under the burner. "I don't feel like going to work today for some reason." He stood by the stove, holding his cup, waiting for the pot to heat up. "You know what, why don't I heat up some milk for café au lait? You want some?"

"Sure," I answered.

When the milk bubbled in the little saucepan, Jay poured it into two waiting cups half filled with coffee. Then he stirred in some cocoa and a little sugar. We sat down at the table, leaning back in our chairs, sipping the smooth, tan liquid.

"When you go to visit Mayer today, tell him I got the oscilloscope to work. I found two cold-solder joints that were the problem." Then, with eyes brightening, he added, "You can tell him it works in marvelous and unexpected ways."

"Tell me," I said eagerly, responding to the mischief in his voice.

"It scares away burglars," Jay announced.

"Get outta here!" I responded in disbelief.

"The proof is as incontrovertible as a Castro convertible," he stated calmly with a twinkle in his eyes.

I waited for him to continue.

"As you know," he lectured, "most of the apartments in our line, from the tenth floor down to the fourth, have been robbed. The crooks got in by coming down the fire escape in every instance. Now, consider which apartments have been burgled: 4A, 5A, 6A, 7A, 8A, and 10A. You notice which apartment has been spared? Ours, 9A. 'Why?' you may ask." Jay took a deep breath for the finale. "Consider this: standing boldly on the desk in front of the fire escape window is an electronic wonder, none other than our oscilloscope."

I stared at him wide-eyed, waiting to understand, so I could "get it," and breathed out in relief.

"The crooks see the oscilloscope and think it's a burglar alarm, so they avoid our apartment. Get it?" Jay laughed.

"Ohhhh, my gosh, I think you're right!" I gasped in delight. Raising my coffee cup, I proclaimed, "Here's to the oscilloscope!"

Jay lifted his cup and took a sip. "Just be sure to tell Mayer when you see him," he said with a faint smile.

My mother rushed into the kitchen just then, looking anxious and absorbed in thought. "*S'iz shpeyt. Ch'miz shoy anpakn, (It's late. I must get ready,)*" she murmured to herself. Then she noticed Jay and me sipping coffee and grinning at each other, and she stopped. Her face broke out in the brightest smile and her eyes glistened. She came over to Jay, held his face in her large, reddened hands, and stooped to kiss his cheek. "Goot mornying, Yankel," she said, just to him, in her Polish-Yiddish accent, keeping her face close to his. The she turned to me and kissed me too. Caressing my cheek and looking into my eyes, she said, "Goot mornying, Maikoo."

Jay and I looked at each other, eyes crinkling at the corners, silently acknowledging this closure to our conversation.

"I'm excited," our mother said, beaming. *"Cho' shoyn nisht ka' gedild. (I don't have any more patience.)* Two months already in the Army." She began filling large shopping bags with corned beef, peaches, some fresh rye bread. "I can't forget the apples." She turned to us. *"K'nayne horeh,* Mayer can finish off five pounds in one time. Two months is a long time," she fretted as she continued to add salami and a jar of dill pickles to the provisions.

"You'll tell me how he looks," Jay said quietly to me, his eyes dimming a bit.

Our mother caught the communication, and her face was grief-stricken. *"Ch'ken es nisht fartrugn, (I can't stand it that you have to work so hard,)"* she said to Jay. "Why does everything have to be such a struggle for my children? *Reboynu Shel Oylem! (Master of the Universe!)"*

"That's just the way it is, Ma," Jay answered the rhetorical question. "You work hard, too. It's alright."

"If I could give you all my strength, I would," she said to him. "I wish you didn't have to work."

And Jay knew it was true. He got up to heat some more milk in the saucepan. "You know, warm milk is very soothing," he said to no one in particular, stirring a spoon in the pot.

◆ ◆ ◆

Jay had always accepted hard choices and their consequences stoically. In his junior year of high school, he came home one day with the message that his chemistry teacher wanted to see my mother at open school night to discuss something with her. She was anxious, and she asked me to go with her because Jay could not take her. She had rarely been up to the high school, an elegant, imposing building in the Federal style. Mr. Kalish welcomed us in, a bit surprised by my presence. But our parents often had one of their children to translate and act as intermediaries between themselves and "authorities."

"Why I asked to see you," Mr. Kalish began, "is because your son Jacob is very talented in chemistry. He has some ideas about the growth of crystals that are very exciting. I think he could compete for a Westinghouse science scholarship. But it would require a lot of time from him and resources from you. Would you be prepared to support him in this?"

My mother had understood the words, but not the intent. "Of course I'll support him. I love all my children," she answered in her highly accented English. She had been surprised by the question. Was it an accusation? She did not know what he had meant by "support," and neither did I.

Jay continued to work at the supermarket after school and on weekends. One afternoon, he took off from work. He came home with several large cardboard cartons, which he deposited on the floor of his room. He opened them up and inside was an assortment of brown jars filled with chemicals, some test tubes, flasks, and glass tubing. He had spent his savings at a chemical supply house.

"Do you know what this is?" he asked me as he opened a jar. "This is potassium permanganate." He relished the mellifluous words.

In the ensuing weeks, Jay spent his free hours heating test tubes and flasks over the kitchen stove. When he ran out of test tubes, he used what was handy. It was not unusual for me to absently open the cupboard for a water glass to be suddenly shocked by the pastel-colored growths in all the glasses.

But there was a limit to what Jay could do at home by himself in the little time he had. He eventually gave up in that attenuated way one gives up a dream that one secretly knows from the start will not be realized. After a while, his experiments became sporadic and without direction. He still announced that he was working toward the Westinghouse scholarship as he dabbled with his powders, long after we all knew it was not to be. Eventually, Jay's jars and test tubes were stored in their cardboard boxes on the top shelf of a kitchen cabinet.

◆ ◆ ◆

"Milk's ready," Jay announced. "Anyone want some?" As he lifted the saucepan from the stove, it slipped out of his hand. He jumped back to avoid the scalding milk, hitting a chair that fell over and clattered the dishes on the table. Jay looked at my mother and me and stifled a guffaw. "History nearly repeated itself," he said with a surprised and tentative laugh.

I wanted to roar but chuckled instead.

My mother let out an embarrassed giggle and averted her eyes.

Jay took a rag from under the sink and cleaned up the spill. "I'd better get to work," he said as he put his dishes in the sink.

"I wish you could come too," my mother said suddenly as Jay exited the kitchen.

Jay turned in the doorway. "Next time," he said, forgiving her. "You'll tell him about the oscilloscope," Jay called to me as he left the house.

◆ ◆ ◆

Jay had always loved milk. He now drank it by the carton. He especially liked it scalding hot, heated up in the enamel saucepan. After it had built up a frothy head, he skimmed off the scum with a spoon. Holding it over his mouth, he chewed it down as if he were eating spaghetti. The hot milk itself he drank in a glass with the metal spoon in it to absorb the heat so that the glass would not break. But his love of hot milk had cost him. My mother told and retold the story.

When Jay was born in Alma-Ata, it was wartime, and there was no *mohel* to perform the *bris*. So, Jay was not circumcised. It worried my mother. As an infant, Jay was so thin and frail. She had so little food to give him. When she nursed him, she barely had any milk, and his sucking was so weak. If he, *chulileh*, God forbid, died, how would he be buried, without a *bris*? At age twenty-two, she had two children, and she was little more than bones herself. But she was determined that they would all survive. *"Ka berayreh hob ich nisht gehat. (I had no alternative.)"*

Day in and day out, she willed herself the strength to do the only work she could find. She rose before dawn every day to load and unload the barges and trains that transported grain in this wheat belt of Russia. Carrying the fifty-kilo sacks of wheat and flour like a pack mule, mindlessly emptying one wagon only to fill another, she strained under the weight. But it was alright. Her slave wages kept her two sons, her husband, and herself above starvation.

There was rarely any meat. Once, in the winter, one of the women who worked alongside her and had befriended her whispered, "Lonya, my husband killed a bear in the woods. There is plenty of meat. If you want you can have some."

My mother agreed. She went with the woman in the night with a knife to cut some meat from the bear. She would cook it for her family. When she reached the hidden spot in the woods, she saw the silhouette of the bear hanging from a tree. As she drew closer, she saw that it had been skinned of its fur. She could not cut any meat from the bear. It looked too much like a person hanging there.

Sometimes she could manage to steal a little flour, and that would help. Once she had been caught scooping a handful of flour into her underwear. It could have meant prison, but she managed to rouse pity in the officials, and they let her go with a warning. This only meant that she had to be doubly careful. There was no other way to survive.

Her husband was a disappointment. He didn't respond to the burning urgency in the same way. He wouldn't work in the transport line like she did. He had survived typhus not long after they arrived in Kazakhstan, and he claimed that this weakened him too much for that kind of labor. Once, he had been forcibly conscripted into an army work gang that would have taken him away altogether, but he managed to escape. As a result, he had to keep a low profile. He got occasional work painting signs, but that provided little. Besides, he took care of himself. He spent his days discussing literature and world events with his cronies, the other Jewish artists and writers who had fled there from Poland.

One day, my mother found him in the street market eating some *smetana*. He stood in the middle of the bazaar, concentrating solely on the pot of cultured dairy in one hand and a spoon in the other. He hadn't noticed her approaching. She startled him with her accusation, "Is this what you do while your babies are starving?"

At the age of two, Jay could only crawl. But things were getting a little better. The war in Russia was winding down, and there was a little more food to be had. And she loved to help her Yankel hold a cup of warm milk in his hands. He gulped it down, wide eyed, as if it were a potion. And he was beginning to pull himself up on two legs. It would not be long before he started walking. There was now a *mohel* in the village of Illi, where they lived. Jay was still young enough, and soon he would be strong enough for a *bris*.

One day, she was washing diapers in a pail in front of the house. A small pot of milk for her children's lunch was heating on the earthen stove in the yard. She watched Mayer, not yet four, sitting open-legged on the ground, digging the earth with a stick. Jay crawled naked in the brilliant sunshine. *The warmth will do him good,* she thought. She wrung out a diaper and turned to put it on the clothesline. When she turned back to the pail, she saw that Jay had pulled himself up against the stove, and he was reaching for the handle of the pot. Before she could run to grab him, Jay pulled the pot over. He let out a fierce yowl as the scalding milk poured over his groin and thigh.

When I was five, Jay's uncircumcised penis was a source of wonder to me. When I saw him naked, his tubelike member, which narrowed almost to a point, had a certain majesty. When he walked, it shook and trembled like a divining rod. Like the top of an exclamation point, it made a statement. One evening, when we were getting undressed for bed, Jay sat down to demonstrate its mysteries to me. We sat on the bed with only shirts on, our legs akimbo. A layer of taut brown skin stretched from Jay's left thigh to his crotch, like the map of an uncharted continent. His penis rested on the tight, round walnut of his eight-year-old scrotum. With two fingers of both hands, he pulled back the prepuce to reveal the pink pearl of his glans, which was bathed in a thin milky fluid. I had seen his glans before, when he had an erection. Then it had bolted out of its sheath, angry, red, and insistent. It was a sight to behold. As I sat, my legs apart, facing Jay, I looked at my own shriveled mushroom cap of a penis and admired his adornment.

But Jay had mixed feelings about his endowment. "I'm always the different one," he often said to Mayer and me. His feelings of being set apart only intensified when Mayer began to study for his bar mitzvah when he was twelve. We were in Paris then, and the Hasidic *melamed*, or teacher, my father had engaged had suggested that Jay and I learn Yiddishkeit at the same time. The three of us sat at the table in size order from our teacher. The *melamed*, with thick beard and earlocks, took out a flat silver case from the breast pocket of his black kaftan. He selected a cigarette. Then, with his pocketknife, he cut it in two and placed one half back in the case and the other half into a holder. After he lit the cigarette, we could begin to learn to read Hebrew: *ah, bah, gah, dah, hah . . .*

The *melamed* did not stay long enough to see Mayer bar mitzvahed. He left for America. But he did stay long enough to teach us considerable portions of Genesis. He alternated between twirling the beard hairs under his chin and the ritual fringes of his *arbah kanfos*, his *tallis* smock, as we read the story of Abraham and translated it into Yiddish.

"You see, God made man imperfect," the *melamed* explained. "He left a little piece of unnecessary skin to stand for that imperfection. It is up to man to perfect himself. Abraham marked his covenant with God by circumcising himself, showing that he was ridding himself of his imperfection. From the moment of Abraham's act, the mark of one's acceptance of the covenant, of being a Jew, is the act of *milah*, circumcision. A male who is not circumcised is not a Jew."

Both Mayer and I turned to Jay as if we had been slapped in the face. Jay could only look down at the table.

A few months later, at the age of eleven, Jay went to the hospital. He had convinced my parents to let him have a *bris*. I only found out about it when Jay returned from the procedure. He was lying in my parents' bed, hovered over by my parents and two bearded men in black hats and kaftans who looked like our *melamed*. When they left the room, I sat down next to Jay. He showed me his underwear, all stuffed with gauze and cotton. We laughed at the bulge.

"Does it hurt?" I asked.

"Very much," he answered. "But now I am like you."

◆ ◆ ◆

My mother and I left the house, loaded down with shopping bags full of reminders of home for Mayer. "We better hurry or we'll be late," she fretted as we rushed toward the 145th Street subway station. As I shuffled clumsily with my bags, I noticed Jay weaving his metal cart between the parked cars and traffic. He did not see us as he pushed and prodded the overloaded wagon at breakneck pace.

My mother and I just caught the bus from Port Authority to Fort Dix. As we rode past the marshlands of New Jersey, speeding toward Mayer, my thoughts kept turning to Jay. I envisioned him bounding up tenement stairs, loaded down with overstuffed brown bags. Then I saw him, the supposedly sickly child, alone in Brunoy.

One day, the authorities of the sanatorium had decided on mass tonsillectomies for all the chronic patients of the infirmary. "They give you gas, and you fall asleep," Jay had told me. "You have strange dreams. You wake up with a terrible sore throat, and then they give you all the ice cream you want."

When he was let out of the infirmary that last time, Jay taught me how to climb the tree in back of The Small House.

"The trick is not to be stuck trying to get to the first branch," Jay said. "If you notice, the second branch is not much higher. But there are knotholes and small stumps of branches you can grab hold of to get you to it. From that point it's easy."

Jay encouraged me to try it, describing the sights, the fields, the roads, the distant houses, and the peaceful feeling at the top. Many times, I tried to grab the holding places to get to the second branch, but to no avail. Jay eventually lost interest in helping me with this. However, I was determined to experience the serenity at the top.

One day, when everyone was at lunch, I tried again. I clutched each hold despite the pain in my twisted fingers and the stinging scrapes on my legs. Triumphantly, I made it onto the second branch in the noon stillness. From there, it would be easy, Jay had said. And at first it was. The branches were spaced almost like steps that circled the tree. But then as I climbed higher, the tree became thinner, and it began to sway under my weight. Climbing higher became extremely frightening, as a stiff breeze buffeted me. But I doggedly continued. As I secured myself at the top of the tree, holding on tightly to the few scrawny branches around me, I looked for the sights Jay had described. But all I saw was a stubbly plot of land and the edge of the woods. The idyllic fields, and roads, and houses were not there! He must have imagined them. I guessed he needed to imagine them.

I could not balance myself on the swaying branches; I was too frightened. I gripped them for dear life. And climbing down was ever so slow and frightening.

As the bus to Fort Dix rolled onward, I imagined Jay calmly perched at the top of the tree as it swayed precariously under the force of the wind, reassuring himself that he was alright. He knew he could balance securely in the arms of his tree for as long as he wanted to. He could even find the road to Paris, maybe. If only he had known where my parents had moved to.

My mother sat beside me, lost in anticipation of seeing her eldest son. My own thoughts turned once more to Jay, bent over his grocery cart, lurching swiftly along Broadway, a solitary figure challenging the whizzing cars for a piece of the road.

And I thought, *If you find a child in the road, how do you know if it's abandoned?*

CHAPTER 3

◆ ◆ ◆ ◆ ◆ ◆

My Future Foretold

I had done it again. I had run the gauntlet. It was only one block from our building to the subway entrance, but it had filled me with dread. When my mother jostled toward the subway station on our way to Mayer, shopping bags banging against our legs, I scanned the streets, praying that no one I knew would see me. I had spotted Jay in the streets, straining against the weight of his cart, totally focused on his goal. His life was hard compared to mine. He looked so small against the backdrop of the shabby buildings and the menacing cars. He did not see us as he lurched behind his load.

But it was not Jay's glance that I was worried about. I was afraid that I might be seen by one of the few students from my yeshiva who lived in this neighborhood. At any moment, one of them might appear in the distance, dressed in his Sabbath suit and elegant hat, walking placidly and serenely next to his shining father. I would see him grow suddenly disquiet, not sure of what he had seen. Then he would stare at me, open-mouthed, as I wore my casual clothes and my yarmulke, carrying my bags into the subway on the Sabbath. If someone like that were to see me and report me, not only would I be kicked out of school, but worse, I would be exposed and humiliated.

I hope I made it, I thought as I rushed down the subway stairs to anonymity. I put my bags down in relief as my mother bought the tokens. I took my worn skullcap off my head, folded it in thirds, and slipped it in my pocket. Now I was the other me. With my head covered, I was the yeshiva boy. With my head bare, I was someone else. My mother turned and saw me take off my yarmulke. She registered my action by averting her eyes and busying herself with the bags and tokens.

Hers was an act of discretion, less to spare me embarrassment than to acknowledge the inconsistencies of living.

I stared at the passengers on the train, and later I studied the people on the bus. I tried to see myself through their eyes as I traveled bareheaded. They seemed to hold no judgments in their stolid expressions. In yeshiva, I felt judged at every turn, if not by others, then by me. As the wheels of the bus hummed along the highway pavement, my mother sat hunched over, lost in thought. Vivid images seemed to flicker in her eyes. I turned to watch the moving New Jersey landscape.

As the bus rolled toward Mayer, I imagined a weight being lifted from me. In my mind's eye, I saw myself being imperceptibly transformed from a puffy-eyed and besieged boy, stooped under the weight of my yarmulke, into a gangly teen, with brown locks that sprouted untamed and free from my uncovered head, indistinguishable from countless other boys my age.

In reality, I could not switch so readily from one existence to another just by removing my yarmulke. Whether I wore it or not, I was peering out from under a shell, berating myself for my hypocrisy and indecision. I stared out of the bus window at the dull landscape, and I saw myself clinging to the top of Jay's tree, swaying one way and another in the wind.

I clutched my hand around the yarmulke in my pocket and held it tight. Removing my skullcap from my head always evoked a mixture of relief tinged with regret and failure in me. Despite the admonitions, it was easier to break the Sabbath than to bare my head. I broke the Sabbath regularly when I pushed the elevator button, turned on the TV, or fried eggs on Saturday morning, all while wearing my yarmulke.

The yarmulke is only a custom, but the Sabbath was commanded to us on Mount Sinai, I scolded myself.

A minhag brecht a din—a custom overrides a law, I retorted. *God will forgive my honoring custom over the Sabbath.*

But will God forgive you for fearing man more than Him? Who commits the greater sin, the highwayman, who confronts his victim and plunders by the threat of death from his weapon, or the burglar, who robs a house in the dead of night, never disturbing the occupants? The burglar is worse. The highwayman fears neither man nor God, while the burglar fears man above God. You are like the burglar. You cover your head to hide from man, but you don't care that God sees you transgress His Law.

No! My yarmulke is not for hiding. It sets me apart. It makes me a visible part of God's people.

An empty gesture. It is the following of God's commandments that makes you part of His people.

But my yarmulke proclaims Who is above. Sh'ma Yisroel! Hear o' Israel! And it reminds me that He is near. And that lets me ask Him so many questions.

An empty argument. You want to take it off more and more.

An empty argument. He doesn't answer.

But I'm still hoping.

My heart twisted with each turn of the argument. As the bus droned on, I could only sigh. Maybe today I would be hiding under the cover of my bare head.

My mother turned to me, her eyes suddenly glistening, as she pointed to a road sign that read Fort Dix. She laughed in anticipation. Mayer was waiting for us, wearing his crisp khaki uniform, spit-polished shoes, and military cap. He looked strong and confident. My mother leapt at him and threw her arms around his neck. She kissed and kissed his cheeks, hardly believing he was finally there. "Mayer! Mayer! Mayer!" she cried.

Mayer grinned, his eyes squeezed shut, his face turning red. With one arm around my mother's shoulder, he walked over to where I stood, barricaded by the shopping bags. With his free arm he patted my shoulder. Then he took a quick glance at the back of my naked head. "Looking good, Michael," he said as he picked up the brown bags from home.

Mayer took a large bite of his sandwich as we sat at an outdoor table in the quiet, countrified setting that surrounded the barracks. "I sure miss this," he said as he took another mouthful of the corned beef and pickle on fresh rye bread. "But you didn't have to bring all this. They feed me well here. It may not be home cooking, but there's lots of food, and it's surprisingly good. Napoleon said an army moves on its stomach, and they sure believe it here."

"So, what is it like?" I asked, as I tried to take in the regularity of the rows and rows of buildings and to grasp the importance that the vastness of the place commanded. I wasn't sure if it was meant for the likes of us.

"I love it. I can breathe here," Mayer said boldly. "Their first job in basic training is to disorient you and make you jump to the sergeant's orders. They want to mold you into a reaction machine. The sergeant calls, you jump. No thinking. They wake you up at all hours of the night to go bivouac. You have to be prepared at any time. Then you run with sixty pounds of gear on your back. You learn pretty quickly not to straggle, or you'll be playing catch-up all night, running while everybody else is resting. You learn to march with precision, and you learn to make your bed so that a quarter bounces off it. You clean your rifle as if your life depended on it, because it might. Your rifle becomes your closest friend. And you go through amazing survival courses, scaling walls, climbing over obstructions, swinging from ropes. The physical exhaustion feels good."

"*Vus di bist du adorchgegangen! (What you went through here!)*" My mother shook her head, confused by the pride she felt.

"It was fun, Mom," Mayer assured her.

"Some of the guys I've seen here are really big," I challenged him. "They must set a pretty hard pace."

"It's all about will and endurance," he answered, pinning me with his good eye.

"What's it like shooting a gun?" I asked, looking away.

"It's not a gun; it's a rifle. Would you believe I'm a marksman?" he laughed, hardly believing it himself. "Not having to close my other eye is an asset." Breaking the silence that followed, he added more soberly, "We were trained to fire many kinds of weapons, even to run drills with live ammunition whizzing overhead. That was not just for battle training. I think it was to check out who had talent for that kind of thing."

My mother gasped. "You could have been killed. *Noch git az cho' nisht gevist. (I'm glad I didn't know.)* I wouldn't have rested one minute."

"Your worry is a little late," Mayer responded good-naturedly.

My mother looked suddenly wounded. She turned away so we wouldn't see her face swelling with tears. She smoothed the folds of her skirt.

"And do you have talent under fire?" I asked Mayer, both of us oblivious to the effect that Mayer's words had had on our mother.

"I do," Mayer answered cockily. "But I'm starting Signal Corps training this week. Electronics. That's the kind of talent I'm interested in exploring."

"Jay found the cold-solder joints in the oscilloscope," I remembered to say.

Mayer sighed. "Tell Jay I miss him," he said softly. "I was hoping he would come today. He needs to get out of his rut for a little while. He would like it here." Then, with a burst of cheer, he turned to my mother. "How about it, Mom? What would you say to having two soldiers?"

"Cho' shoyn genig gelitn, (I've already suffered enough,)" she responded coldly, a tense sadness descending over her face.

"I'm sorry, Mom. What did I say?" Mayer sighed.

"I'm sorry too," she said, not looking at him. "I've had enough of armies in my life."

When it was time to go, I could tell my mother wanted to hug Mayer and kiss him and cry and say she would miss him, but she couldn't let herself. She stood apart from Mayer, avoiding his glance.

Mayer walked over to her and tried to turn her around to face him, but she wouldn't let him. So he held her shoulders to his chest and said, "Let's have a real goodbye, so I can say a real hello next time."

Then my mother turned around. She held her son close and cried, "You know I always meant the best."

◆ ◆ ◆

We came home to the heat of the city. My yarmulke once again covered my head as we climbed the stairs out of the subway station. Cars heaved down Broadway as we walked from the subway in the early twilight. Soot and exhaust fumes hung low in the summer air, trapped by the buildings. My eyes scanned the sidewalks anxiously for any of my schoolmates who might be straggling to the evening services that would end the Sabbath. We entered our apartment, and my mother went wordlessly into the kitchen to empty the bags Mayer had asked us to bring back. My father lay asleep, half on and half off the couch, illuminated by a lamp. His open mouth was visible beneath the Yiddish newspaper he still held. In his undershirt, with his pants loosened, and his legs crossed at the ankles, he formed a familiar sight of bunioned feet, belly, mouth, and nostrils. He looked dead, except for his soft, rhythmic snoring. He stirred as I walked into the room.

"*Shoyn tserik? (Back already?)*" he startled. "*Geloyb tse Got. (Praised be God.)*" The newspaper fell to the floor as he sat up, his face creased with sleep, his eyes the size of a bird's. He shuffled into the kitchen, holding the ends of his belt in one hand as he rubbed his tousled head with the other. "*D'host epes ts'essn? (You have something to eat?)*" he greeted my mother, who was putting fruit into the refrigerator.

"*D'host gevart uf mir? (You waited for me?)* I just walked in the door. *Ch'bin nisht dan meshures, (I'm not your servant,)*" she shot back.

"*Nayn, nayn, stam gefreygt, (No, no, I only asked,)*" he mumbled.

My mother began emptying another shopping bag as my father fastened his belt.

"How did he look?" he asked her, now fully awake.

"He looked fine," she said dully, answering only the direct question.

He beamed. "For a Jew to be in the American army is a great thing," my father proclaimed with genuine enthusiasm. "In some countries, we had to fight for the right to be in the army. This means he's a full citizen of this country!"

"I hope we haven't lost him," my mother responded, closing the refrigerator door.

◆ ◆ ◆

I closed the door behind me in my parents' bedroom and sought out the armchair crammed in the corner between the dresser and the window. This had served as my place of refuge since the time we had moved into this apartment. Rarely was I intruded upon here as I lay sprawled out, with my head on one soft arm of the rose-colored chair and my legs over the other. Here is where I spawned daydreams about the future. Here is where I fulfilled my wishes. Here is where I constantly reviewed my life, measuring it against my yearnings. And here is where I stayed motionless, in a near stupor, for hours on end, my body too numb to move.

I flung myself into the chair. The visit to Mayer had left me agitated. I sat with my body pinned against the back, my hands gripping the arms of the chair as if I were moving at high speed. Mayer had broken out of his boundaries. I thought of what he had said before he had left home. Had he become what he was not? Had he decided to become someone else and then simply changed? Or was he simply reclaiming who he once had been?

In Brunoy, when he was nine, Mayer had tagged along behind the boys his age, with his shoulders hunched, his head bent. This was not so when he played out his adventures. Mayer knew more about American Indians than anyone. How he got this knowledge I didn't know, but he often went bare-chested, and he put bands around his sinewy arms. With a solitary feather in his headband, he stood erect as he championed the Indians' right to exist. Other boys did not join him in his cause, but Jay and I were willing Comanches and Apaches. He taught us reverence for the land, and we took only what we needed. We hunted bison with our bows and arrows. We harvested wild maize. Mayer led us to a clay embankment he had found in the old, drained pond, and we fashioned tomahawks around our decorated ash-wood handles. With war whoops, we rode our mustangs into battle against those who would not share the land. We took many scalps with our tomahawks.

Most important to me, Mayer provided us shelter in the woods. As Jay kept lookout in the treetops, Mayer wove strips of fresh bark and leafy branches around scrub tree trunks to make walls. Then we thatched the roof with pine boughs. As we sat in the earthen coolness of our hut, we pretended to smoke peace pipes made from hollowed-out horse chestnuts and maple switches.

It was the spring before his tenth birthday when Mayer's head was shorn in Brunoy. When my mother found out about the humiliation, she stormed up to the sanatorium determined to bring him home. He came home later that summer, and Jay followed in the fall. Jay was eight, and he took to school right away. But Mayer, at age ten, returned from his first school day distraught. My mother scraped together the money for a tutor. Under the watchful guidance of this gentle and patient old woman, Mayer began to read, and he roamed even more freely between his knowledge and his imagination. His head swirled with *Fanfan la Tulipe* and *Les Trois Mousquetaires,* and he swept Jay and me along. As D'Artagnan, Mayer gave us a code of honor: All for one and one for all. He led us into noble battle in the cause of France.

That last September at Chateau Rose in Les Andelys, three days before we were to set sail for America, we played out our final battle. After protracted dueling with the treacherous and invisible foe, we stood on a small promontory overlooking the main house. Fire burned in his eyes as the thirteen-year-old D'Artagnan surveyed the landscape that had been a home for us and that we would soon abandon.

D'Artagnan spoke eloquently to his two loyal musketeers in knee pants and heavy leather shoes, as we stood in size order to his right. "We have fought our final battle. We have vanquished the enemy and restored the king to his rightful throne. Now we can throw down our swords. Our work is done."

Jay and I drew our maple swords from our belts and threw them on the ground, ready to accept the anonymity of peace.

Then D'Artagnan said, "Let us lift up our wine goblets and toast this great victory. But first, let us stir in some poison, for we have reached the height of glory, and now we can die."

We quaffed the poisoned wine and fell contented to the ground, affirming the glory of life in death.

Mayer brought his sense of adventure with him across the ocean. A few months after we were settled in a surprisingly idyllic, suburban-like section of Pittsburgh, Mayer begrudgingly acknowledged that this was a good country, and he decided to bring a gift offering to his new homeland. One late winter day, he sat down at the enameled kitchen table, a thick brown notebook in front of him, and, from memory, he began to transcribe word for word what he had enjoyed as a great French classic. He wanted to unveil the book of Tarzan to his new countrymen by spring.

He would have loved to act out the jungle adventure, but Mayer's kind of noble play did not translate well in his adopted land. To most boys he met, he seemed uncomfortably different.

"You want play Tarzan?" I heard him ask a group of boys in the schoolyard one late fall day.

"No, I can see that in the movies," answered one of them. "Pretend is kid stuff, kid."

"*Foosball*—soccer?" Mayer countered.

"What's that?" asked another, tossing a softball into his large leather mitt. "How about baseball?" he asked, waving the ball in front of Mayer's face. "I'll lend you my glove."

"OK!" Mayer said, grinning, using this most blunt and friendly American expression.

But Mayer had no depth perception with only one good eye. He ran around the asphalt outfield, his arm outstretched, missing every shot that came toward him.

"He's so goofy," one of the boys laughed as Mayer swung the bat clumsily, well ahead of the pitched ball.

He walked off the field when he saw the others losing patience.

"Tankyoo," he called out as he waved to them, although they seemed already to have adjusted their play and forgotten him.

◆ ◆ ◆

Try as he might, Mayer found no heroes in cowboy movies or baseball to help him connect with the well-meaning acquaintances he met, and his awkwardness became as accented as his English. He had been the outsider here as much as he had been in Brunoy, until he met Heinz. Heinz was a bold-as-you-please fourteen-year-old. He wore a cut-off felt hat that looked like a small crown, like Jughead's in the Archie comics, complete with a dazzling collection of commemorative pins.

As often as not, Heinz wore a striped T-shirt, dungarees, and sneakers, as he walked jauntily along. Unlike other boys, Heinz seemed charmed by Mayer's view of things. He laughed at Mayer's mixed-up sentences. Heinz loved to laugh. He pointed to the miniature Heinz pickle and tiny Heinz Ketchup bottle on his hat. "Heinz is a big name in Pittsburgh," he said with a laugh.

Heinz showed Mayer the wonders of Pittsburgh. He didn't mind if Jay and I tagged along. One early summer Saturday, Jay and I, brown sandwich bags in hand, accompanied them on their trek to Schenley Park. Walking along the road, we imitated Heinz and Mayer as they stuck out their thumbs whenever a car passed. A large black sedan stopped. The four of us piled into the back seat of the cavernous car. Turning around in the front seat was Sandra with the dark curls and dark eyes, the girl who sat next to me in class. Her father smiled through his pipe and took us out of his way to the park.

There were people everywhere, picnicking or sunning themselves, but there was still room for us to slither through the woods, scale rocks, and run along the paths. My brothers and I had salami sandwiches washed down with water for lunch. Heinz had peanut butter and grape jelly on white bread with a bottle of cherry pop. Mayer winced and teased him that he wasn't eating lunch but candy.

"It's good!" Heinz answered, offering each of us a bite of his sandwich.

The combination of tastes and textures was incongruous, as bold and unself-conscious as this accepting new country.

"Does anyone have money?" Heinz asked.

Mayer dug into his pocket for the dime he had brought.

"Take your little brother on the pony ride," Heinz said.

The three of them watched from behind the rail as I sat in a western saddle atop a pinto pony, imagining it was mine. I felt Jay's eyes following me. He looked both pleased and sorry he was too old for this.

Heinz had two bathing suits in his knapsack, so Jay and I waited as he and Mayer went swimming. I watched them return up the path. Mayer was listening to one of Heinz's stories as they walked. Mayer seemed different. His laugh was gentle, and he didn't walk with his shoulders hunched. Rather, his posture was relaxed, his skin wet and shiny, as he sauntered easily toward Jay and me.

As evening approached, we dug a small pit using sticks and flat rocks. Mayer took charge of making the fire. Out of his knapsack Heinz took a small metal contraption, and he placed the grate over the fire. He opened a can jaggedly with a special blade on his knife. On the grate we roasted franks Heinz had brought, while the Heinz-branded can of baked beans bubbled over the heat.

It was getting dark when we doused the glowing embers and covered them with dirt.

"Can't thumb it now." Heinz shook his head. "Too dangerous. Won't be able to see the cars coming if we stand in the road."

We walked all the way home, against traffic, single file on the sidewalks and dirt edges of the roads, Heinz in front and Mayer bringing up the rear. My mother was watching television with Mrs. Federman when we walked in the house. She jumped up and greeted us with a sigh of relief. Surprisingly, she did not look angry. As we recounted our day, she actually seemed excited for us, although she tried to hide it.

"I told you they probably had to walk all the way home," said old Mrs. Federman from her couch, holding her Raleigh cigarette between her yellowed fingers and keeping her eyes on the television.

"It's late. Go right to bed," my mother commanded, trying to sound stern.

We went upstairs dutifully, glad for the reprieve, although she rarely scolded any of us. Jay's and Mayer's beds were next to each other, while I had a cot against the facing wall. We lay in the dark, exhausted but unable to sleep. Jay was on his side, turned to Mayer, his head propped on one hand. He laughed as one by one he reviewed the events of the day with him.

"Yeah," I responded in my new slang into the darkness in witness to each detail.

Mayer lay on his back, his hands under his head, resting on the pillow. "*C'etait chie*—It was fantastic! I think this might work out." He sighed contentedly.

On weekday mornings, Heinz routinely stopped by the house, and he and Mayer climbed the hill to school, gesticulating and laughing. Mayer now had a paper route, along with Heinz, complete with little red wagon.

I watched Jay watching them. He was getting used to sharing Mayer. "Mayer's not the same," he would say. "Maybe that's good," he would add with a wistful shrug.

We watched Mayer put aside his fantasy adventures for the real adventure of everyday life.

◆ ◆ ◆

I twisted uncomfortably in the upholstered chair in my parents' bedroom, as if I were unwillingly strapped into it. I struggled in my heart. Could I break out of my boundaries? Would I have needed to if we had stayed in Pittsburgh? I would certainly have been different. Would that have been for the better? Almost certainly. How could I be sure?

I considered the Midrash about Elijah. The prophet was traveling with a young disciple, both disguised as beggars, when they stopped at a rich man's house to ask for lodging for the night. The rich man grudgingly let them stay in his stable with the animals. In the morning, Elijah asked his disciple to repair a wall that was crumbling along the border of the rich man's property as a gift for his kindness. The prophet and his student traveled on, and as night fell again, they stopped at the hovel of a poor farmer and his wife. They welcomed the two strangers into their home and shared their evening meal with them. Then the couple gave the men their own straw bed, while they themselves slept on the earthen floor. Upon leaving their hosts in the morning, Elijah ordered his disciple to slaughter the poor couple's only milk cow. The young man did as his teacher ordered, but he was deeply disturbed.

"How can you reward the rich man so well for his stinginess and take away the livelihood of the poor couple who shared all they had with you?" he asked.

Elijah answered, "Had the rich man restored the wall himself he would have discovered a treasure buried in it, and he would have been all the more confident in continuing his hard-hearted ways. The poor couple's cow was about to die suddenly. Had that happened, they would have had nothing for it. Now they can at least start over with the proceeds of its meat. I gave all of them their due, for the future is foreshadowed but not foretold."

Everything that might have been is lost! The future is foreshadowed but not foretold, I thought with bitter irony as I lay sprawled and motionless, helpless against the weight of my own body as it pressed into the fabric of the easy chair. The sacks beneath my eyes filled with loss. What would I have been like had we stayed in Pittsburg? My daydreams were a continuous loop that repeated itself day in and day out.

I would imagine myself in the schoolyard in Pittsburgh, playing softball with the guys, swinging the bat, running after the ball, making the catch, exhilarated by the strength in my adolescent body. After the game we would sit, rousting about, shoulder to shoulder, leaning against the chain-link fence, drinking our soda pops.

I would see myself as a young man in a light T-shirt, chinos, and tennis shoes, running freely down Black Street to Sandra's front door. I would hold her hand as we would sit on her front porch swing. I would be laughing, laughing unself-consciously.

But that day I had seen Mayer, and my wish-fulfilling dreams were not enough. We had lived in Pittsburgh for less than a year, scarcely more time than it takes someone to be born. I mourned my stillborn future. The images of how things might have been that repeatedly flashed before my eyes had lost their life, at least for today.

CHAPTER 4

◆ ◆ ◆ ◆ ◆ ◆

My Pittsburgh

Pittsburgh was not at all what any of us had imagined. Before we left for America, I had heard that it was a big, grim, industrial city, but we would live better there. I had imagined myself living in Pittsburgh, playing in a large courtyard surrounded by looming gray concrete walls that enclosed a small patch of gray sky. I would have a bicycle, and I would ride in circles on the concrete pavement.

When we arrived, my parents said the city was dirty, and my brothers agreed. But my impression as an eight-year-old was quite different. In Paris the streets were washed down every day, but inside our building, the walls were dank and decayed. And there were no remains of bombed-out buildings in Pittsburgh. In Paris, Jay and I often played in the foundations of missing houses, wondering if there might still be dead bodies hidden in them this long after the war.

Before the Hebrew Immigrant Aid Society had found us our apartment, we stayed in a hotel downtown. It was a wonderful place. All five of us stayed in one room, but it was softly carpeted, and we had our own bathroom, something we had never had before. I loved lying in the green tub, with the warm, clear water shimmering around me. It was a welcome change from Paris, where I stood in a galvanized metal washtub while my mother poured water on me from a kettle.

When I looked out our fifth-floor, curtained hotel window, I saw men in suits and hats rushing by and cars glinting in the crisp autumn sunlight. On our street corner was a newspaper stand that was manned by two Italian boys. My brothers and I befriended them with gestures and the few English words we had learned. The papers were stacked on plywood on top of milk crates. When the boys were in school, they left the stand unattended. People would pick up their papers and drop their pennies on the plywood. Or they would make their own change for the nickels and dimes they left. The boys shrugged in puzzlement when we asked if anyone ever stole from them.

Our social worker, a genial older man with a moustache, took us to see our new home on Black Street in what was for us his luxurious dove-gray 1953 Plymouth. I sat in front with my mother, staring at the shiny chrome grill of the radio, imagining I was driving as we rolled smoothly to our destination. The street we were to live on charmed me with its two-story houses, front lawns, and porch swings. A little girl roller-skated on the slate sidewalk bordered by grass on either side.

Our house stood right next to the entrance to the schoolyard. We would literally have to hop over a low metal railing behind the backyard to get to school. We would live on the second floor. We had four rooms off a narrow landing. I had never seen such clean, freshly painted white walls or stained-glass decorations in the windows of people's homes.

We had been there only moments when two men in a pickup truck loaded with furniture stopped in front of the house. One wore a straw cowboy hat and the other a baseball cap, and both looked strong in their dungarees and plaid shirts with rolled-up sleeves. They brought in our two cardboard valises. Then they set up a kitchen table and chairs and put together some beds. They came back several times until it got dark, bringing dressers, lamps, a stuffed chair, and clothing "for the boys." They wished us a good night and a hearty welcome from the members of the synagogue on Nagley Avenue.

From the first moments and through the early months on Black Street, Mayer and Jay struggled to maintain their sense of themselves as French. The fruit had been more succulent, the pastries more delicate, the buildings more graceful, the sidewalks wider, and the skies bluer in Paris. Besides, French was such a lyrical and subtle language. It would be hard to give it up for the loud and coarse-sounding English. Mainly, they tried to hold on to the identities they knew. But this welcoming country gently seduced us all, and, despite their deprecating comparisons, I knew that deep down my brothers shared my feeling that this was the best place we had ever lived. And even in the short run, we were willing to be led into its ways.

My first days in third grade at the Rogers School were a wonder to me. To see boys and girls in the same school, and in the same class, was astounding. What's more, they were free to move about the room and to talk to each other and work on "projects" together. I must have been used as some kind of current events or geography lesson by the teacher when I first entered the class because all the children came up to me to introduce themselves.

One girl in particular shocked me in her boldness. She had black finger curls and wore a checkered dress with short, puffy sleeves and puffy skirt. "Hi," she said with a bright smile, looking me directly in the eyes. "I'm Lucy. I like you. Do you like me?"

I was speechless, and I averted my eyes in embarrassment. I could not express this feeling. In French, one said, "*J'aime*," and in Yiddish it was "*Ich hob lib*," I love. I knew no feeling or word in either language for this milder gradation of "I like."

I was paired with Marvin, who understood Yiddish and spoke a hobbled version of it. He explained many curious things to me in the first months before I learned to speak English well. One day, the entire class lined up and solemnly marched to a janitorial passageway behind our classroom. I whispered my puzzlement to Marvin as we stood pressed against the tile wall.

He explained in his cryptic Yiddish, "There's a plane over us with a bomb. And maybe . . ." He arched his eyebrows and nodded his head sagely.

I was more confused than before. We repeated this air-raid drill several times during my stay in this class. For some unfathomable reason, we also practiced contorting our bodies under our desks.

I soon learned the nuance between "like" and "love" in my class. I liked the lively and bouncy Lucy, but I loved Sandra, with her dark eyes and her red, red lips. She spoke slowly and softly, and she laughed easily. Her movements flowed with an inner calm, a way about her I had never been aware of before. But I loved Darlene even more. Her gold-blond hair was parted in the middle and ended in two ponytails, except when she changed it to ringlets and left me breathless. She had liquid blue eyes, an upturned nose, and lightly freckled cheeks. She was thin and pale and always wore pastel colors. I knew intuitively, even before I saw her walking her golden cocker spaniel puppy, that she was my American ideal. For a short time in that ever-changing class, I sat next to Sandra, but I sent a Valentine's Day card to Darlene.

There was little academic pressure for me in school. The work was introduced at a leisurely pace. After two years of schooling in France, I had learned long division, and I could write simple script compositions in ink. Here, they were just getting to the times tables, and they were block printing sentences in pencil. I had plenty of time in class to observe the other children. I learned their movements and their expressions. I studied the gestures and singsong of their language. I discovered that not knowing English very well gave me a good deal of freedom. I could interpret and respond to what was said to me as I wished.

"Would the class president and the class council please come up front to decide our Thanksgiving presentation," the teacher said.

I went up as well, and no one objected. I didn't understand a thing, and I kept quiet as George, our tall and handsome class president, held forth.

My brothers had similarly novel experiences, and we shared our discoveries. Jay said to me in French, quite impressed by what he had learned, "You know that when you say *tankyoo* to somebody, they have to say *yoowayco*. If they don't, they're not polite."

We practiced the word and looked for opportunities to say *yoowayco*.

One afternoon, Jay came home with several dimpled white balls. "Look at this," he announced. "I got these in a field a few streets up the hill. Can you believe that grown-ups play a game with these small balls? It's called golf. They seem to lose the balls all the time," Jay said. "I found these in the bushes."

"Show me," I said.

We walked up to the golf course. Two men and a woman, who were wearing flat round caps with pompoms and who were equipped with large leather sacks containing metal and wood sticks, were standing in front of us. The woman took a majestic swing and her long plaid skirt and a little white ball went flying into the air. The men patted the woman on the back and smiled as they started walking.

I had followed the arc of the ball in the blue sky, and I saw where the ball landed, although it was no longer visible in the distant grass. I ran swiftly to retrieve the ball and brought it back to the golfing party. "I have it!" I shouted gleefully in French as I handed it to the woman. "It isn't lost!"

Jay explained to me why we were chased off the course.

◆ ◆ ◆

In the early days, Mayer, Jay, and I explored our new neighborhood together. People didn't mind that we crossed their backyards. They greeted us and started conversations. In one backyard, Jay found a friend. Bernie was generous. He let us use his bicycle, and, even more special, his archery set. This was nothing like the rough bows and arrows we had made in Brunoy and Les Andelys. We admired the sleek lines of the laminated bow and the metal-tipped arrows with their colorful feather vanes. And there was actually a target. In another yard, I found a swing set, Arnold and his younger brother, and their dog, Snowball. Bernie's parents soon invited us to his birthday party, and in the spring, Arnold's parents drove us all to the circus at Forbes Field.

Not long after we arrived on Black Street, to my young mind, the most astounding thing happened. One afternoon, Jay and I dropped in on Bernie to see if we could use his bow and arrows. Bernie was in his living room with his mother. He was trying on a costume made of shiny red and yellow fabric, a clown mask, and a funny wig. He looked dazzling.

"I'm going to be Clarabel," he said. "What are you going to be for Halloween?"

"Qu'est-que c'est Halloween?" I asked Jay.

He shrugged in puzzlement.

"Come back after dinner," said Bernie's mother. "You'll go with Bernie."

We returned with Mayer, and Bernie's mother gave each of us a mask and a large brown paper shopping bag. About a dozen children, ages five through fourteen, some in complete costumes, others in simple masks like ours, were gathered at the corner of Black and Chislett Streets as twilight descended. Together we swarmed from house to house, shouting "Trick or treat!"

People gasped at the assortment of goblins who lurked in the light and shadow of their porch lights, and they filled our bags with candy bars, candied apples, popcorn balls, and Indian corn. Twice my brothers and I ran home to empty our bags and to return to the fray. As we ran to rejoin our small horde of children, my mask was hot with breath, and the autumn air chilled my face. I peered out from behind foreign eyes as I cut through the night that was illuminated by the glow of streetlamps and windows.

When the evening's foraging had ended, Mayer, Jay, and I sat at the kitchen table with our parents looking on, staring in wonder at our huge mounds of candy, the gifts of strangers. We had heard of Mardi Gras in France, but we had never participated. Once, when we first arrived in Paris from Poland, when Mayer was eight, my mother had taken him to a Purim party for refugees sponsored by the Rothschilds. She had sewn him a red Cossack costume for it. It was not long after his injury, and she wanted to make him feel special and cheer him up.

Mayer had come home from the party unenthusiastic and handed me the large cellophane bag of candy he had received. He didn't like sweets. Now Mayer sat in front of his mountain of booty and shook his head in disbelief. He told Jay and me to pick what we wanted from his pile and divide the rest between us.

"Can you understand this?" he said. He turned to my mother, who was looking on pensively, and he guessed at her thoughts. "In Russia, did you ever think we could come to such a day?" He laughed.

My mother smiled through pursed lips and sad eyes. Every happy occasion evoked twinges of sadness in her. She bent her head and turned away briefly, as if trying to shake some unwanted image from before her eyes. *"Ich vinsh ach aldes gits. Chapt aran mit bayed hent,"* she said with forced cheer. "I wish you all that's good. Grab it with both hands."

CHAPTER 5

◆ ◆ ◆ ◆ ◆ ◆

Lubavitch Winter

One evening toward late November, when we had been in Pittsburgh fewer than two months, my brothers and I were returning home from exploring the less familiar parts of our new neighborhood. It was beginning to get dark early. We had tramped through the golf course and also down scruffier streets and alleys on the other side of Negley Avenue. The air was crisp and pungent with the smell of decomposing leaves on the lawns and in the gutters. As we rounded the corner of Black Street, my brothers talked animatedly. Faint vapor trails danced around their mouths, heralding the colder weather to come. But we were warm in our new matching heavy blue jackets that would serves us through this winter and likely the next.

"School isn't bad here," Jay suggested. "They go rather slowly, though. I think they're at a level that's a year behind the schools in France. They play a lot and waste so much time on things that aren't important. But the kids are nice, and the teacher lets them talk while they're working."

"I think they're two years behind the schools in France," Mayer offered. "I don't know how they can compete with Europe," he fretted, dangling on the edge of loyalty to his new country. Then his face brightened. "But it's nice to have girls in your class. That sure is better than in France."

"And how!" Jay exclaimed.

They chuckled and elbowed each other and gave each other knowing looks.

Jay turned to me with a leering look. "And you, Michael, you have a little girlfriend, I bet."

"Leave me alone," I blurted, my eyes cast down to the ground. I could feel my face blushing.

Jay and Mayer roared and elbowed each other again as they nodded in agreement about my romantic interests. Then they grew quiet. I was relieved that they would not go too far in their teasing.

"Halloween was great," Jay reflected, as we drew closer to the house.

"If they do this for Halloween, what do they do for Christmas?" Mayer wondered aloud.

"There is another holiday ahead. Next week, I believe. Its name is Tangivin," Jay responded.

"Ah, yes. You're right," Mayer caught himself quickly, a bit upset that he had slipped in his awareness of the customs of his new homeland.

"I know that too, but what is Tangivin?" I asked.

Mayer and Jay shrugged. "I don't know," they said in unison. Then, immediately they both shouted out, "Philippine!" In a burst of laughter and excitement, they pointed index fingers at each other as each claimed to have said "Philippine" first and had won the French version of the game of Jinx.

Their voices suddenly dropped to a near whisper as we reached the gate to our house. The landlord of this two-family house had complained that we were too loud, and our parents had warned us that he could kick us out. We climbed the carpeted stairs to our second-floor apartment with exaggeratedly soft steps. Mayer gave me a cross look as, no matter how I tried, I still clomped with each footfall.

"*Ot zenen zeh! (Here they are!)*" our father said as we reach the landing. He grinned at us as we poured into the kitchen. Curiously, he wore a yarmulke as he stood behind the table with a man we've never seen. The stranger's name was Lazar. Under his yarmulke he had red hair, and he had red *payos* behind his ears. A scraggly tuft of red beard covered his chin. He was thin and intense. He smiled at us with piercing eyes that seem to hold a surprise that I was hesitant to discover. Our mother stood in the corner, her lips pursed, her arms folded under her breasts. Her eyes darted from one to another of her sons, but she said nothing. I could usually read her face, but this day her thoughts were well hidden.

"Here, put on these *capelech*," Father said, handing each one of us a yarmulke.

Lazar handed my brothers and me each an *arbah kanfos*, the oblong garment with *tsitsis*, or fringes, at each corner. "Jewish boys wear these," he said in Yiddish, beaming with pride. Then he laughed and his eyes sparkled.

"They know, they know!" my father said, nodding and smiling.

We knew what the *arbah kanfos* were. In Paris, our *melamed* had made us say the *modeh ani*, wash *neygl vasser*, put on the *arbah kanfos* over our shirts, and bless and kiss the *tsitsis* before each lesson. We now put them on compliantly for Lazar.

"*Ch'hob giteh nayes far ach, (I have good news for you,)*" my father laughed happily. "Tomorrow morning you're all starting yeshiva!"

I stared at my father, trying to understand the meaning of his words, trying to discern from the yarmulke on his head, which he had never before worn in the house, trying to divine from his darting, not-quite-embarrassed eyes whether he thought he was doing us a kindness with this rare and unwelcome intersession in our daily lives. I barely knew what a yeshiva was. The idea of going to one had not been discussed with us before, and it would not be discussed now.

My brothers and I stood silently, looking blankly at each other, each with our own unspoken thoughts. For myself, I imagined what my classmates would think when I no longer appeared at the Rogers School. What would the teacher do with the pencils and the notebook in my desk? Would my classmates be hurt that I had just left without a goodbye? Would they think I really didn't like them? The truth was that I had begun to feel welcome and almost comfortable, and I had begun to imagine that I might one day feel I really belonged. I pictured my class going on, with me not there, a palpable void in the room.

The next morning, instead of jumping the fence into the school-yard, greeting our lively classmates, we waited for a large yellow school bus to pick us up. It was a novelty at least. We had never been in one before. Inside, it was less interesting than I had imagined. It was drab and dirty. I was assaulted by the acrid smell of leather mixed with rotting food. As the bus took off with a jolt, I was thrust into one of its flat, Spartan seats. The bus went through its paces of lurches and stops, and I became lightheaded and nauseous as exhaust fumes pervaded the back of the bus. We were the first passengers on what was to be an hour-long ride of stops, starts, and fast turns as we picked up other boys on our way to the Lubavitcher Yeshiva. None of the other boys seemed to notice us as they boarded and took their seats. Most didn't even acknowledge each other during the monotonous journey.

The school itself was in a dilapidated mansion-type building. Lazar was there to greet us the first day, but the last we saw of him was when he escorted us to our classrooms. I was placed in a Chumash, or Bible class, with seven other boys my age, where I was to spend my mornings. Secular class was to be held in the afternoons. The other pupils were already in their desk chairs when I was brought into the small, drab, gray room. They resembled the children at the Rogers School, except they were all boys. They also wore the same kind of flannel shirts and corduroy pants, but they all wore yarmulkes. Some had *tsitsis* protruding over their belts. A couple of them had long *payos* that dangled from their otherwise closely cropped heads. The teacher, a young man with a dark beard and tired eyes, a rumpled suit, and a wide-brimmed hat, welcomed me by assigning me a seat and handing me a book opened to the page being studied. The boys looked at me with blank expressions, as they waited for the rabbi to continue with the lesson. The instruction was rather straightforward and dry. The teacher stroked his beard and listened to the boys take turns reciting and translating passages from Leviticus. Some read in a flat, neutral manner, while others rocked to the rhythm of their singsong recitations.

The morning droned by slowly. It was afternoon when we were dismissed, and the other boys streamed out of the room. Some rushed to the yard, which was no more than a dusty, patchy lawn in back of the building. Others headed to the lunchroom. I followed with paper sack in hand. The lunchroom was a dingy space in the basement with long tables covered with shiny red oilcloth.

"Some of the boys like to play in the yard first before eating their lunch. Would you like to join them?" the rabbi asked, mistaking my quietness for shyness.

I kept my head down and shook my head no.

"Then come have lunch with the other boys in the class. You'll get to know them. It won't take long. You'll see. You'll like them."

I nodded in agreement and sat at a table with my classmates, my eyes still averted.

The rabbi sighed. "Do you have dessert?" he asked.

"No," I answered.

"Have a candy bar on me," he said, pointing to a display.

"No thank you," I responded.

"Have one. *Sheym zich nisht, (Don't be ashamed,)*" the rabbi encouraged.

"I don't know which one I would like," I answered.

"Just pick any one."

I picked a candy bar to be polite.

The other boys were loud and raucous and ignored me, which was just as well. I had no curiosity about them. What I was thinking is that I would no longer be able to hop the schoolyard fence and eat lunch at home in our little kitchen with my mother and my brothers. Mayer and Jay had a different lunch shift, so I would not see them until the long bus ride home. I finished my sandwich and washed it down with water. Then I discovered that I didn't like my Clark Bar. From the first bite, it was a mixture of incongruous flavors and textures that left a confused taste in my mouth.

The yeshiva was a mixture of incongruous feelings for me. Every morning we studied prayers and Chumash. The time droned on. I struggled to keep up with the lessons. I tried to feel some enthusiasm. *This is what a Jewish boy needs to know,* I kept telling myself. But my Hebrew reading was poor. I had had so little practice of what I had only begun to learn in Paris. I stumbled over almost every word. I struggled to translate Hebrew words, whose meaning I didn't know, into English, which I was just learning. I was confused and bewildered. I began to feel myself resist all of it. But some things evoked such an air of mystery that they drew me in. I was captivated by the prayers: *Thank you, God, for making the sun rise every morning. Thank you, God, for not making me a heathen. Thank you, God, for not making me a woman.*

In the afternoons, we had "English." All secular subjects were lumped under that name by the boys. Unlike the religious classes, in which there were only a small number of boys, placed by age and knowledge, many students of varying ages and grade levels were packed in one large classroom for "English." We sat in rows of bolted-down desks, each of the four rows constituting a different grade level. The size and apathy of the students seemed to increase with each row, as I looked from the compliant third graders to the indifferent sixth graders on the other side of the room.

Every day, the teacher, a small, energetic elderly woman who was clearly not Hasidic, greeted the students with a cheerful expression and the day's assignments that she had neatly written in four columns on the blackboard. She called me by my first name. None of the other teachers or boys here did so. I had gotten to like this more personal appellation used by my teacher and the children at the Rogers School. So, I liked her.

This singular woman teacher at the yeshiva, who struck me as having the frailty and vivaciousness of a small bird, began each afternoon with renewed hope as she attempted to engage the boys. And no matter how difficult that was, she usually maintained her composure. I marveled at her effort to give three rows of students independent work as she instructed the fourth row. But she was usually unsuccessful. A number of the boys, especially the older ones in sixth grade, seemed to ignore her much of the time. They made jokes, talked across the room, and shot spitballs. Some boys brazenly opened their Hebrew notebooks to do their religious homework rather than classwork. The noise level rose as the afternoon progressed.

Sometimes the teacher attempted a lesson with the entire class. On one particular day, she tried to teach a poem. As she read, her chest heaved with feeling. She had a faint smile, and her eyes were hopeful.

The younger boys listened with curiosity, but the sixth graders started to make fun and throw the entire class into fits of laughter. The teacher came close to tears. To the cheers of the older boys, she turned her back to the class and walked out of the room.

Several minutes later, one of the rabbis entered the room. The din turned immediately to hushed silence. With a cross look, the rabbi lifted a finger in the air and admonished, *"Derech Eretz!"* (Respect!) He stared around the room at the suddenly chastened boys before leaving dramatically. The teacher, who was waiting in the hall, returned sheepishly. She looked embarrassed as she began to speak. We did not go back to the poetry. Instead, we did seat work in arithmetic. This was a safe subject; most of the boys were interested in math instruction. The class remained quiet and attentive to their work for the remainder of the class.

Within a few days, the noise level and contempt in the class returned to their old levels. I felt sorry for the teacher. I thought of the other gray-haired woman who had been my teacher at the Rogers School, how calmly she would talk and suggest, and how eagerly the class followed her directions. One particularly rowdy afternoon in "English," I turned to a gentle fourth grader who sat across from me. I tapped him on the shoulder to get his attention above the roar.

"Why are they like this?" I asked him.

"They don't think this is important," he replied. "The school only has 'English' because they have to. It's the law."

◆ ◆ ◆

Within a month of starting yeshiva, we moved. Mercifully, it was literally down the block from where we were living. Our landlord had become angrier and more threatening every day. Our parents could no longer convince my brothers and me that we were the cause of his complaints about the noise. The truth was that the conflicts between my parents that had initially subsided with the diversion of being in a new country had resumed full force.

On one such occasion, my mother started with determination, "You've got to find work!"

"Haybst shoyn vidern un? (You're starting again?)" my father asked rhetorically, half dismissing her.

"You can't sleep all day or disappear till all hours!" she retorted, her voice rising sharply.

"What do you think I do when I'm not here?" my father protested, his voice rising a notch.

"You've found some other good-for-nothings to play cards with again. You promised me before we left for America that you would stop your card playing!" she screamed.

"I'm out all day looking for work!" my father responded, his voice rising almost to the threshold of screaming.

"What was wrong with the job HIAS got you last week?" my mother demanded. "It paid good money. How long can we stay beggars taking charity? That was supposed to end when we left Paris."

"I couldn't last on that job. I was there two days, and it exhausted me."

"You didn't even try!" she accused.

"They had me climbing on scaffolding high in the air, in the wind. Do you know what that's like? I can paint signs, but not on that kind of platform. I'm not a young man anymore. That work would kill me," he now shouted as he pranced from one foot to the other, while my mother shook her head, not listening. She was ready to resume her litany.

"Before we left for America, you gave me your solemn word— *'T'kias kaf*—that you wouldn't play cards anymore. 'In America, people don't play cards in the cafes,' you said. 'I'll find real work,' you said."

"What am I supposed to do, stand around wringing my hands?" he thundered. Then, in the moment of silence that followed, his voice grew calm and his eyes saddened. "What kind of work can I get here in Pittsburgh? I can't speak the language. They called me 'Hey, Charlie!' I didn't know what they wanted from me when they talked to me. I'm fifty-seven years old. I'm too old to balance on scaffolds, and there's no place here for a Yiddish writer. In New York, maybe I could find work. But they brought us to this forsaken desert!"

Then my mother turned her back on my father and started crying.

My father sighed. Composing himself, he left the room, his Yiddish newspaper under his arm.

◆ ◆ ◆

The new apartment my father found for us was in a large old house that had a deep front yard and a huge backyard. The house had a covered front porch that ran the length of the facade and was equipped with awnings, wooden rockers, and a porch swing. The house itself wasn't pristine and precious like the previous one, but it was so much more comfortable and informal. The landlady lived on the first floor, and we occupied the second. We had a large kitchen and bath, and the rooms were spacious. The three wide living room windows had pretty stained-glass inserts. All the rooms were off a central landing, with no front door to mark off our apartment. The landlady's son and daughter-in-law had to walk through our landing to get to their attic apartment, which also had no front door. This arrangement didn't bother me or anyone else. After all, we all used the entry foyer of the house, which opened into the owner's living room on the left and revealed her kitchen for all of us to see beyond the staircase.

There was such a relaxed feeling about the house. Mrs. Federman, the landlady, was an old woman whose gray hair was done up in a tight bun. She spent much of her time watching television through horn-rimmed glasses while she smoked Raleigh's. Her gouty legs and heavy shoes were propped up on the couch that only she occupied. But there was another couch and an easy chair in her living room, and she invited us to join her. Her apartment soon became an extension of ours, at least to me. We didn't have a television at all, and hers was the latest model large-screen console. I watched anything she watched, but she also let me change the channels when her favorite shows weren't on. She was very tolerant. She never worried about my breaking anything, even her two-year-old granddaughter's hobbyhorse, which I liked to rock on, and which at my age of eight I was too big to ride.

Many times, I galloped down the stairs, stomped down the hall, and slammed her kitchen door on my way out to the backyard. My mother scolded me for the noise and commotion, but Mrs. Federman calmed her. "He's only a child," she said gently.

I learned a lot of English watching TV shows with Mrs. Federman. One show in particular puzzled me with its peculiarity. "Buzz and Bill" had a daily afternoon program called *The Buzz and Bill Show* with patter that seemed to have a humorous bent, although I usually didn't get it. The two light-haired young men always wore identical light-colored suits, and they featured a discordant kind of music they called jazz, which was also puzzling. For an entire week, after they had performed a particularly rhythmic and repetitive song and dance routine, I asked everyone I knew what "crazy, man, crazy" meant. I could get no satisfactory explanation and decided that in America some words changed meaning depending on how people used them. *I had better be careful with English words,* I thought.

Buzz and Bill were fond of saying that their program came to us from Pittsburgh, where the Ohio, Allegheny, and Monongahela Rivers meet. That was nice to know, and I wondered where they met and what they looked like. Something else they said actually shocked me. They were "comin' to you from just north of the Mason-Dixon Line." I had learned at the Rogers School that this was the line that divided the South from the North, and the states that used to have slavery from those that did not. And it was clear, even without the teacher saying it, that slavery was cruel and evil. In our home, we remembered our own slavery in ancient Egypt. And my father had one day commented that slavery was America's biggest shame. I hadn't known that we were so close to that border. The proximity made me uncomfortable. Why would Buzz and Bill mention being close to the Mason-Dixon Line? Were they proud of this? If they weren't, why weren't they ashamed enough not to mention it? *Maybe it has something to do with the music,* I thought, giving the jovial characters the benefit of the doubt.

The thought that America had once had slavery, and not so long ago at that, made me uncomfortable. What kind of place was this new country I was growing loyal to? At the Rogers School, the white and black students seemed to congregate in separate crowds. An assembly that had been called for the entire school the first week I was there hinted at things unsaid. I sat next to Marvin in the auditorium. He translated the gist of the speeches for me into Yiddish.

Three black youths, who looked too old to be in the school, the principal, and two other official-looking men sat on the stage. The young men were being honored for saving the life of a baby. They had been walking by a house when they had noticed smoke coming from it. They rang the fire alarm and then ran into the building to see if anyone was inside. They had found the infant in its crib and carried it out to safety. Now the boys were being given awards for heroism. At one point, the entire auditorium broke out in laughter when one of the boys answered a question. I turned to Marvin for an explanation.

"He said the flames hadn't reached the child because it had wet itself. That's why everybody laughed," Marvin responded.

As my class lined up to leave the auditorium, I thought about the implausibility of the statement about the wet baby. I dismissed it as an embellishment. But the rest impressed me. These boys had put their lives in danger to rescue a child. They were heroes. Before coming to America, I had seen black people only two or three times before, while walking in the streets or riding in the Metro of Paris with my mother. They were tall, imposing, and mysterious to me, with their strong dark faces, full sensuous lips, and brilliant white eyes and teeth. I had heard Yiddish poems that had described them in warm and exotic terms. It was clear that here in America many whites did not share such a view. Yet the school was trying to remedy that. I did not lose faith in the America that had led my father to kiss the ground after we had disembarked at Pier 86 in New York a month earlier.

In the late afternoons before dinner, I watched *Captain Video* and cartoons, but I liked some of the evening shows the best. While my father fell asleep upstairs reading his newspaper, my mother, my brothers, and I sat with Mrs. Federman in her softly lit living room quietly watching *Life Begins at Eighty*, *Your Hit Parade*, *Loretta Young*, and *Private Secretary*.

Before I started yeshiva, I would sometimes go over to Marvin's house after school. He loved *Howdy Doody*. He waited excitedly for it to come on, and when it did, he ignored me almost entirely. I couldn't understand why anyone over the age of three would like this show. It was embarrassingly dumb to me, and it quickly led to my not going over to Marvin's. When I was switched to yeshiva, I came home too late to see him in the afternoons. We weren't really friends, anyway. *He just helped me out in school because the teacher asked him to,* I told myself.

◆ ◆ ◆

I tried consciously to get used to the ride home from yeshiva, but it made me dizzy every day. I had to sit in the back of the school bus at the end of the school day because I was the last one to get on and the front seats were taken. The bus bounced higher, the curves were more jolting, and the fumes were more visible and caustic in the back.

One day in late January, as the bus lurched and bounced, my body revolted. My head began to spin. I gripped the steel bar above the seat in front of me. It was cold and stinging, and I shuddered with a chill. I bent over as my stomach roiled. Then my mouth hit the bar as the bus hit a bump. I felt sharp pain in my teeth, and my lip immediately puffed up. The acrid taste of the metal in my mouth put me over the edge, and I vomited all over my pants, my shoes, and the floor of the bus. The driver must have heard me retch because he made an unhappy-sounding comment and yelled back at me, asking if I was alright. But he didn't stop. The boys who were still on the bus immediately moved away from me. Mayer, who always sat in the front with Jay, came to get me. I sat between my older brothers as they talked.

"It gets worse every day," Mayer said in French, so no one would understand him.

"This is not a school. It's a waste of time," Jay agreed.

"We have to get out of there. I didn't come to America for this," Mayer added, holding me around the shoulder.

CHAPTER 6

◆ ◆ ◆ ◆ ◆ ◆

Fate and Choice

The Sunday after visiting Mayer at Fort Dix, I rode my bike down the steep hill from Broadway to Riverside Drive. I turned right and pedaled uptown along the tree-lined street, the pungent scent of the damp sycamore bark filling my nostrils.

The cemetery wall at 153rd Street marked the southern border of Washington Heights. Most of my school colleagues lived there, mainly around 181st Street, near the school and synagogue. I rode up the Drive all the way to the new tennis courts at 165th Street. Young men and women, who might have been doctors and nurses from the nearby Columbia Presbyterian Hospital, were dressed in white outfits and were prancing and swatting balls with their rackets. Little children with pink faces and identical outfits cantered in circles on the adjoining grassy knoll and were being photographed by their father who was dressed in a plaid button-down shirt and Ivy League pants. Two older women, dressed in light cotton summer dresses, their gray-streaked hair tightly pinned, sat on a bench and talked politely in German.

This is where I turned around. I could go no further. Here Riverside Drive ended at the Henry Hudson Parkway. To ride up all the way to my yeshiva required turning up 165th Street, fighting the sharp cobble-stoned incline, then pedaling against a continuous succession of hills. I had neither the stamina nor the will to reach that destination, although I wondered what my classmates were doing with their summer vacation. During the school year I spent almost ten hours a day with them, but in the summer, they vanished from my life. I did not matter to them, and they did not matter to me.

I rode back down Riverside Drive. The stretch between 153rd Street and 135th Street was my territory. The benches along the Drive here were always more deserted than those further uptown or downtown. This hadn't always been so. When we first moved into our neighborhood, there were still white people living between the west side of Broadway and Riverside. They congregated on the benches to take in a bit of gossip and catch the cool breezes off the water. On hot summer nights, the crowds were as thick and noisy as flocks of pigeons. The bench-sitters were mostly old, but there were some children who clung to their parents or ran around the trees. The light from the streetlamps and the ice cream trucks combined with the lights from Palisades Park across the river and lent a subdued carnival atmosphere.

No longer. Now, this part of the Drive was mostly desolate. The benches were always empty. An old black man, wearing a herringbone coat and cap more appropriate for a cooler season, walked slowly along, keeping silent counsel with a graying dog. Three boys of assorted sizes moved at a lively pace along the shaded sidewalk. The one with the basketball talked animatedly, turning and dribbling, as the trio bopped toward the stairs at 148th Street that led down to the playground. It was a long way down and back up. They would walk more slowly on the way back up from the playground.

You had to negotiate two long and steep sets of stairs, cross the trestle over the train tracks, and traverse a tunnel under the Westside Highway to get to the playground, ball fields, and handball walls along the river. If you clambered along the rocky embankment at the edge of the water, you could get to the rotting remains of the wooden piers. Five years before, when I first moved here, men and boys still cast their fishing lines and threw out their crab traps on the brown, splintered piers, which smelled of pitch and oozed tar in the sun. Now the docks were closed off. Jay sometimes came with me to the playground when I was younger, but now, when I went, it was mostly by myself. When I wandered down to the river these days, it was mainly to feel myself against the familiar wind.

In the springtime, when I was eleven and twelve, I would save up twenty-five cents to buy a paper kite and a spool of string at Manny's, and I would join an assortment of adults and children alongside the grassy square between the playground and the handball walls. It was barely a trick to launch our kites. There was usually a strong and steady breeze in March and April. All you had to do was hold the kite against the wind and pay out the line slowly, and the paper diamond, with its rag tail whipping around, champed at the bit and rose steadily into the sky against the backdrop of faraway buildings, high on Riverside Drive.

Sometimes in those days I used to watch the older boys and young men in their sneakers playing half-court basketball. As I stood behind the basket, one of them would occasionally motion to me to join them. I didn't realize that I had "next" by virtue of standing in that particular spot. It was an oddly freeing feeling, racing around the rectangle of play. Scuffing and scraping my leather shoes on the asphalt, a young white boy in a yarmulke, hovering close to the ground, passing the ball to tall, young black men. They passed me the ball and let me shoot when I was open, even though they knew I would miss the shot. But I was good at stealing the ball on a pass or a dribble. I could never read the emotions on their faces, but they called me "Hands."

When we had moved into our new and larger apartment on the same floor of our building, in the fall after my bar mitzvah, my brothers and I found a samurai sword, several soapstone vases, and two framed Japanese prints. The sharply tailored men who had regularly visited their parents who had lived there had recently moved their mother into a nursing home after their father had died. They must have been in the Pacific Theater during the war. We also found several old tennis rackets. The gut strings of the rackets had popped in several places, but they were still good for hitting balls against the handball walls by the river.

One blustery late winter day, just a few months earlier, as I was hitting balls against the wall, a well-dressed man in a brimmed hat and black coat got out of his car in the parking lot and brought his little boy, not much more than a toddler, over to the handball court. He had obviously gotten off the highway to let the child out of the car so he could run around a bit in the chill air. The child, a beautiful boy with a shiny brown face and bright white eyes, dressed in a navy cap with flaps tied beneath his chin, a matching winter jacket, and baby jodhpurs, kept running after the ball as I hit it, making it impossible to play. So, I began throwing the ball to him. He squealed as he ran after it and threw it wildly at me.

The man never smiled, but before he left, he thanked me for playing with his son. "I'm a minister," he said.

I nodded. It was awkward, almost embarrassing that he felt he had to explain to me who he was, that it was safe that he was talking to me. "I have a racket in the trunk of my car that's a little better than the one you're playing with that you can have." We walked over to his car. He opened the trunk and gave me another wooden racket. "Well, I thought it was in better condition," he said. His license plate read Alabama. I knew he felt he had to give me something for playing with his son, so I took the racket.

As I now rode my bicycle along the Drive, I thought of the man in the black coat and hat, standing and watching his little boy as the wind carried the ball. Somehow this image was tied to a jarring experience I had recently had. I had been delivering groceries on Friday afternoons to an old, gaunt woman who lived by herself in a large apartment on Riverside and 145th Street. I had to walk slowly behind her as we trekked from the supermarket to her building. She held the heavy entry door as I lifted the cart up the steps into the lobby. When we entered her apartment, she crumpled into her kitchen chair as usual. But this time, she just sat there, staring at me intensely as I unloaded the brown paper sacks onto the table. I had looked at her, wondering if I had done something wrong.

"You know," she said slowly, deliberately, and with an unfathomable expression. "My grandmother was a slave."

I did not know what to say. It was a profound shock. I could only feel grief for her. After a long silence between us, she said, "I'm sorry. I'm keeping you," and she handed me my quarter tip from her purse.

After the viaduct that ended at about 130th Street, I turned right, down the sloping path that led into Riverside Park. The park above 125th Street was scruffy and unkempt, designed for hard play with its baseball fields, playgrounds, and handball walls. The area I now rode through was more genteel, designed for quiet activities with its sloping lawns and meandering walks. Along its tree-lined promenades, from the 90s all the way down to 72nd Street, there were rows of ornamental cherry and apple trees that bloomed in a blinding pink-and-white profusion that overwhelmed the senses in the spring.

There were few people out this morning. A student type with a crew cut sat under a tree with a book. A young couple in matching white socks and penny loafers strode hand in hand along the promenade. She wore a yellow sweater and a blue plaid skirt. Her silken auburn hair quickened my pulse. She looked like one of the perfect girls on the back cover of *Scholastic Magazine*. "Beautiful hair, Breck." I always felt like I was entering a different country when I walked or rode here, half expecting that someone would ask me what I was doing here.

One recent Saturday, Aaron, my one friend in yeshiva, and I had walked down the Drive from his house at 153rd Street to 120th Street. He too noted the difference in the people in this area as we walked along the shaded sidewalk and stared at the well-dressed crowd that thronged the benches. We were dressed in our Sabbath suits, and maybe this emboldened Aaron.

"I'd really like to find out about these people. Some of them are professors from Columbia University. Some of the people who live in the big buildings here are rich. They have apartments of seven or eight rooms and still have servants."

"Get outta here!" I said, not believing him.

Aaron was always saying these incredible things that couldn't be true. He lived in a one-bedroom apartment with his parents, his younger brother, and his grandmother. What made me most uncomfortable was that he envied people. He acted like an outsider, always proverbially knocking at doors and looking through windows.

"You never believe me, but I know I'm right. Let's find out about these people. We'll pretend we're from our school newspaper and say we're interviewing people for an article, so we can talk to them," he urged.

Aaron was always proposing doing things that embarrassed me or at least made me uncomfortable. "I'd rather not," I said.

"Oh, come on. What can they do to us?" he responded.

"Why don't you just go up to them without your cockamamie newspaper story if you want to talk to them so much?" I retorted.

"Nah! Why would they talk to us then?" he argued. Then he added, "You've got to be the one to talk to them. You're good with people."

"You come up with these harebrained ideas, and you make me carry them out," I protested. "What do you want to ask them anyway?"

"Oh, please," he pleaded. "You start and I'll jump in," he promised.

We were beyond the age when he could persuade me with the promise of a Three Musketeers bar or Potato Stix as he did when we were younger. So, without answering my question, he took my arm by the elbow and boldly turned me toward a man sitting on a bench. He was an older gentleman, dressed in a tweed jacket, a plaid shirt, and a bowtie. His long, craggy face was crowned by a wave of salt-and-pepper hair that swept across his forehead. The man lifted his gaze from his *New Yorker* as we approached him. With gray eyes he looked at us through round, gold-rimmed glasses.

"Pardon me, sir," I said in my best Mike Wallace. "We write for our school newspaper, and we're doing a story about people who live in the Columbia area. Would you mind if we interview you?"

"Not at all," he responded. He looked a little amused as he put down his magazine.

"Have you lived here long?" I asked, not knowing what I would ask next. Aaron stood behind me. I hoped he would have an idea.

"A number of years," he responded, waiting for the follow-up.

"And do you like it here?" I continued, after a pause in which Aaron had said nothing.

"Very much. I came here from Iowa, if you know where that is. This was quite a change. I teach anthropology at the college," he said, motioning toward Broadway and Columbia.

"Anthropology. That's very interesting," I said. I was about to ask him what that was when Aaron shot out from behind me and squared to face the professor.

"And did it take you long to feel you belonged here?" he blurted out with great force of urgency.

"Not really," answered the professor, taken a bit by surprise. "You see, I was welcomed into the intellectual community, you might say. It doesn't have geographical boundaries. And there are other ways you can join a community." He looked hard into Aaron's eyes. "When President Eisenhower became president of Columbia back in 1946, he signaled his intention to be part of the community by attending services at Riverside Church over there." The professor said pointedly, "You boys must understand that. You study Bible and Talmud and pray with your fellow congregants. You might say that you have your intellectual and spiritual and social communities all in the same group. In that way, you belong to a triply close community, don't you?"

"I guess so," responded Aaron, the corners of his mouth down-turned and bitter. His face could never hide his emotions.

"But you don't have to be part of only one community," the man on the bench continued. "You can sample all of those around you. For instance, Riverside Church there has an organ recital on Saturday after-noons at three o'clock. Everyone is welcome. You might go. They are quite wonderful."

"I don't think we're supposed to go into a church," Aaron responded.

"He was a smart guy," Aaron said after we left the man to his *New Yorker*. "Nice, too. He knew we weren't school reporters, and he talked to us anyway."

❖ ❖ ❖

I turned the key in the door and maneuvered my bicycle into the apartment. My mother sat at the kitchen table, her arms folded about her, leaning on both elbows. She stared at nothing in particular as she hummed softly to herself. She startled when I entered the room.

"Did you have breakfast?" she asked. "Jay is still sleeping."

"When did he come in? I must have been asleep."

"You fell asleep in the chair," she laughed. "I couldn't wake you, so I carried you into your bed, just like when you were little."

"You carried me?" I asked, disturbed and incredulous. I was bigger than she was. When she was out in public, at five-foot-six, even taller with her long, dark hair done up in a swirl and just a touch of the reddest lipstick, in her high heels, she looked strong, youthful, and radiant. Her exuberance was contagious when she laughed out loud. But when I intruded upon her in her private moments, especially when she sat at the kitchen table, with only her thoughts for company, at age thirty-nine, she looked old and broken. She was fond of saying, "My children are growing older, and I'm growing old."

"Do you want to go back into traction?" I admonished her.

She laughed shyly and waved my concern away with her hand. "I've carried heavier loads than you." Her eyes began to look off somewhere.

"I'll have a roll with butter," I said quickly, although I had already eaten breakfast.

She practically leapt from her chair to the breadbox. She rarely did anything halfway. I was relieved that she had not responded to my inadvertent lead about the traction, and I wanted to divert her from thinking about the heavy loads she had carried. Any stray word or phrase might be a land mine that could launch her into reveries and stories about the past. An expression or incident would catch her up, and she would flash on a memory. Then, almost unwittingly, she would make a comment. "My father used to say that . . ." or "You should have seen my brother Simcha . . . " or "My mother was stricter than my father." And, if she found a willing audience, she began in earnest with, "Before the war . . ." or, "In Russia . . ."

I loved my mother's stories. To me, they were epics in black and white about a time in a time warp. It had existed just a moment ago, yet it had disappeared eons before I was born. With a few words and the soft modulation of her voice, my mother could sweep me into the images of her life. But her stories were dangerous. I had to struggle with myself to resist them. They were like a drug. I wanted to be sucked into their vortex, no matter how often I'd heard them before. But I had to keep her away from them, for her sake, for all our sakes.

"Good morning, everyone," Jay announced in a cheerful lilt. Bare-chested and barefoot, and in his chinos, he walked regally into the kitchen. He had had a good night's rest. "And how is the sack of potatoes this morning?" he addressed me.

"You were there? Why did you let her carry me in?" I accused him. "Why didn't you shake me or slap me awake?"

"Believe me, I wanted to give you a good smack, but Mom wouldn't let me," he said with a smirk.

My mother placed a plate with a buttered roll on it in front of me. "Here you are, my little sack of potatoes," she said, grinning as she caressed my face.

"Actually, you looked more like a hulking carcass," Jay demurred as he poured himself a cup of coffee from the pot on the stove.

"Don't say that!" my mother said in a strained voice. "*Meh tur nisht zugn aza zach, (It's forbidden to say such a thing).*"

Jay reconsidered, to please her. "Alright. You looked so cute when she carried you in her arms like a baby." He smiled disingenuously. Then his perplexed eyes darted from my mother to me. "I offered to pick you up, but she wouldn't let me."

"You looked just like a baby, with your pouting mouth and your red cheeks. You were having a bad dream. *Vayn nisht, (don't cry),*" my mother smiled pityingly. She believed in the power of revelation in dreams, but she did not ask if I remembered mine, which I rarely did.

"You're still the baby in the family," Jay said, teasing. "You were the baby in your family, too, weren't you, Mom? Did your mother carry you to bed when you were fourteen?"

"My mother . . . My mother . . ." Mom's face trailed off, and her eyes glazed over.

Jay realized too late that he had done it, that he had sent her back. His face turned sullen. He took out two eggs from the refrigerator and smashed them into a bowl. He began to whip them furiously.

"By the time I was born, she was so tired," my mother began, suddenly haggard, not facing either Jay or me. "She was my father's second wife. He was a widower, and she raised my father's three older children. I was the sixth child born to my mother, and she was no longer young. We were very poor. There was so little she could find joy in. She didn't want much for herself, but she couldn't dress me properly, and I was her last child. My father was a tailor, but there usually wasn't enough money for the cloth. She didn't ask my father for anything, and he didn't say a word. What could he say? She wanted to be good, but she rarely found the strength to say a kind word to me. She always had a hard expression, not because she was hard, but because she was so disappointed in life. Only before Passover did she liven up. It gave her hope, I think, to see the world waking up. I loved her very much."

My mother turned to look at Jay, then at me. Jay had begun whistling softly, as the eggs popped and sizzled in the frying pan. The bite of soft roll stuck in my throat as I tried to swallow. We turned to face our mother. She looked small and vulnerable. She raised her eyebrows and smiled through pursed lips. She sensed the tension, and she was embarrassed.

"Oh, but she wanted the best for me, and so did my father," she continued, trying to be positive. "I was the only one to finish school to the eighth grade. When I was born, Poland was free, and I was so proud to learn in a Polish school. And I went to Beis Yankev, too, to learn what a Jewish girl should know. And after, I went to the Zionist program to learn modern Hebrew. None of my brothers and sisters had that." She was trying the best she could to lighten the moment.

"So, you were spoiled, like little Michael here," Jay chimed in, relieved.

"Yes, I was spoiled. Like Michael." She laughed, her eyes moist and distant.

❖ ❖ ❖

My mother told me I was born with a cowl of skin covering my head. That covering, a God-given yarmulke, was a sign of good luck among Jews. And I always considered myself the lucky brother. It seemed a given to all of us that Mayer and Jay would struggle but that I wouldn't.

They had lived through the hardships of the war. I had not. They were each scarred by injury. I was not. They had spent years in orphanages, away from our father and mother. I had not. Until my brothers returned from Brunoy, I felt almost like an only child. In fact, I had my mother practically to myself until then.

When I was just two, we were in Poland, and my mother and I spent the summer in the country village of Tuszyn-Las. My brothers had been sent away somewhere, while my father came from Lodz at what seemed like unpredictable intervals. We had a sparsely furnished room, with a soft bed that I shared with my mother, even when my father came to join us. It was a small room but brightly lit. When the sunlight came through the curtains, the walls took on a mint-green hue that I tasted with my eyes.

Most days, my mother packed a blanket and lunch, and we picnicked by the side of a field, under a tree. She spoon-fed me *smetana* from a jar, and the cool, creamy taste played on my tongue. She held strawberries by their stems, and their juice stained her fingertips red as I bit into the gold-flecked, crimson fruit. Her hair was pulled back and fell in curls, revealing the oval contour of her face, with its pale, penciled lips and fine, straight nose. Her hollow cheeks and curved eyebrows gave emphasis to her large, dark eyes. I studied the roundness of her eyelids and the upward sweep of her lashes as she sat on the blanket, sewing little buttons that looked like hats onto the green sweater she had just knit for me. She wore the blue dress I loved, the one with the gold and red medallions, which rose and fell with the breathing in her breast, and whose pleated skirt fanned out in front of her on the blanket as she worked.

Some days, we were joined by another young woman who had a daughter, who was also two. We were supposed to play together, but the little girl and I had little interest in each other. We hovered around our mothers as they talked on the blanket. One day, the women were lost in conversation. The little girl played with her mother's hair. The sun was high in the sky, and its strong light bounced off the leafy vegetation that was sprouting in rows in the pungent, loamy earth in the field.

I wasn't noticed when I wandered into the shade of the stand of trees behind the blanket. In only a few steps I traversed the little woods and found myself in a grassy clearing surrounded by brambles and more trees. *No one knows where I am,* I thought. *I should get back or they might leave without me.* But the clearing was inviting, with its tall grass that tickled my calves and knees, and with its buzz of flies that punctuated the stillness. As I began to walk, the spongy feel of the earth beneath my tread felt like the chest of some giant living thing. "With each adventurous step," it said to me, "you may walk on me. Don't worry; I will hold you up."

At the other edge of the clearing, I found a gravel pit. It was as wide as it was deep, which was about three times my height. *Should I climb down and see what it's like inside? I might not get out,* I thought. The giant had stopped talking. I sat at the edge of the hole and let myself down into it. The sand and gravel cascaded around my feet as I slid to the bottom, barely maintaining my balance. Gray sediment filled my sandals and reached the cuffs of my short socks. I looked up and traced the circumference of the pit with my eyes. I could see the disheveled stalks of grass congregating along the edge and the scraggly limbs of trees protruding their fingers into the blue sky.

I could not tell how long I had been down in the pit, but I was anxious to get out. I took a step and another, but each time I slid back down to the bottom, with streams of sand and stones running over my sandals. I repeated my attempts several times, each time with more force, but I only succeeded in bringing down more dust and gravel. After a few more futile efforts, my breathing grew heavy. I coughed from the dust. I had never exerted this much energy before, but I was still stuck. Maybe no one would find me. They would look for me but would not see me down here.

With desperate force I lunged into the embankment, clawing my fingers and my sandals into the gravel. My knees scraped on the grit, and my voice growled in my throat, as my fingers finally grabbed the grass at the rim of the pit, and I pulled myself out by clutching the hair of the mouth of the sleeping giant. I looked down at my adversary. His swirling mouth no longer moved.

I was surprised at how close the blanket was when I walked back from the clearing. My mother and her friend were still talking. "Look how dirty you got playing in the sand," my mother said when she saw me, and she brushed off the dust from my hands and legs. She was unaware of what had happened to me. On the walk home, I clutched her fingers tight.

At night, I slept securely in my mother's bed. But when I woke up too early in the morning, my mother brought me to the landlady next door and went back to bed. I watched the old woman do her housework. Sometimes, she would leave me to my own devices in the yard. It was surrounded by a masonry wall that had a tall, closed iron gate. I would scrape a stick along the ground, making ruts in the brown earth. Or I would chase the chickens, interrupting their pecking in the dirt, to hear their squawking and the rustling of their flapping wings.

One night, as I was falling asleep, my mother sitting next to me in the soft light, the door to the room opened. It was my father. My mother shot up from the bed. She hissed some angry words at him. He responded in whispered, pleading tones. The bed sank as he sat down on it. He had a faraway, cold, metallic smell about him. His large round hands reached out toward hers, but her white hand swatted his away. She hissed some more. He pleaded again. I didn't remember falling asleep when I woke up early in the morning. My mother was lying asleep, facing my sleeping father, with her back toward me. She woke when I stirred. She wordlessly put on her robe and took me and the clothes she had prepared for me to the landlady. Then she returned to the room and closed the door behind her.

I sat in the doorway of the large shed at the end of the yard. The sun glared down on the rust and black chickens that busily clucked and pecked the ground. Some chicks with yellow fuzz peeped and ran and scattered and regrouped in a repetitious cycle. The door to the house opened. With one hand, the old woman held her apron swollen with feed. She shut the door behind her. The hens swarmed around her, pecking at each other to get closer, squawking in anticipation. With a sweep of her hand, she sprayed handful after handful of grain into the yard as hens, yellow feet racing and red-crested heads bobbing, fanned outward toward the scattered meal. A few brazen young birds took brief flight and tried to land on the diminished stores in the old woman's apron. She smacked them away, and they fell on the mottled backs of other birds that were only slightly discomfited by the brief encumbrance to the pursuit of their interest.

Her apron now empty, the old woman walked slowly through her flock. She stopped and, with a swift motion, she grabbed an unsuspecting hen by the throat. She picked it up with her veined hand and held it away from her body as the fowl flapped its wings desperately, pleaded and squawked, and lashed out with its taloned feet. The woman brought the struggling bird to the large sand pile near the iron gate.

With one hand, she held the animal by the neck, while with the other she reached for the long sharp knife that was hidden in her apron. The hen's squawks became shriller as its wings flapped furiously, and its feet claw the sand. With one swift stroke, the old woman ran the knife across the bird's feathered gullet, and the shrieking fell silent. In its place came the soft, whispered explosion of air escaping the bird's severed throat, and the sputter of living red blood geysered above the beaked head held in place by the woman's hand. The gush of blood spattered and changed to a sickly brown as it hit the sand. With wings still beating, the bird buried its own life force in the dirt with its scaly, yellow, taloned, clawing feet.

I watched as the old woman carried the unlucky hen by the feet back to the house. Its wings were extended, and its head dangled loosely from its nearly severed neck smeared with red. The other hens barely raised a flutter as the woman parted them like a muddy roiling sea. They were intent on their own task of pecking at the grains, and they did not notice their fallen comrade being taken inside.

Soon the door opened again, and my parents emerged. My father squinted in the glare of the sunlight. His dark, curly locks sprouted from his head like wild grasses. His searching eyes were set in shadows on his handsome face. He saw me. He came toward me with my mother at his side. He had a rested smile, and he looked confident as he walked. She was calm and silent.

He picked me up and held me in his arm. *"Un vus macht mahn Menacheml hant? Bist git geshlufn?" (And how is my little Menachem today? You slept well?)* He kissed my forehead. I jerked back from the prickles of his chin, and I reached for my mother. He laughed and handed me into her soft arms.

◆ ◆ ◆

"I am not spoiled," I protested, placing my plate in the sink for my mother to wash later.

Jay took a mouthful of coffee, chewed, and swallowed. "Alright," he said, weighing my statement. "Maybe not spoiled, just pampered." He guffawed at his own wit.

"Cut it out!" I shouted, trying not to laugh.

"It's alright that you're pampered. We want it that way. Someone has to be. It might as well be you." Jay brought his cup of coffee to his lips. Small chuckles escaped his mouth as he tried to put his lips to the rim. His eyes were focused on the cup. Concentrating too hard. He looked up sheepishly. "I'm only kidding. You know that, don't you?"

"It was an accident of fate that I was born the youngest," I responded.

"Ah, but you don't believe in accidents of fate. What's that poem you like to recite?" he asked. "'We are the architects of fate, working in the walls of time.' Something like that, isn't it? 'Architects of fate.'"

"Yes," I answered, discomfited by my contradiction. "But I didn't choose when I was born," I stammered.

"Talmud Chochem! (Talmud scholar!) You who study the meaning of words!" Jay's voice grew louder to help his words penetrate my consciousness. His eyes were wide open now, alive with a sudden excitement. "The poem doesn't say *I* am the architect of fate. It says *we*, all together, collectively. And it doesn't say *my own* fate, just fate in general. I am the architect of your fate as much as you are the architect of mine!"

I was about to thank him for making it my fate to be pampered, when we both became aware of our mother. She sat stooped over the kitchen table, a cup of coffee suspended in one hand. She had a distant look as she shook her head.

"What choice did I have? I had to leave home. I tried to stay. What was there for me there? I had finished school long ago, but I could find no work. We didn't have a piece of bread in the house. When I told my father I was leaving for Lodz to learn to be a hairdresser, I could see he didn't like it. He lowered his eyes and didn't say a word. He knew I couldn't stay. My last day at home, my father looked up from his sewing machine as I stood in the doorway. I don't know if his eyes said he had failed me or that I had failed him. He didn't get up to kiss me.

"My mother couldn't get out of bed when I said goodbye. She was too sick. I hated to leave them, but what could I do? I didn't have a proper dress on my back. She understood. She squeezed my hand. If she had said . . . if only she had said, 'Stay,' I would have stayed. But they knew we would all starve together. Their silence was telling me to go. I was only eighteen! I was still a child! They were telling me to go. I think my father was relieved that he would have one less mouth to feed. They needed so little for themselves. They were so tired. I was the last child at home. All my brothers and sisters had left. I didn't want to leave them! I had no choice!"

"You had no choice, Mom," Jay echoed quietly, trying to be reassuring. But his face bore the signature of doubt. To him, everyone always had a choice. "Those were very bad times," he said to convince himself as much as her. "When was it, 1938, 1939? The war was coming? Try to remember the good times. You told me there were good times."

"Oh yes, there were good times." She smiled, but she still had a trancelike expression. She often let herself be guided in her reveries, so long as it kept her in the past. "Konin was a nice town. There was little tension. We were called Christ killers, but mostly it was quiet. We had our own organizations we could belong to. We had sports clubs and youth groups. And I always took out books from the library. I liked reading romances best. And sometimes I gathered the few *groshen* to go to the movies with friends. I was in love with Nelson Eddie and Herbert Marshall.

"And I was blond like gold." She laughed and touched her hair. "My hair got dark when I got older. I loved school, too. I was a good student, but I was rebellious. They used to taunt me with '*Greeneh kanarek, arup fin marek, aran in keyler, aros a geyle. (Green canary, so contrary, went into the cellar, and came out yeller.)*' I was very tall for a girl, and I stood out. The teacher always noticed when I talked in class. She punished me by making me stay in her coat closet. One day, during recess, I went into her closet and nailed her galoshes to the floor. When she went to put them on, she couldn't get them off the floor. She asked every student if she had done it. When she came to me, I told her the truth. She said that as punishment I would have to kneel before the crucifix in front of the class. I told her I would kneel, but with my behind to the cross.

"So my father had to come to school. He had to apologize for my insult to the Catholic faith, and he had to pay for the galoshes. I felt bad about that. He worked very hard, and he didn't have money for such foolishness. But when I finished school, he paid for me to study modern Hebrew at the Zionist organization. My sister was jealous. It was a lot of money for us, and he had never spent like this for her. He said, 'She's the youngest, and she asked.'"

"So you *were* the pampered one," Jay said with forced cheer.

"You were the lucky one, like me," I added for effect.

It was the wrong thing to say. Her eyes welled up. "Yes, I was the lucky one," she said bitterly.

Then she became silent. Jay and I looked at each other. There was no way we could escape now. We sat, waiting, wanting to hear and, at the same time, dreading what was to come. Our mother began again.

"When the Germans occupied Lodz, all the Jewish men fled. Your father, too. I met his sister Sarah in the street, and she asked me to come stay with her. Why should we both be alone? Then the Germans normalized life. They allowed everything to go on as usual. Stores opened; trolleys ran. Yes, there were incidents, but mostly things were quiet at first. And the men began returning home. Sarah's husband came home. He was a kind man, and I continued to stay with them. Your father was last to come home.

"When he returned, he caused a sensation. People were standing in the street, staring at him. He was filthy from head to foot. His eyes were wild. His hair flew from his head as if he had been caught in a windstorm. He wore the same clothes he had on when he left, and he looked as if he hadn't taken them off in the weeks he was away. Under his arm he was holding something wrapped in an old, sooty newspaper. He wouldn't let go of it. What could it contain? When he was finally persuaded to release it and the newspaper was unwrapped, we found an old, moldy loaf of bread. We could never get him to tell us what had happened to him.

"Soon, he returned to his old self. And he began working for the Germans. They needed skilled laborers, and your father was a capable sign painter. We moved back to our apartment. Things were better for us than for other people. Because of his work, we had extra rations, and he brought food to his sisters and mother when the Germans threw him a scrap. But more and more, there were attacks on Jews. One afternoon, a soldier who had taken a liking to your father whispered to him. 'You better run away. Tomorrow we are rounding all of you up.'

"Your father came home and told me. Maybe it was something he had seen when he had fled, but he said there was not a moment to lose, and we had to risk everything to escape. We told all the relatives. I pleaded with Sarah to come. She said 'We can't leave now. We'll wait for the morning when we can get money out of the bank.' Your father told her there wasn't time, that she couldn't wait. But she didn't listen. None of them listened. They didn't believe it.

"Your father said to me, 'Just take some clothing and whatever money there is, and let's run to the Russian side.' I decided to take the bedding, pots and pans, and the silverware. He argued with me that it would slow us down, and he wouldn't help me carry it. So, I took it and carried it myself. He yelled at me that I was being foolish. Our lives were in danger, and I was worried about bedding! If we were to be seen, it would give away that we were running. I was already pregnant, but I was strong, and I didn't slow us down.

"When we came to the river that was the border with the Russian side, it was night. The men in the boats laughed as us. They wouldn't risk their lives for our few *złotys*. But they bartered for some pieces of silverware. We crossed the river in a small boat. It was dark. It was the beginning of winter. I was afraid that the men in the boat would kill us and throw us overboard. But they lived up to their word. When we got to Bialystok, we stayed in a place they used for storing carriages. The first months of Mayer's life, he lived in a barn.

"There were other Jews like us who had fled to Bialystok, and your father got word that the safest place to be was Kazakhstan. That's where the Russians had stored many of their treasures, and that was the last place the Germans could get to. But Stalin had other plans for us. He sent us to Siberia to work as his slaves. Newborns like Mayer died there in a short time. But a kind of miracle happened, if you can call it that. When the Germans attacked the Russian side of Poland, Stalin released the Polish refugees and let them go where they wanted. People said he needed our guards as soldiers at the front. We traded the down comforter we still had to be allowed to get on a freight train that was headed to Alma-Ata. It was the things I brought that kept us alive." She turned to Jay and me and looked at us pleadingly. "Why didn't they listen to us?"

"You had to go, Mom," Jay said softly. "It was the right choice."

"Do you want to take a walk with us, Mom?" I asked. "We can go down to the playground. You should see the things that Jay can do on the parallel bars."

She startled. "What time is it? I have to get ready for work. It's late." With that, she sighed and pushed herself upright with her hands on her thighs. Then she rushed into her bedroom to change into her bakery clerk uniform.

CHAPTER 7

◆ ◆ ◆ ◆ ◆ ◆

Deceit

Could it have been at the moment I saw Mayer's blood spattering like swollen drops of rain on the worn wooden stairs in Lodz when I was two that I learned deceit? I am certain that it was shame even more than horror that taught me to hide in that instant. It was also shame that was powerful enough to obliterate memory and to set and reset the borders of what is and what is not.

Self-deceit hides blame and failure and shame. Would my father have felt shame had he really faced the meaning of his actions toward my mother and toward his children? In his poems, he wrote about love and longing and joy and pride. He wrote about sadness and loss, never about guilt and regret.

Shame and obligation went together in my life. I was the special child, the one my mother clung to when she sent Mayer and Jay away. I knew the pleasure and the cost. I was her companion, her little cavalier, her consolation, her *Menacheml*, and she demanded nothing more from me. I struggled not to be overwhelmed, and part of me went into hiding.

When I had breathed in the expansive air of America, in sooty Pittsburgh of all places, it had reached into the hiding places of my shame and had begun to clean them out. In America, one could be bold and open in one's desires, as bold and blunt as its language and people. "Hi, I'm Lucy. I like you. Do you like me?"

After leaving the Lubavitcher yeshiva in Pittsburgh, I felt very awkward returning to my third-grade class at the Rogers School, where I had earlier found a home. When I had left without a goodbye and had gone to the yeshiva, I had rejected this welcoming society, and I was now embarrassed, even though it had not been my choice.

The class was already in session when I came in, and all the children were working at something at their desks. "Michael is back with us," the teacher announced.

The children looked up. Some said, "Hi," with no strong reaction. I sat in the back until the teacher rearranged the seating, as she liked to do periodically, and I sat next to beautiful Sandra, who loved to talk and laugh.

Spring came, and with it the soft, sweet scent of flowers and mown grass on the front lawns of the houses on Black Street and the quiet that was only accentuated by the chirping of birds and the sporadic sounds of muffled voices. I wore floppy shirts and a light jacket that let the cool breezes in and dungarees and sneakers that I didn't have to worry about dirtying or damaging. Easter approached and instead of watching the passion plays at the movies, as we had done in Paris, Jay and I took the shiny dimes our mother gave us to buy live chicks from the local butcher. One could buy a living thing for a dime! We looked into the box in the store window that held more than a dozen birds that were dyed in bright colors. Jay selected a small purple one, and I took a larger green one. Ironically, he called his Samson, while I named mine Peewee. We kept our living things in separate boxes by our beds, except when we let them play together, which meant that they just stood next to each other with startled-looking eyes, just peeping.

Feeding them was not easy. They did not respond well to the dry oatmeal we placed in front of them, and we tried to force feed them with tiny pieces of meat. After a few days, Samson developed a bulge in his throat. His downy feathers began to fall out, and soon after, he died. Jay wrapped him in a paper napkin, as if in a shroud, and buried him by the fence in the backyard without additional ceremony.

"I think the dye killed him," he said. "It wasn't that I handled him too much, do you think?"

Peewee was larger and stronger, and he survived more than a week to the point that the dye wore off his more mature feathers. He pecked at the oatmeal and drank the water from the saucer in his box. Holding him in both hands, I dashed through Mrs. Federman's kitchen door to take him to the backyard where I could watch him scratch and forage about in the dirt. I was sure he would live at this point. I had fantasies of raising chickens in the backyard, and I would become rich selling their eggs. Alas, Peewee developed the same lump in his throat and died in the second week I had him. I buried him in a shoebox in the backyard, near the kitchen steps. I checked daily to reassure myself that no animal had dug him up.

I loved living in Mrs. Federman's house. I loved the fact that she was there on her living room sofa with her gouty legs propped up, smoking her cigarettes, and paying me no mind as I flung open the front door and bounded up the stairs to our apartment. I loved the large, open rooms and the stained-glass inserts in our living room and bathroom windows. I loved that Mrs. Federman's son and daughter-in-law walked through the landing through our apartment to get to their attic apartment. I loved their two year-old daughter, Penny, with her pigtails. I loved watching over her. She was like the little sister I had always wanted as she followed me around. I loved running down to the drugstore to get Mrs. Federman her cigarettes whenever she wanted. I loved coming home at lunchtime from my school up the street and finding Mrs. Federman and my mother looking so serious as they watched *Search for Tomorrow*, "brought to you by new, blue Cheer."

I wound down almost every evening watching Mrs. Federman's Dumont with her, squeezed into her second couch with my mother and brothers, or stretched out on her fuzzy, dull-brown carpet. I had not known a really old person before, and I was beginning to feel what a steadying thing a grandmother could be.

My brothers and I had learned to tolerate the tension between my parents. We were able to escape into our own preoccupations and the outside calm. My mother's loud sobs and plaints and my father's eventual screaming defenses did not rattle Mrs. Federman as they had our former landlord. In the brown light of her living room, she comforted my mother and mediated with my father. Between puffs on her Raleigh cigarette, she spoke bluntly in her Americanized Yiddish. "She loves you." *Puff.* "You love her." *Puff.* "Be good to her." *Puff, puff.*

One afternoon when Mayer was working his paper route, Jay and I returned from looking for golf balls and found our father packing a valise.

He moved into a furnished room about two blocks away. I would see him several times a week when my mother asked me to bring him his mail. The room was small and dark, with heavy curtains, a rug on the floor, a tall maple dresser, and a single bed. Once, I entered the room as he was sitting on his bed, staring at the contents of a can of beans that he was heating up on a hot plate for his supper. He looked up at me through distended, hangdog eyes.

"*Zits (Sit)*," he said, pointing to the bed next to him.

I remained standing, lightly swaying awkwardly in place.

"*Nie, vus hert zech? (What's new?)*" he said quietly in anticipation.

I shrugged.

"*Vus macht di mameh? (How's your mother?)*"

I didn't want to tell him that she seemed more lighthearted in the weeks since he'd gone. The songs she hummed to herself as she stood by the sink were brighter. And she laughed more easily when my brothers and I told her something, which we were eager to do more often.

"*Zi's git, (She's fine,)*" I said noncommittally.

He nodded with an understanding smile and shuffled his mail. I was torn. I missed him. I missed his earthy man's smell and the texture of his presence in the house. There was always excitement about him, although I could not describe why it was. Perhaps it was his paradoxes. He wrote poems about his children, but he did not read them to us. He clearly cared about us, but he ignored us. He made promises to my mother—"*Ich geb dir di hand t'kias kaf! (I give you my solemn word!)*"—but he was often just trying to get away. Did this man of words remember, even moments later, the words he had just spoken? This caused enormous tension between my parents, and it infected us all.

Now, as he sat stooped over his mail, the top of his head looking small, round, and vulnerable, I felt sorry for him. I felt disloyal and ashamed.

My thoughts flashed back to the time in Paris when my mother had paced and fumed in the dingy room where we ate. The table had the plate and silverware that she had left there for emphasis from the night before when her husband hadn't shown up for supper. He had been out all night and was not home yet in the middle of the day.

"*Ch'vel dos nisht fartrugn!*" she raged and sobbed at the effrontery. "I won't tolerate this, I won't survive this!" Mayer, Jay, and I stood by, our faces tense and worried, with nothing to say to soothe or distract her.

The key turned in the door. We stood in a semicircle, a seething woman and her twelve-year-old, ten-year-old, and seven-year-old sons, lying in wait as their man walked through the small hallway and into the room.

My mother grew calm, now having a place to focus her fury. "*Vi biste geven, ts'al d'riches? (Where were you, damn you?)*" she hissed.

"I told you I was going to a gathering of writers at Yanasovitch's," he stammered unconvincingly. "It got very late, so I stayed over. The metro wasn't running that late. There was no way to contact you."

"And you stayed there through the middle of the next day, didn't you, you *parshevater ligner! (You slimy liar!)*"

"I couldn't just leave. I took him for a coffee at Republique," he retorted, beginning to sound indignant himself.

"*Shtik menuvl vus di bist! (Piece of shit that you are!)* You stand here and lie to me and to your children!" She turned to us, her eyes ablaze. "Tell him what he is. He's betrayed you too. Tell him!"

Looking at my mother as much as at him, my brothers began to walk toward him. I followed, conflicted but complicit, staying a step back. "Liar! Traitor!" they shouted, walking menacingly toward him. My father backed up toward the table as my brothers, and I following behind them, hovered closer. "Liar! Traitor!" Jay and Mayer screamed, and I echoed them more softly. "Liar! Traitor!"

My mother closed in, too. "Show him how it hurts. Hit him!"

My brothers raised their arms hesitantly. "Liar! Traitor!"

That's when my father had grabbed the knife from the table. "Stay away from me! I'll stab you all!" he screamed.

We all backed up at the threat.

And that's when I felt the most pity for my father. He looked desperate and alone. I was ashamed for him and for myself. I had taken sides and abandoned him, although I had not wanted to.

The room suddenly filled with a heavy silence, until my mother broke it with "*Durak! (Idiot!)*" and left for the other room, where she sat on the edge of the bed and cried, "*Reboineh shel oylem, farvos hoste mich gelost leben? (Master of the universe, why did you leave me alive?)*"

My father put the butter knife back on the table. Without looking at us, he went into the small kitchen, where I could hear him pour some coffee grounds and water onto the eggshells in the small saucepan and light the gas hotplate with a match.

Mayer and Jay looked at each other with furrowed brows and shrugged. We had made it through another storm.

Now my father sat on the narrow bed in his furnished room in Pittsburgh and opened one of his letters with a small kitchen knife. "Here," he said, ripping a section of the envelope with the stamps of Eva Peron on it and handing it to me. "Give this to Mayer for his collection. It's from Argentina." He smiled apologetically. "*Kenst shoyn gayn. (You can go now.)*"

In the next month my father vanished. When I asked my mother where he was, she answered with an air of finality, "He moved to New York." A quick exit for him. I had known such exits before.

Life was calm, even more so than it was when he lived down the street. The outdoors beckoned—exploring streets and backyards, riding Bernie's bicycle, trailing baby Penny behind me in the front yard, catching fireflies in jars in the evening as my mother sat on the porch steps, riding the ice cream truck and ringing the bell, for which my brothers and I got several pints of ice cream in "payment" from the ice cream man. Running into the kitchen after a morning of meanderings, I always found my mother by the sink or stove, ready with lunch. She now had a case of soda pop delivered each week to indulge us, something my father had dismissed as a waste of money.

My mother no longer looked infuriated or sad as she had been so much of the time. She didn't start sentences with the accusation, "Your father . . ." There was no tension over the unexpected when I entered the house. Yet my mother was mostly pensive. She huddled with Mrs. Federman in whispered conversations.

Early in the summer, after we had gotten along without him very well, my mother announced that she and I would be traveling to New York to "talk things over" with my father.

We boarded a Greyhound Bus, which made many stops and took eleven hours to get to Port Authority in New York. My brothers stayed with Mrs. Federman, which meant they had all the freedom they wanted to hang around with Heinz while I was in New York.

One night, I stayed with my granduncle Sam, a distinguished-looking, craggy-faced septuagenarian who lived in a dark and plush apartment on Riverside Drive in Washington Heights. He had come here in about 1905 and had paid his dues. He was now a "designer," which meant he designed women's coats for a firm on Seventh Avenue. His younger brother, Morris, who looked older and sicklier, did the same.

Uncle Sam and I had dinner at friends of his, which meant eating TV dinners at snack tables, a novel but pleasant experience for me. The next morning, we had breakfast at a diner, a wonderful experience. In the afternoon we went to see the movie *The Egyptian*.

My parents reunited, and we would move from idyllic Pittsburgh to the drab confines of a Harlem apartment in New York City. And from then on, I would live mainly in the little boxes of my mind.

My brothers and I once again said goodbye to people we had grown to love. Gathered on the stoop of our home and on the front lawn, we laughed with Bernie, Heinz, and Arnold and his dog, Snowball, from across the alley. We hoped one day to see them again. I said goodbye to two-year-old Penny, whom I would not get to see grow. Yet again, I did not get to say goodbye to my school friends. It was the end of summer, and by sheer happenstance, since it had never happened before, we would arrive in New York in time for the new school year in early September.

My father had written my mother that he had found a nice apartment in Manhattan, a bus ride from his new job. She did not have to bring any of the furniture or dishes or pots. That would be expensive and unnecessary. The new apartment had furnishings from the previous tenant who had moved out.

I said goodbye to the wooden kitchen table with its enamel top and the wooden chairs with their seats covered in red vinyl plastic. I said goodbye to the big walnut dining room table, whose rich, warm grain I could feel viscerally, and to the green velour and hobnailed *fauteuil*, or easy chair, that often enveloped me in the otherwise empty living room. I said goodbye to the tiara-like stained-glass inserts that sparkled with color in the large living room window and in the window of the white-tiled bathroom where Mayer, Jay, and I took our once-a-week baths, reusing the water as much as possible because it was expensive for Mrs. Federman to heat it. I said goodbye to my parents' bedroom set that had so charmed me with its thick maple, orange-brown chest and dresser and its four-poster bedstead with its knobbed posts with carved pineapples on top. I said goodbye to Mrs. Federman as she lay stretched on her couch in the brownness of her living room, a Raleigh in the curled fingers of her hand. I kissed her wrinkled cheek for the first time.

"Goodbye," she said through moist eyes. "Be a good boy."

My father picked us up at Port Authority. We crammed our valises and bundles and all five of us into a large Checker cab that took us uptown.

From external appearances, 3569 Broadway was an elegant ten-story tan brick building that had seen better days. It had an impressive front entrance of ornamented steel and glass. There was lobby furniture and mirrors in the marbled lobby. Three crystal chandeliers and wall sconces were signs of past glory. There was a service elevator and a passenger elevator. We took the Serge passenger elevator to the ninth floor and made a right turn to Apt. 9C. My father opened the door to a dark and deteriorated four-room apartment.

We crossed the transom and the narrow entry hall, past the kitchen, and we put our valises and bundles on the worn-out linoleum floor in the completely empty living room. We were in total shock at the gloom and shabbiness. At first, my mother did not say a word. She walked to the small kitchen and surveyed the rickety kitchen table and chairs where we could eat, if we did so two or three at a time. Its window looked out onto the wide shaft between the two columns of the front of the building, and its oily white enamel walls reflected light at this time of day. She yanked at the kitchen cabinets and drawers whose doors were so encrusted with years of paint that they could not fully open or close. She shook her head in disbelief when she saw the few filthy pots and the odd assortment of cutlery and mismatched dishes. A dirty frying pan and a small coffee pot were on the grimy narrow stove.

The three main rooms seemed freshly painted a dull drab green and their floors were covered with linoleum that had worn through in many places. Yellowed and ripped shades adorned every window. The living room was somber, despite its large window that faced the shaft. Its size was adequate, and its wall moldings were appealing. At the end of the living room was a long hallway that led to two bedrooms and the bathroom. My parents' bedroom, halfway down the hall, also faced the shaft and was dark despite its large window. Facing the door in the room was a scratched and dented brown metal bedstead topped with a bare box spring and a stained mattress partly covered by a sheet and a bare pillow, clearly where my father had slept. An old oak dresser with a mirror whose silver backing was partly worn away was up against the opposite wall. One of its curved drawer doors, its dovetail joints barely together, was nearly falling off.

We walked down to the bathroom. It was tiled and painted a shiny pink, and it had all the equipment. The tub was inset into the checked tile floor, and it had a showerhead. The claw-footed tub at Mrs. Federman's did not. At the end of the hall came the large room that was to serve as the bedroom I would share with Mayer and Jay. It was the only bright room in the house. It had three wooden single bedsteads and lumpy mattresses pressed head to foot against two walls. There was no dresser, only a narrow closet with a mirrored door. Against the wall that spanned across part of the two large windows was an old brown walnut buffet table.

"Don't open the window too wide," my mother warned. "It's very high up, you could fall out."

At least this was something good. We had never lived this high before. The view out the window faced out onto tenement rooftops and beyond. This was the nicest room, and the only one with a bit of cheer. Mayer and Jay, making the best of it, picked their beds, the ones that most faced each other. I was left with the one at the foot of Jay's bed, facing only a wall.

"*Shayn, yo? Groys!* (Nice isn't it? Big!)" my father said, grinning with his arms wide open and unaware of the effect of the place on the rest of us.

"You brought us here to this?" my mother hissed. "*Burich Habu!* A fine welcome! A fine new beginning!"

My mother raged after we had looked at every room in shock. As she began to try to organize our belongings into a semblance of a home, she fumed quietly. She had gotten herself stuck again. "Where are we supposed to sit? Where are we supposed to eat? Where are the boys supposed to do their schoolwork?" she fumed at my father.

With the intercession of an older writer friend of my father's and of my granduncle Sam, my father promised to spend on furniture. My mother had the wooden floors under the linoleum sanded and varnished, and they turned out to be beautiful oak. In the next few weeks, my parents bought a showroom sample green satin couch, a gently used rose-colored armchair, a gray Formica dinette set, an oriental-style area rug, and a clunky green convertible chair that would become my bed.

I would sleep in the living room so my older brothers could have their own room. They would feel they were not just an add-on to me, I supposed. In the next few weeks, we would become the proud owners of a twenty-one-inch Dumont television in its richly grained mahogany console and complete with rabbit ears. It was placed in the corner next to my pullout bed. When I needed to go to bed but Mayer, Jay, and my mother would want to watch TV a little later, I went to sleep in Jay's bed and my mother would later carry me into my own bed, fast asleep.

All the people who lived in our building were white and mostly Jewish, although it soon became clear that the majority of them would soon be moving out. "The Jews are moving out, so we're moving in?!" my mother hissed at my father.

The street was a different thing. The big apartment buildings on the west side of Broadway down to Riverside Drive were all occupied by whites. On the east side of Broadway and beyond, the inhabitants were all black, with the exception of a few Hispanics. The stores on both sides of the street were white-owned. The islands in the middle of Broadway, with their scruffy shrubbery and trees, seemed to be the *de facto* boundary of white and black. Once most whites began to move out of the big apartments and buildings, landlords would fill them with lighter-skinned Puerto Rican families who were just migrating from the island to New York.

In the first week in our new home, Mayer and Jay took to exploring the new asphalt and stone neighborhood together, and I was left to wander on my own. I walked down the steep slope of 146th Street to Riverside Drive. At 148th Street was a wide, elegant balustrade with a staircase that led down to a trestle over railroad tracks and then to a tunnel under a highway to a playground, a basketball court, ball fields, parking lots, and large grassy spaces.

Beyond these was the Hudson River itself. Massive flat boulders, glistening with mica schist, stood as bulwarks that bordered the vast, gleaming, and majestic waterway, with its myriad ripples and splashing sounds. I clambered down the rocks to the water's edge. The strongest sensation from the river was its smell. Its delicate watery, muddy scent was periodically accented by the pungency of raw sewage that could be seen floating and desecrating the river I now adopted as my own.

I came across two black boys, about age seven and nine, who were fishing off the rocks. They had shiny blue fishing poles with reels. They were busy throwing out their lines and reeling them in, rarely leaving them in the boreholes that were found in some of the flat granite boulders. I was transfixed. I had never seen anything like these rods.

"Where did you buy them?" I asked.

The older boy first shrugged. "Manny's Candy Store," he then answered.

I knew this was improbable. I had been to Manny's across Broadway near 148th Street. It had a dizzying assortment of small toys and objects for kids, but not fishing rods. America was a country of dazzling gadgets, from the baseball gloves I had seen when we first arrived in the States, to the fancy bows and arrows and the red wagons of Pittsburgh, and now to the shiny fishing rods of my new Manhattan home.

I moved on, running and skipping across the jigsaw puzzle of the flattened boulders, enjoying their silver gleam, careful not to fall into the larger cracks between them, until I came to a pier that jutted out into the river at 155th Street. I could see the silhouettes of men standing or sitting at the end of the long wooden expanse. I walked out onto the rotting and splintery red-brown timbers, infused with pitch that gave off a pungent smell of hot tar. The planking was deceptive, frailer than it looked, and I fell through some boards and scraped my leg.

I wove my way carefully to the end of the pier. Some old back men were standing about, tending to their long, impressive fishing rods. Two men sat on the edge of the pier, their feet dangling down. One yanked a line from the water and pulled out a wire cube. He opened the trap and carefully corralled a blue crab and threw it in a bucket where several others were contained. I had never seen such creatures before.

"What will you do with them?" I asked him.

"Eat 'em!" he answered. "Used to be easier to get a mess of them," he added as he put some baitfish into the now empty trap, set it, and tossed it back into the gray-green water.

I wondered if people got sick eating things from this wounded river. Still, I felt I could belong in this place where I had already seen new things that captivated me.

My father again decided we would not go to the public schools in the neighborhood. The next day, Mayer, Jay, and I traipsed behind him to several yeshivas in Washington Heights about two miles north. One accepted the three of us as scholarship children, refugees.

I had been in the Lubavitcher Yeshiva in Pittsburgh, but Yeshiva Samson Raphael Hirsch was different. When I met Mr. Jacob Breuer, the principal, he was an impeccably dressed and polished man with an easy manner. He didn't try to peer into me when he looked at me with a playful smile. He answered in a charming, lilting English that had a slight British intonation when my father had spoken to him in Yiddish. He knew German well, for this school was part of the German-Jewish community in Washington Heights, and he could have responded in that language exclusively, but it seemed he was addressing my brothers and me as much as he did my father by using English. "Your sons went to school in Europe. They teach at an advanced level there. We'll put the younger ones up a grade, and the older one will be in our highest grade, where he should be by age."

I began my first day in yeshiva with some initial pleasant reactions. The school was housed in a modern building, and, unlike the Lubavitcher Yeshiva, it had real classrooms, with modern desks like the ones we had in Pittsburgh. The teacher, Mr. Lowenthal, was a clean-shaven young man with a pleasant disposition and a chatty style. The class was all boys. We were to start the study of Talmud. This was the first time the class would be studying it, and most of the boys looked excitedly at each other, proud to have reached this level. They were giddy, but they tried to look mature. They had all had Mishnah the year before, and now they were to begin what for Orthodox Jews is the ultimate study of Torah. The Pentateuch, the five books of Moses, is the written tradition. Talmud, or Gemara, as it is usually called, reflects the oral tradition, the explication of the Pentateuch and the laws, rituals, and customs that are said to have been handed down by Moses orally at Mount Sinai and that also emanated from its close analysis.

We began the tractate *Bava Metziah*. After the morning of bewilderment, with a type of page I had never seen before and words that sounded like Hebrew but were not and that I could not read because they did not have the vowel markings I needed, I told Mr. Lowenthal that the class was too advanced for me. I barely knew how to read Hebrew. "Please put me back a grade," I asked him before lunch, and he nodded, looking as if he was judging me.

Mr. Lowenthal was also the teacher of my fifth-grade afternoon secular class. There was a lively bustle as clusters of boys talked to each other and found desks on their side of the room and the girls on the other. Two boys caught my eye. Leslie was a very bouncy boy, who smiled and talked to anyone who'd listen. He tried to barge in on the cliques of boys, but they rebuffed him. Another boy just stood in the middle of the room. Aaron was an odd-seeming, freckle-faced boy who wore a foppish blue blazer, gray slacks, blue bowtie, and blue beanie cap. He smiled and nodded grandly at no one in particular, and no one paid him any mind.

I felt some excitement about seeing if I could keep up with the work in the fifth grade. Mr. Lowenthal called the class to order. All the children took their seats. The teacher began talking, and everyone listened quietly.

"Good afternoon. I know most of the boys from the morning, and I'm sure I will get to know all of you better as we go through the year together. On the board, I've written the list of supplies you will need in my class. Try to get them as soon as you can."

I had a new pencil case and a new notebook, and I knew that was all I was likely to get from my parents.

"We will be doing reading, writing, arithmetic, and American history," the teacher continued. "I will now pass out the books you will need. I have checked each one of them, and they are in good condition from last year's class. I expect you to have them covered with book jackets by tomorrow. I don't care if you use brown paper bags to do it or fancy store-bought covers, but you must treat the books with respect because you will be learning from them."

The afternoon went by quickly as Mr. Lowenthal handed out mimeographed sheets of work for us to do. "I want to see what you know, so do the best you can," he said.

I saw that I could do the multiplications easily. I could also do some of the English grammar. The reading was a little advanced for me, and I could only understand some of the questions about it. But I felt confident I would be able to catch up. I had my doubts about the morning religious studies, but I was relieved that the afternoons would be interesting and that I would like what they asked me to learn.

Three abreast along the sidewalk, Mayer, Jay, and I walked home from our first day of school that early September day, two miles down Broadway from Bennet Avenue and 184th Street back home. The streets and stores and people along Broadway seemed bleak and drab, and the September heat was oppressive.

Mayer said, "I'm not going back there," and Jay sighed in agreement. The yeshiva was not for them. Our father would not succeed in this trick again. I had mixed feelings. I didn't like the morning religious studies, but I sort of liked my teacher and the work in the afternoon. As we walked home, I envisioned Pittsburgh, and I decided I would rather be in public school. My older brothers would speak for me, too.

When we got home, Mayer, his eyebrows furrowed and his back straight, spoke in a loud, determined voice. My father didn't argue or stand up for his decision. His eyes sad, he just shrugged. *"Tit vus ir vilt,* (Do what you want,)" he said and walked off with his newspaper.

◆ ◆ ◆

The next day, we registered at public school. I would go to the school two blocks from home. Mayer and Jay would go to Stitt Junior High School at 164th Street, Mayer in ninth grade and Jay in seventh.

The entrance to my new public school, PS 186, was on 145th Street between Broadway and Amsterdam. From the outside, it looked like an old chateau with a gabled tiled roof and a raised courtyard in front. It reminded me of the house we had lived in on Rue Guy Patain in Paris. I was hopeful.

An unsmiling older woman behind a tall counter in the main office signed me into the fourth grade. She barely looked up as my mother struggled to fill out the registration card. My mother and I climbed the staircase with its thickly painted wrought-iron railings. Its gray stone treads were worn down—by how many children over how many years, I wondered.

On the second floor, we walked down the long, narrow hall with its high windows on one side that lighted the ashen yellow-beige walls. The high, dingy white ceiling had age cracks and pockmarks and dangling, peeling sheets of paint. The dried-out, painted floor creaked with our steps as we walked slowly, looking for the right room number.

My mother's eyes looked worried, her eyebrows arched and her mouth pursed. I smiled at her and nodded to reassure her that this would be fine. She did not say a word as she knocked on the classroom door. The door was opened by one of the children, as the class was already in session. The boy looked curiously at me and returned to his seat without saying hello. My mother, looking uncomfortable and uncertain, bent down to kiss my cheek goodbye. She handed me the admission card and, as I walked hesitantly into the room, coaxed me to hand the card to the teacher.

The teacher sat at her big, blond wood desk and took the card in her bony, spotted hand. She was an older woman with a sallow, wrinkled face topped with a faded auburn wig that looked more like skeins of matted wool than hair. I began to feel anxious. It wasn't that she was old. She just looked very tired and disinterested in me. Her face had no expression as she read the card. She did not tell me her name or ask for mine. She simply pointed and said in a reedy voice, "That will be your desk. Put your notebook and pencil case inside it. But take them with you when you go to lunch and at the end of the day or they might get stolen."

I slid into my seat and lifted the top of the old-fashioned desk bolted to the floor. I was repulsed by the smell. I hesitated to put my things inside it because it was so dirty, with old chewing gum pasted to the sides and bottom. The desk was similar to the ones I had in Paris, except that there was a hole where the inkwell had been in my old school. Instead of a soft patina, this drab-brown desktop had names and crude pictures etched into it. I looked around at the bare walls of my new classroom. They were the same faded and sickly color as those in the hall. Ragged and threadbare oilcloth shades hung from the tall windows.

The teacher, with a sweater draped over her shoulders, walked slowly down to me with a clomping tread, carrying several sheets of yellow-lined paper in her hand. She spoke with her cracked voice. "Copy the problems on the board and then do them. You can do them, yes?" she said, barely looking directly at me before she walked slowly back to her desk.

I took my new, shiny clear plastic pencil case out of the desk. I looked at the problems on the blackboard, and they were all simple addition. I turned to look at the other children in the class, and I noticed that I was the only white child. All the rest were black.

There were boys and girls doing various things. A few were copying the problems or already working on them. Three girls in the farthest row were smiling and whispering to each other. Then there came a burst of giggling from them that dissipated as quickly as it started. One boy near me sat at his desk industriously doodling. Another boy rested his head on his folded arms on his desk. The teacher said nothing to all of this. I was in shock. *What kind of class is this? Is this the level of work for fourth grade in New York?*

I began to copy the problems. I debated with myself if I should do them as multiplication problems instead of addition, so the teacher would notice that this is too easy for me.

The teacher sat at her desk. She did not look up from whatever she was reading until the noise level grew a bit loud. She then looked up. Calmly, and without getting up from her desk, she said loudly, "Quiet please," and the children complied. Then the rising wave of noise began again. Eventually, the teacher closed her newspaper and got up from her desk. The children looked up at her, waiting for what she would say. I looked up too, hoping she would say something interesting.

"I want four children to come up and solve any four problems on the board," she announced. "Who wants to?"

A few hands rose, but the teacher only picked two of the children with their hands up. She picked two other children who seemed to try to recede into their desks. One of the hesitant boys made an error in his solution at the board, and a few hands immediately shot up to correct it. The teacher called on a girl with large bright eyes, pinned-up pigtails, and a pretty pink dress to come up and help the boy out. She seemed pleased to explain the error and solve the problem.

"Very good," said the teacher, and she smiled faintly at the girl as she returned to her desk. The two boys and the other girl at the board explained their problems and solutions. "Good. You may all return to your seats. Arithmetic is now over," the teacher said. Her heavy-heeled shoes thumped noisily on the floor as she walked over to the blackboard all the way to the right where ten spelling words were listed in a neat manuscript. "Copy each word three times," she said as she sat back down at her desk.

To me, the words were suitable for second grade. I had harder words in third grade in Pittsburgh. *Maybe the teacher just wants to keep the children busy,* I thought.

I felt agitated. It is as if light sandpaper was rubbing against my skin. But I did not get out of my desk as the morning droned on. The other children in the class took turns raising their hands, asking to go to the bathroom or to get a drink of water. I thought they just wanted to get out of the room for a while. Lunchtime finally came. I trudged down the stairs along with my classmates and swarms of kids streaming from other classes. I looked forward to going home for lunch. I wasn't hungry, but I needed to exhale. I was exhausted.

When I got out of the school building and onto the street, a boy I recognize from my class greeted me. He had dry, ashy skin and matted hair, and no expression on his face. "Hi," he said. "Can I come with you for lunch?"

He had nothing in his hands, so I knew he wanted something to eat at my house. I felt bad. I realized that he did not have lunch waiting for him at home. But I did not know him. I didn't trust him to come home with me. I stammered something, and I was embarrassed to say no to him. He turned on his heel and walked away without another word.

The afternoon was the same kind of busywork. "Write a sentence with each of the spelling words," the teacher instructed. The children complied as best they could. I looked over at the desks of some of the children near me. Some could do the writing, but others could barely copy the words. The teacher walked between the rows of desks, but I didn't see her stop to check to see who needed help. She said, "Very good" to a few children as she meandered.

As the day drew near to a close, several children clamored to play a game. "Hide the eraser! Hide the eraser!" they shouted, bouncing in their seats. The teacher finally agreed. One child was chosen to hide his face in the corner of the room while another hid a blackboard eraser under one of the children's desks. At the signal from the teacher, the child in the corner ran madly about the classroom, trying to find the eraser before the class could count to ten out loud. Then, another two children were chosen to play the game. This continued until the school day was over.

I walked the two blocks home, my head swimming. I felt defeated. I couldn't stay in this school. *It's not a school!* I was infuriated. My father had won out, and I would have to return to the yeshiva if I wanted to be in a real school.

◆ ◆ ◆

The next day, I was placed in Rabbi Cohen's fourth-grade religious studies class. Rabbi Cohen had a kindly face, concerned eyes, and a strong nose accentuated by a well-trimmed, bristly black moustache. His navy-blue double-breasted suit jacket hung open around him, giving him a casual air despite his starched white embossed shirt, gold silk tie, and sparkling cufflinks. The class was bustling. It was not like my Pittsburgh public school class, but it had girls in it, and they seemed cheerful and busy in their half of the room.

The boys worked in pairs on reading and translating sentences from the Biblical book of Exodus. *This will be manageable for me,* I told myself. I had studied some of Exodus in the Pittsburgh yeshiva.

Rabbi Cohen assigned me a seat in the boys' section. I was surprised to see one of the boys from my fifth-grade secular studies class there. It was Aaron, the odd-seeming, freckle-faced boy with the blazer and bowtie from the first day of school. He was still wearing the same outfit, including his beanie cap. Aaron grinned intensely as he acknowledged me. "You, too," he seemed to say, looking pleased that he was not the only one in the class who had been left back.

Rabbi Cohen asked me if I had *davened*—prayed—yet this morning. I honestly told him no. He quickly gave me a *siddur*, the prayer book, and gestured for me to stand by the eastern wall, where several other boys and girls were praying. I worried. My Hebrew reading was halting. I did not know what prayers I had to read. I knew a few from my previous experience, but not many of them or what their order had to be. I did not know where to start or when I could stop.

I felt myself growing anxious. I would be against this wall all morning, every day. I began to read a group of repetitive prayers I had learned in Pittsburgh, namely the "*Shelo Asani*" prayers. Among them, I said, "Thank you God '*shelo asani*,' that you did not make me, 'a heathen,' 'a slave,' 'a woman.'" In other prayers I said some words I recognized and I mumbled others, thinking that in time I would learn to read them all. I looked over the shoulder of the boy who was praying next to me, and I began to turn the pages along with him. I mumbled more than I read. I *shockled*, or swayed, like I saw the other boys do.

Suddenly a voice shouted out from the boys' half of the room, "He's not praying! He's faking!"

Bewildered, I turned around and saw that it was Aaron who had shouted. Animated, with fire in his eyes and a leering smile, he pointed his finger at me. "Look! Look!" he shouted, turning to the other children and Rabbi Cohen. Panicked and devastated, I gasped for air. I only regained my composure when I saw Rabbi Cohen tell Aaron to be quiet. He told the other children to resume their work. As I continued stumbling over my words, I determined that from then on, I had better tell Rabbi Cohen every day that I had davened at home. Perhaps I would never learn the prayers, but I would not face humiliation again.

From that moment on at Breuer's, there was never a time that I did not feel I had to watch my step, when I didn't feel that someone would catch me not knowing something that would disclose that I was not religious. If that happened, I would have been kicked out and would have had to go to the dreaded public school. Beginning that morning in Rabbi Cohen's class, I started to feel like an outsider at the yeshiva. But this was not solely due to my own anxieties. In actuality, no one tried to include me. My classmates all seemed to have already picked out their friends. Most had been together since kindergarten. This was a tight-knit German-Jewish community, and I was not a member. Their families were closely connected by their synagogue, their German language, and their Washington Heights neighborhood. Many of my classmates who were born in this country spoke English with a German accent. "Do you hev *milshting* or *flaishting"*—dairy or meat—"for lonch?" I would hear one ask another.

From that first morning in Rabbi Cohen's class, despite his kindliness, I felt trapped in isolation and guardedness. I became more tense every day as I began to live in the silence of my own thoughts. Over the ensuing months, I became more and more an observer. Although I tripped over reading, I listened intently every day as Rabbi Cohen explained many things in his gentle way, from translating the Bible text we were studying to telling us the story of the weekly Torah portion that would be read in synagogue on the coming Sabbath. In time, I was calmed by his kindness and his soft words of instruction.

One morning, a girl who was praying against the classroom wall walked up to Rabbi Cohen, her open prayer book in her hand. "I know I don't say the prayer '*Shelo osani isha*—Thank you God for not making me a woman,' but should I say something else instead?"

Rabbi Cohen crouched down to look at the little girl. He thought for a moment. With sincerity on his gentle face, he said to her, "You can say '*Shelo osani ish*—Thank you God for not making me a man."

The girl looked at Rabbi Cohen. "But that's not printed in the *siddur*," she commented.

Rabbi Cohen nodded and smiled at her. "That's true, but you can say it anyway."

The child was much relieved, and she went back to the wall and her prayers.

I was taken with Rabbi Cohen's quiet fervor as he explained a beautiful prayer to us. I learned from him what it means to be a Jew: "*V'ohavto es Adonoi Elochecho b'chol l'vovecho, uv'chol nafshecho, uv'chol meodecho.*" You will love the Lord your God with all your heart, and with all your soul, and with all your might. *I will try to do that,* I said to myself, *because of my kindly melamed in France and because of you, Rabbi Cohen.* This was what my father wanted me to learn, although he did not practice our faith at home.

Mr. Lowenthal called the afternoon secular studies class, known as "English," to order. Except for one boy, none of the other students greeted me or showed any curiosity about me whatsoever. It was Aaron, the same boy who'd tried to expose me in the morning.

"Hi," he said to me with his toothy, wide-mouthed smile and watery eyes. "Do you want to sit next to me?"

"I already have a seat," I managed to say, my eyes averted.

"OK," he said, without reaction. "I'll see you tomorrow at lunch!" he called out and returned to his seat.

CHAPTER 8

♦ ♦ ♦ ♦ ♦ ♦

Parents, Entrances, and Exits

Nothing was ever simple. My father sat at the dining room table, rapt in concentration, forcefully banging out a gentle poem with the middle finger of his right hand on what he called his "*klap* machine," his banging machine. The curly whisps of graying hair that rose from his slightly thinning crown were like the flaming ideas that streamed out of him. His fervent images and prayers wafted heavenward as he pressed them to the keys of his *klap* machine. His watery eyes, which only now were beginning to show the creases of his sixty-three years around them, were fixed on the paper that jerked by in front of him as he banged away and as he shut out the world around him.

His Hermes Baby Yiddish typewriter was spattered with flecks of paint from the store posters he painted at the same table. Sign painting and writing—the Word was his calling. His prominent brow, his sensitive face, his lusty laugh, and his beautiful wife were his calling cards. He had a lyric voice, and he was sought out for his words.

"Chaim Leib, write a *retsenzia (a review)* of my book!"

"Chaim Leib, we'd like to publish these poems."

The impassioned speeches he made in front of hundreds made him a hero to me. Now he sat in the midmorning light, banging at his keyboard and looking at the letters that formed from right to left on the paper in the typewriter carriage, and he ignored me.

During the past two days, now that school was out for the summer, he hadn't ignored the extra pair of hands I had provided as he fabricated a large sign for a jewelry store on the Lower East Side. Deftly, with a pair of metal snips, a simple saw, and a hammer and nails, he had just fashioned the twenty-foot sign out of tin and wood. It was my job to bang the galvanized flathead nails along the seams of the sheets of tin.

"Space them evenly," he cautioned, only half-looking at my efforts as he mitered the corners of the wooden frame.

His knees buckled with every step as we strained under the weight of the giant placard, carrying it out of the store to the street. With the aid of simple pulleys he had rigged, we hoisted it. Passersby stopped to gaze at the old man and his young teenage son seesawing the looming rectangle into place above the storefront.

"Ease up on the rope," he called down from the ladder as he secured the sign onto the hooks he had previously embedded into the brick of the building facade. With that done, he ascended the ladder once more with a large brush and sure strokes, and he quickly painted the tin surface light blue.

"*Genig far hant. Cho shoyn nisht ka koyech, (Enough for today. I don't have the strength,)*" he said, wiping the paint spatters from his face and hands with a turpentine-soaked rage.

We rode the subway home with few words between us. My father read a Yiddish newspaper.

The next day, we returned to do the lettering. Holding a last for balance and a can of paint in one hand, with simple, steady strokes, my father drew the outlines of the three-foot tall letters. By eye, he made them all the same size and perfectly plumb.

He felt the ladder move, and he yelled down to me, "*Halt di layter! (Hold the ladder!)*" He wasn't as secure anymore in being up on a tall ladder. His age was catching up with him.

Soon it was my turn to go up the ladder while he held it. I filled in the letters he had outlined. "Up and down strokes only! Put more paint on the brush!" he yelled up, as he wiped his round, sweaty face with a wrinkled handkerchief.

My father went back up to put the *trompe l'oeil* shading on the sign. Afterward we looked at it from a distance. It had turned out very well, we commented with satisfaction. It was then that I noticed that the word "jewelry" was misspelled.

"No, it can't be," my father protested.

"Yes, the way you spelled it, it's a store of Jews, not jewels." In the colors of the Israeli flag, the sign read: *Israeli Jewlery.*

My father rummaged in his pocket for the piece of paper with the text the store owner had given him. He was relieved. The storeowner had written the word incorrectly. My father could not be blamed. He didn't know English, after all!

"I would fix it now, but I can't paint over the wet letters. I hope the *balebos*, the owner, doesn't notice until he pays me. I need the money now. I'll keep this piece of paper, just in case."

After the storeowner inspected the sign, he paid my father with a satisfied look, because indeed the sign was beautiful, with its stylized Hebrew and English white letters, with dark-blue shading that presented them in high relief against the light blue background.

We went around the corner to Isaac Gellis. His salamis were famous—Send a salami to your boy in the army. We never ate out. This was a rare treat—in payment for my help, I supposed. Besides, we had worked well past lunchtime, and we were hungry.

"I'll fix it another day," my father said, chomping on his sandwich.

"At least it's not as bad as the one in the fish store," I said with a smirk.

At this, my father convulsed with laughter. He had the kind of laugh that he held in, so it reverberated and rippled inside him. His eyes were closed tightly and his body shook uncontrollably. The year before, he had made a sale poster for the fish store in our building. Instead of writing "Fish Sticks" on it, he had written "Fish Stinks." The sign was in the window for three days before a customer brought it to the attention of the fish monger.

"You know, my father was a wonderful sign painter," my father said once he regained his composure. "He was the best one in all of Poland. His signs were commissioned around the country. Actually, he was a great artist. Once, he had to paint a sign for a large creamery in Lodz. When he was there, he carved a lion out of a huge block of butter. People who walked in the door and saw it were frightened because of looked so lifelike.

"He didn't start out as a sign painter. He was a scholar. When he married, he was given a living allowance so that he could go on with his learning. When his wife's father died, the stipend ended, and he was forced to open a grocery store to make a living. One day, he decided he needed a sign for his store. After it was finished, it looked so beautiful that other storekeepers asked him to make signs for them too, and his career with vegetables was over. But he still studied Talmud deep into the night. It stood to reason. He was descended from the great rabbi of Chechenov, and before that from Yosef Caro, the medieval sage who wrote the *Shulchan Oruch*. You know, on your grandmother's side, we are descendants of the Grand Rabbi of Lodz."

"So why weren't you a Talmud scholar, Tateh?" I asked him.

"I was. I was considered an *illui*, a child prodigy. And I got *smichah*, rabbinical ordination, at the age of sixteen. But then I discovered the larger world—Shakespeare, Ibsen, the Russians like Tolstoy, Pushkin, and Gorky. All of them had been translated into Yiddish. After that, I had to be a writer." Then he added, "I could interpret *Gemara* and I could paint signs, but not like my father. He was a great man." My father's eyes moistened briefly, and then the flash of emotion that had just gripped him was gone as quickly as it had come.

"I guess I don't have the family Talmudic ability," I ventured.

"You'll do fine," my father answered mechanically, his thoughts already elsewhere. *"Kim, lomir gayn. Ch'bin meed. (Let's go. I'm tired.)"* He stood up. The discussion was over.

As I now watched my father immersed in his work at the dining room table, pounding on his little metal typewriter, it occurred to me that he had created the jewelry sign with the same concentration and intensity as he used when he forged words into poems. And when he researched information about the lives and works of myriad Yiddish writers for their biographies in the *Lexicon*, the biographical encyclopedia for which he worked, he did it with incredible urgency. I wished I could find passion and resolve like he did, that I could tune out what was irrelevant to me like he did, that I could draw from the well within me and create something beautiful like he did.

Yet, he had said he was a lesser man that his father. And his father could not be likened to the revered Chechenover Rebbe, who was not as great as Yosef Caro, who came before him. And I thought about Abraham and Moses, whose greatness could never again be achieved. Surely, as time progressed, we were all diminishments of those who came before us. Occasionally, facets of our elders would glint on the souls of the fortunate among us, allowing them to shine in some way.

I could see that pieces of my father's gifts had been distributed to my brothers and me. Mayer was granted his passion for reading and ideas and knowing countless details. Jay had garnered a fine hand that let him carve and draw and paint beautifully. And I had received the love of playing with words. Together we did not amount to our father, and, certainly, we could never surpass him.

Perhaps Mayer and Jay had diverted their interests to the sciences to sidestep comparison with him, just as our father had chosen poetry as his calling in deference to his father's Talmud learning. It was not avoidance of competition as such, although it was not in their nature to want to behead the father king. It was more silently giving him his due. Maybe Mayer and Jay hoped that in his silences toward them, he was giving them a nod as well. In any case, having obtained independence so young by virtue of their time spent in children's asylums, their father's praise and encouragement had long ceased to be a motivating force in their lives.

For my part, when my father cast more than a momentary glance at me, it was always welcome. I expected little more from him than my brothers did, but I needed him more. Perhaps this was because I had spent more time with him than they had.

My body had been changing for a year by now. For the past year, every day had brought new small changes in my face that I could see in the mirror. I had never known most of my relatives, whether they were uncles and aunts or cousins or grandparents. They were annihilated in the war or died before. My parents had few pictures of any of them. As I looked in the mirror every day, I searched for my family in my face. Did I look a little like my grandfather today, or was it a lost uncle whose features I saw, or was it my grandmother's expression that suddenly came through? I had no control over these changes. I wanted to look like Mayer, but every day I looked more and more like Jay. This was frustrating. But I was glad to look in the mirror and see the traces of what I knew were the features of my lost family, and that gave me solace.

◆ ◆ ◆

My memories of my father from before I was five were sketchy and episodic. From that age on, I had a continuous stream of recollections and wishes. I think they began with the evening he came to collect me in Brunoy.

My parents had placed me in Vladeck Heim in Brunoy when I was four and a half, because the house on Rue Guy Patin in Paris, where they lived communally with other writers and artists, was being closed down. My mother later told me that the Rothschilds had provided the building for artists and writers displaced from their homes by the war. By its appearance, it seemed to have been a former school. Each family was given a room that had enough space for a double bed, a bureau, and a hotplate. Some rooms could hold an additional army cot or two for children. Most were small. When my parents came from Poland, they felt their older sons, ages six and eight, would be better off in the children's asylum than in the small room they had been granted. At the age of three, I stayed back with them. Mayer would sometimes come home for a visit, but Jay was thought to be sickly and rarely came home.

The house in Rue Guy Patin was a remarkable place. There were conference rooms where famous Yiddish writers came from all over the world to hold court. The large communal dining hall also served as an auditorium for musical recitals, theater events, and painting exhibitions. The throng and activity of our neighbors and their children, whom they had managed to keep with them, spilled from every room and out into the large, gated courtyard in front of the building. The house throbbed with life, even when it held the hushed gatherings and echoed the staccato speeches that honored the recent dead.

Most important to me among the many people I came to know was a man named Aschendorf. He was likely in his forties. His sad, lined face and wavy hair gave his visage the semblance of rippling water, and his eyes and mouth were so sharply drawn and accented that they seemed to float. He had lost his entire family—even children, I suspected—in the war. He spent his days doting on me. My mother sometimes let him take me for walks. I walked holding his hand.

One day, Aschendorf placed towels in the crack at the bottom of his door and turned on the gas on his hotplate. By chance, my father passed by his room and smelled gas. He pushed in the flimsy locked door, shut the gas, and opened the windows wide. Aschendorf didn't forgive my father at first. As the neighbors took turns watching over him and feeding him, I overcame my fear and stood in his doorway. He lay in his bed looking as pasty and gray as his name, which meant "village of ashes."

"*D'host mich ba'avelt, (You've wronged me,) Chaim Leib,*" I heard him moan softly to my father, who stood by his bed.

When he recovered, he spent even more time with me. I rode on his shoulders, held his large, fleshy hand, and observed his downturned mouth and beaten eyes. As he bounced me on his knee, I kept wondering if he would turn on the gas again.

I said no emotional goodbyes when I left the house in Rue Guy Patin, neither to the house, nor to Aschendorf, nor to my parents. I was excited about going to Brunoy while my mother and father looked for other housing. I would be with my brothers. It was a trade-off I was willing to make. I would stay in Brunoy about half a year, since my parents had little money, and it took them a long time to find a new place—two rooms that were not much bigger than the single room in Rue Guy Patin.

My mother missed her children, and when they settled in, my father came to get me. At least he would bring home her youngest. The other two boys would have to wait until they could afford to house and feed them. They had been promised a third room down the hall from the two they occupied. Five years after the war was over, they were still living from hand to mouth, almost as if the war were still on for them.

When he came for me in Brunoy, my father packed up my few clothes on the shelf by my bed in the long dormitory where I and some twenty-odd four- and five-year-old boys and girls made a temporary home. He took me to the railroad station where we waited in the cold autumn air. It grew dark at an early hour in October. I didn't know if he had stopped to see my brothers or whether they knew I was leaving. I did not get to say goodbye to them, nor to anyone else I had become fond of. But I did not regard that as unusual. I had grown used to the abrupt comings and goings of people in my life.

My father shook me awake from a deep sleep when the train reached its destination. I rose to find I had wet myself. I shivered with cold as we walked and my wet underwear chafed against my skin. My father did not notice my condition. When we stepped into the night outside the train station, he hoisted me onto a military-type truck where we sat on benches along the side panels, the dark canvas making a tent overhead. The other passengers of the makeshift bus were just silhouettes and streaks of amber light as I sat huddled close to my father, looking up at the bristles of his face, taking in the outline of his jaw and smelling the damp pungency of his wool coat mixed with the mustiness of his body. I held on to his arm, and I thought, *This is the man I belong to.*

When I awoke the next morning, my mother smiled at me and made me a bowl of steaming farina with a dab of butter in it, just the way she knew I liked it, but my father was gone. The new place was small and shabby, but it was much better than the cramped room on Rue Guy Patin. It had two rooms, a green-tiled potbelly stove, and a tiny kitchen with its own sink with running water and a two-burner hotplate. It wasn't the grand rooms of Brunoy, but anywhere my mother was, was home. I didn't ask her where my father was. I quickly remembered that he made even more abrupt entrances and exits than my brothers did.

My mother and I spent the day together. We walked along my new street. On one corner was a bakery with exquisitely decorated pastries. The pies were topped with golden cardboard crowns. The aroma of the confectionary sugar and fresh bread wafted out onto the street. On the other corner was an *épicerie*, a grocery store. The smells of coffee and spices and cheese that escaped the door filled my nostrils.

We crossed the wide intersection where five streets converged. On a side street, beyond the wide Boulevard Barbès, was a bustling open-air market. The stalls of established merchants opened up from the houses onto the street. Pots and pans were hung from the ceiling of the housewares store that was packed with boxes of merchandise. Hog maws, singed and scalded pink, impaled on steel hooks, looked almost human and stared at me with jealousy behind their blank eyes above the butcher's stall. Pushcart peddlers hawked fruits and vegetables that had come right from the farm that morning.

A man with bulging muscles and a smiling moustache sold eggs. "Eggs, straight from the chicken to you. Still warm," he barked at us. "Fresh, fresh, fresh!" With that he took a pin and pierced both ends of an egg. He offered it to me. "Go ahead, drink it. It's still warm." I backed away. "Nothing to be afraid of. Nothing to be afraid of." With that, he lifted the egg over his head, and, with an exaggerated motion, he cracked it with his hand and let it slither into his mouth. "Ahhh!" he exclaimed.

We moved on. We walked from cart to cart, stopping at those where the fruits and vegetables struck my mother's fancy. The peddler women's shrill voices advertised their wares: "Last tomatoes of the season! Green Canadian apples! Baby cauliflower! Fresh peas!"

"I'll make you a *jardinière* with a little butter. You'll like that," my mother said to me, referring to a light vegetable soup.

I spent the rest of the day looking out the front window of our apartment onto the street, staring at the people and after the occasional car that wended its way along the cobblestones. My mother cleaned the barren rooms, and she talked to me as we shucked the peas for my *jardinière*. As the light faded, I was getting sleepy from the indolence when she bade me put on my coat to leave the house. We crossed Barbès and entered a café.

"*Kim shoyn ahaym, (Come home already,)*" she said to my father who was engrossed in a game of cards.

"*Ch'bin di minit arangekimen. Ch'shver, (I just got here. I swear,)*" my father stammered in excuse.

The men at the table averted their eyes and shook their heads. My father got up from the table and followed my mother home. "I walked from publisher to publisher all day," he protested.

◆ ◆ ◆

During the months that followed, my mother and I made daily out-ings to the open-air market. She had me link my arm in hers as we walked jauntily along the wide sidewalks of the boulevard. "My little cavalier," she called me with a laugh that warmed me all over. I imag-ined myself her escort and protector. I sometimes accompanied her to her friends Madame Therese or Madame Adela. They bent their heads close as my mother whispered confidences to them I should not hear.

By the spring, when I was nearly six, she allowed me to play in front of the house. After a few days, when I came upstairs, I confessed that I had gone past her limit and onto the next street. "I didn't tell you you could!" she scolded. Then she added, "Go no further than that."

So it went with regularity until, dressed in knee pants, heavy shoes, and falling socks, I spent most of my days exploring all the streets of the neighborhood by myself. There were few cars, and I felt no dan-ger. If my mother worried when I left the house, I never knew it. She appeared pleased that I was going out to play.

I climbed the hill all the way up Rue de Clignancourt, where we lived, and traipsed down the terraced park that cascaded from the Sacré-Cœur. I watched children play with hoops and other whirligigs, as their mothers and grandmothers sat by. I would often get lost along the side streets, looking at the grimy building facades with their tall windows and dark painted shutters for signs of familiarity. I never grew too anxious because I knew I could find my way back home by going continuously downhill from Sacré-Cœur. When I got home, I always found my mother alone. Her face would brighten when she saw me at the door.

In the evenings, she would often ask me to get a baguette from the corner bakery but to first fetch my father from his card playing at the café on Barbès. I would find him seated with several other men, shuffling and reshuffling his hand of rummy. I could tell how he was doing. When he was winning, he laughed and joked over his pile of small change. When he was losing, he sat hunched and worried. I knew that playing cards was very important to him.

He didn't drink, but once he bought me a sweet green drink from the bar. On the way home he asked me to tell my mother that I had encountered him coming out of the Metro. I didn't want to take sides, but I could not lie to my mother. Almost every night there were loud arguments about where my father had been. He protested unconvincingly, and he swore, with his hand on his heart, that he would change. My mother usually ended up crying.

My mother had threatened to leave him if my father didn't publish. Many times I heard her admonish him.

"An article or a poem in a journal here and there is not enough if you want to call yourself a writer. With all your scribblings you have enough for a book. You let your children out more easily than your poems. Are you afraid your readers will take them from you if you let them out? A fine purveyor of culture you are!"

"Leave me alone already," he answered dismissively as he turned the pages of his newspaper.

But my mother would not let go. "You call yourself a *kultur treyger*? *(a purveyor of culture?)* What are your accomplishments? A speech now and then? A few words in print? How could anyone respect you as a writer?"

"You don't know what you're talking about," he responded without emotion, his face buried inside his newspaper.

With this, my mother tore the paper from his hands. "*Shtik nevayle! (Piece of offal!)* "Look at me when I'm talking to you. I swear to you, if you don't show something for all your dawdling, I'll leave you. I'll take the children and vanish from sight. You'll never see us again. That you understand, don't you?"

Now my father's anger was engaged. "You peasant girl! What do you know?" he thundered. "When I picked you up off the street, you were nothing. You were studying to be a hairdresser! I elevated you to society. But you still know nothing!"

With this outburst from my father, my mother became silent. She had cornered him and roused him to react with anger of his own. She began to cry quietly, not from the wound of the words, which were flung about with regularity, but because she knew that she had touched him.

My father's tone softened. His own anger made him uncomfortable. "It's hard to get money to publish a book," he said softly.

"You're able to raise money for artists and other writers to publish their work. You love to do that. There's no shame in asking for yourself," she said, her eyes averted, lest looking at him directly would signal renewed confrontation to him and the end of this real conversation.

"*Bist gerecht. Ch'bin maskim, (You're right. I agree,)*" he answered.

With that, my mother wiped the tears from her flushed face.

◆ ◆ ◆

My mother took to sending me with my father on his outings, when he allowed it. It was exciting for me. I tagged along with him to conferences, to publishers, and to meetings with writers. He seemed pleased to introduce me. These people made a fuss over me in ways my father never did. They greeted me loudly, picked me up in the air, and made me laugh. I especially liked going to the big hotels when important guests from the Yiddish world stayed there. We would sit in the elegant lobbies, and they would order me egg salad and ham sandwiches on soft white bread cut into little triangles.

Most days that I was with my father, he said very little to me. He was pleasant enough but matter-of-fact when he directed me or answered my questions. In the spring we sometimes spent hours sitting at a little table outside the café on Barbès. He sat, intently writing on sheaves of paper with his red-flecked black fountain pen, while I sat next to him, observing the creases in the arm of his jacket jump to the rhythm of his writing motion. Lots of things happened on Barbès. One day, a large contingent of *gendarmes*, wearing steel helmets and holding nightsticks, assembled on the corner. I disturbed my father with a question.

"There might be an Algerian demonstration," he said quietly, turning back to his papers with no further explanation.

I looked forward to it with curiosity and anxiety, but it didn't happen. Mostly, I amused myself by watching the few cars, trucks, and taxis that occasionally rolled by.

A most interesting thing happened in the early evenings. Large packs of hundreds of men wearing suits, berets, and raincoats would ride by on bicycles. Some had briefcases rigged onto their back fenders. Others carried long baguettes under their arms. Occasionally, a bicycle would ride by with one man peddling and another riding on the handlebars. The bicycles always seemed to travel in hordes. They looked like swarms of giant black insects. Suddenly, one swarm would come to a complete halt at the traffic light. Then the swarm that was waiting its turn slowly cranked up to full speed and rolled away *en masse*. Some of the cyclists jockeyed for position, almost as if this were a race and not just rush hour.

One particular time, my father actually paid full attention to me, and it caught me by warm surprise. We were sitting at his usual table, my father's black locks of hair falling over his eyes as he made animated flourishes with his pen. I sat, dangling my legs, staring at an Algerian man at a nearby table as he packed little sacks of peanuts from a pile in front of him. My father noticed me staring. He got up and bought me a sack.

As he cracked open a peanut and split one of the kernels, he whispered to me conspiratorially, "Inside each peanut you can see Stalin and his moustaches, he said with a sparkle in his eye. Then he ground the peanut between his teeth.

As he returned to his writing, I opened each peanut kernel and experienced the peculiar pleasure of crunching down on little Stalins and sharing this secret with my father.

Many days, I would only see my father in the morning. He would rise from the lumpy bed where my mother was still asleep and grin toward me in the crib, which I still slept in at the age of six. *"Bist git geshlufn? (You slept well?)"* he would greet me.

Then he went to the narrow little kitchen, and I could smell coffee boiling in the small enamel saucepan. I got up to watch him pour it into a cup, using a spoon to catch the grounds and the broken eggshells that absorbed the bitterness before they fell into the cup. As often as not, he would be out the door before my mother rose.

◆ ◆ ◆

At night, until I fell asleep, I lay on my back, knees up, in my crib. I often lay staring at the shadows on the wall that were cast by the light from the single light bulb that dangled from its wire in the other room, as my mother sat at the bare table, waiting. I heard the angry, sharp, whispered screams that she addressed to the empty room. "You think I'm your slave? No! You must answer me!" she railed.

One night, she woke me, shaking me roughly. "Get dressed. We have to go somewhere," she said in a desperate tone.

I could tell she had been crying. We clomped down the stairs and into the yellow-black night of the shadowy street. The chill of sleep refused to leave my bones. We crossed the star-shaped intersection to the other side of Clignancourt, where I was afraid to go by myself. Red-lipped women with severe eyebrows and tight dresses slouched in the backlit doorways.

"Who are they waiting for?" I asked my mother.

We walked into a building where a man gave us a key. The room had a heavy feeling, from its thick draperies and red carpet to its commode, modestly hidden behind a waist-high screen. My mother pulled back the brocade spread and rough white sheets and placed me in the bed.

"Now he'll know what it's like," I heard her say before I fell back asleep.

The next morning, she took me to a public bath. The weathered matron in her white uniform filled the two tubs in the white-tiled room. My mother locked the milk-glass door behind her after giving the woman a *pourboire*. I sat in my large white tub, my semi-sunken ship, watching my skin wrinkle as my mother hummed a dolorous tune in the tub across the way. She sighed heavily, her crying echoing against the tile, her large and shapely breasts with their purple-gray nipples heaving with a shudder. Later we wandered around bustling streets, where she bought me a *café au lait* and a *pain au chocolat* before we returned home.

My mother girded herself as we entered our building. She looked triumphant as we climbed the stairs. Her shoulders sank as we entered the empty rooms. Her husband hadn't even been home yet. That night, after a long and tense day waiting for my father, she placed me in the bed beside her instead of in the crib. There would be no room in the bed for him should he return.

I was awakened by deep sighing and the rhythmic depression of the bed. I felt my father's earthy presence above my mother. *"Durak! (Idiot!)"* she cursed him quietly in Polish, as the bed heaved in waves. I kept deathly still and my eyes tightly shut, aware that I was witness to one of life's cataclysmic mysteries.

That night, I dreamed a powerful dream. In the dream, the night was pitch black. I saw my mother dressed in a shroud, standing in the prow of a large rowboat, silhouetted in white against the darkness. She held me, a baby in swaddling, close in her arms as we crossed a dangerous river. The boat heaved with each stroke as a man with bristly chin and leering eyes strained at the oars.

◆ ◆ ◆

On our floor on Clignancourt there lived a couple. The wife had befriended my mother after she had let her store some furniture in the unused room down the hall from us that my parents had just acquired in anticipation of Mayer and Jay returning from Brunoy. This room was not connected to our apartment. My parents had bought it with a small amount of cash and a handshake. My mother hoped to one day buy the room in between, if the rowdy couple that had it would ever move.

The French woman who became my mother's friend was a bit older. She looked sophisticated to me, with her delicately shaped eyebrows, her perfect wavy hair, and her fitted dresses. She spoke only French, and my mother spoke little of it, but they liked each other, and they baked Bundt cakes on top of our two-burner stove. I remember them laughing, and I felt good for my mother. She did not laugh often enough.

With her other friends, like Madame Therese, the German woman with the painted mouth and eyes and flaming red hair who lived with Aaron, the "rich" *shmatah* man, or with Madame Adela, the demure young matron who was her childhood friend and who was married to a rich sweater manufacturer, my mother's intimacies were formed through whispered secrets and pained confessions and the need for solace.

Certainly, I had known her to laugh raucously at parties and gatherings of the Yiddish artists and writers who gathered by word of mouth in the dining hall when we lived in communal housing on Rue Guy Patin or who came by invitation to indulge their humor over schmaltz herring and potatoes and strong vodka in our shabby rooms on Clignancourt. But too often she was sad.

Our neighbor made her laugh. "Madame is so nice," my mother told me. "With the laws of Paris, she could have claimed the room as her own, and we would not be able to take it back. What proof did we have? But she didn't do it. Isn't she nice?"

One day, with reddened eyes, my mother told me that Madame's husband had been diagnosed with cancer. I got a quick glance of him lying in bed, propped up against several pillows when my mother brought over a dish of soup for him. With his thinning hair and sunken eyes, he looked gaunt but serene in his striped pajamas. He accepted the food graciously.

When he died, my mother was devastated. "He was only forty-two," she cried, her eyes brimming with the injustice of it and with the loss that the man's death must have evoked in her.

The front entrance of our small, insignificant building was soon covered with black bunting, announcing that death and mourning were within. Madame's young teenage son came to spend time with us as his mother was occupied with arrangements and visitors. Mayer and Jay, who were home by then, sat against the edge of my parents' bed, looking up at the older boy, who was telling them a joke. He kept repeating the word *"enculer."* I stood near the bed listening. Curious, I asked what it meant. My brothers guffawed.

In explanation, before going on with his joke, the boy made a circle with his left index finger and thumb, and he poked his right index finger through it several times. I was stunned, but I understood right away. I was now in on a great secret. The room now seemed totally quiet as I stood there surrounded by the aura of mystery that was greater than the knowledge that I could never count to the end of all numbers, even greater than the unfathomable awareness that the world existed before I was born.

◆ ◆ ◆

In the spring before my seventh birthday, we had visitors from England. My mother's cousins Sissy and Hilda were older than she was. The two sisters lived together in London and were properly called spinsters. They wore sensible, well-tailored woolen suits and sturdy laced shoes and smiled strangely. Cocking their chins into their throats, they either pursed their lips into curlicues that matched their hair or opened them thinly so that their teeth showed a little. But their eyes always remained slightly sad. They had come to Paris on holiday, partly to see their refugee relative from the Poland their parents had abandoned well before the war.

They stayed in a hotel because we lived in two rooms. One room held a large workaday table and some mismatched chairs. There was also a small, Spartan dresser in one corner that held the dishes. These furnishings stood uncertainly on the uneven and worn-out terra cotta floor. In the corner near the large window stood a little potbellied stove covered in green porcelain tiles. It had a little grating through which the fire stuck out its tongues at me when my mother lit it. The stove was the only heat for the apartment. A calendar with a picture of

Chaim Weitzman was hung on a nail on the wall and completed the air of transiency. This was our public room, where we ate and in which my parents greeted visitors.

The other room was connected to the first by just a doorway. The walls of both rooms were covered with the same peeling yellow wallpaper. The inner room contained my parents' lumpy mattress and box spring hard against one corner. Next to it was the large rattan trunk Mayer had slept on in Poland and on which he had been laid out after he was shot. Then there was a pretty but nonworking mantle and, hugging that, a rickety armoire adjacent to the window. On the other full wall were a tiny closet and the crib I still slept in for want of a bed. Spread out on the splintery wood floor, the old Oriental rug with its geometric designs added the only color to the room. I loved its patterns, and, as one of my few forms of entertainment, I used discontinued coins that I found in the gutter to scoot around its border. There was also a closet of a kitchen by the entrance of the apartment. It held a cold-water sink, a two-burner gas hot plate, and a shelf to store pots and dishes. The toilet was halfway down the stairs. Consisting of a hole in the floor flanked by two foot pads, a water closet with a pull chain, and a supply of old newspaper hanging on a hook, it was shared by the occupants of two floors.

My mother took her cousins to meet her friends at their homes or to sidewalk cafés, where they sipped aperitifs and listened to a chanteuse in the warm afternoons. I often accompanied the three of them, holding my mother's hand. On one outing, we went to an elegant department store. I had never seen anything like it. My mother seemed a little uncomfortable. Maybe we didn't belong in such a fancy place, I thought. The profusion of merchandise and the self-assured crowds were intimidating. Hilda and Sissy were buying souvenirs for their return home. We stopped in the book section, where they perused the art books. Sissy showed me the children's books, and, in English and gestures, she invited me to select a book for them to buy me as a present. I looked at my mother, who nodded her permission.

There were so many inviting books, all with pretty and colorful covers and decorations. My mother hovered over me making seemingly casual comments, trying to guide my choice. I suddenly stopped. I saw a book I really wanted. It was my favorite story, *"Les Trois Petits Cochons (The Three Little Pigs)."* The cartoons that illustrated its pages were so vivid, and when I pulled its paper tabs, some of them moved. I looked at my mother, as I held the book. She surreptitiously shook her head no and moved her head to point to another, more serious-looking and weighty tome on the counter. I was about to put my book down when Hilda, who had intercepted the interchange, took it from me, smiled at my mother, and said in Yiddish, "This is the one he wants. We'd like to buy him this one."

My mother looked at me chagrinned, as her cousins paid for my choice. I felt a strong pang of guilt, but I was also secretly glad and excited. It was the first book I actually owned.

Later, at home, when Sissy and Hilda were back in their hotel, my mother looked at me as I held my book. *"Farfaln, (Too bad,)"* she said as she sat sunken in her chair.

I tried to shrink into the corner, not knowing what I had done wrong. Should I have picked the book she had selected because it was more expensive? Should I have gotten that more mature volume because it would last me longer, like the shoes whose toes we stuffed with cotton that had room to grow into?

"If you had told them that you wanted the book I picked, I would have had something to give to Madame Adela's son, Yeszik," she lectured. "He's your age, but he's more advanced than you. He has older interests. Adela's my childhood friend, but she's also our benefactor. When I don't have a *groschen*, she's the only one I can turn to. Not only do you get Yeszik's hand-me-downs, but she always gives me money for new clothing for you. And you like the sweaters that you get from her husband's factory. It's hard for me to find ways to thank her, and that book would have been perfect."

Now I understood. My mother was right. We had to think about important supplies we needed to go on living before luxuries for ourselves. *"A mentch miz koydem trachtn vegn parnoseh, un noch deym vegn epes hecher! (A person first thinks about providing for his family before he can think about loftier things!)"* she would yell at my father during their many arguments about money. My father had finally published a book, but his work was mainly writing occasional poems or literary articles for newspapers or journals.

I went into the other room and sat down on the floor, leaning against my parents' bed. I thought about the last present my mother had given Yeszik on his birthday in gratitude to his mother. It was a huge metal toy crane. It had wheels and gears that worked. It had a bucket on the end of a cable that you could move up and down. And you could pull a lever and lights would go on. I had played with it when Yeszik got it, but despite its dazzling appearance, I was not envious. It did not fire my imagination, and it became boring to me after a short while. I had no toys of my own, and I had not learned how to play with them.

I looked at my book with little joy. I wanted to feel the full thrill of having it, but I had disappointed my mother with it. Yet, when I opened the cover, I soon got lost in it. I was intrigued by the cleverness of the moving pictures. I liked becoming part of the book by pulling and pushing the flaps and tabs. More important, this book had not been a frivolous choice for me. As I read about the three little pigs, they became my two brothers and me.

I will be the one who succeeds, I thought. *I will value work and protect against an uncertain future.* I studied the placement of the brick and mortar as the third little pig worked with trowel in hand. *This is how you build a house. I will build a house where we will all be together and safe, Mother.*

Michael, age 2, and mother, picnicking in Tuszyn Las (1947)

Michael, age 2, and
Jay, age 5, in Dusznicki
Sdrui holding the bike
Mayer got after losing
sight of his eye (1947)

Michael, age 5, center, in Vladeck Heim (1950)

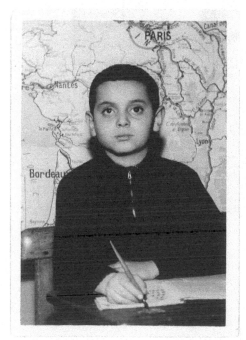

Mayer, age 10, in Paris, attending school for the first time after returning from Vladeck Heim. His hair is growing back. (1950)

Mayer, almost 12, in school photo at end of school year (Paris 1952)

Mother, (Paris. 1951)

Father (Paris, 1951)

Michael and classmates in yeshiva, (Purim 1960).
In front row, second from left, Bernie Gissinger; in second row, first
on left, Sam Schildhaus; in second row third from left, holding award,
Michael Fox; in third row, first on left, Jacob Friedman, who left at the
end of the year. Sam, Bernie, and Michael left the following winter.

Jay at George
Washington H.S.
(Spring 1959)

Michael in Far
Rockaway
(Summer 1959)

CHAPTER 9

◆ ◆ ◆ ◆ ◆ ◆

Paradoxes and Contradictions

At noon, my mother called to my father from the kitchen of our Harlem apartment as he beat out a rhythm on his paint-flecked typewriter, making the dining room table shake. "*Vilst a tepl kaveh, epes ts'essn? (You want a cup of coffee, something to eat?)*"

"*Farvus nisht? (Why not?)*" he responded, getting up quickly from his chair.

In the kitchen, he poured a heaping teaspoonful of instant coffee powder into a cup, poured hot water into it, and stirred slowly with his spoon. As the coffee steeped, from a wrinkled wax paper bag he kept only for himself, he took two pieces of hard stale bread that no one else would eat anyway. From the fridge, he took out a block of farmer cheese and topped the twisted bread slices with two slabs of the soft, flaky white cheese. He then sat down at the gray Formica kitchen table and began slurping loudly from his cup.

"Take a plate," my mother told him.

He ignored her. "Ahhh," he sighed contentedly. "It's hot." As he bit down on a hard piece of bread, it squealed from the pressure of his teeth, and the cheese crumbled all around him, on the table, his clothes, and the floor. "So good!" he proclaimed. His lips were shiny, and his paunch was covered with specks of white cheese. A murmur of pleasure accompanied his chewing. He saw me staring at him. "Here, you want some?" he asked, offering me his half-eaten piece of bread, as if that was why I was looking at him.

I stared, embarrassed by my father's gluttony. When food was in front of him, he became a child. I regarded his unbridled hedonism as a weakness; as it was, I was uncomfortable with my own fourteen-year-old interest in bodily pleasures. I was unable to comprehend how a man who wrote such touching and lofty words could be reduced to a voracious mouth and insatiable belly. Unlike my mother, who seemed to grow distant and sad with each morsel that passed her lips, he ate with concentration and gusto. Yet, he had a difficult relationship with food. He never seemed sure he had enough.

On Clignancourt, in Paris, not long after Mayer and Jay had returned from Brunoy, we received a package from America that contained a can of Spam. "It's pure fat," my mother said. "I can't give this to the boys; it will make them sick."

"There's nothing wrong with it," my father replied, standing in the kitchen, gorging it down in illicit haste, hungrily sopping up the drippings straight from the frying pan.

A major battle between love and anxiety about food raged in him at dinner not long after that. We were all seated at the table. Mayer and Jay were heatedly debating some aspect of the Tour de France. My mother hummed quietly to herself, holding her fork distractedly. There were several large and shiny new coins stacked on the table next to my father's plate. He was hunkered down over his food when he suddenly shrieked, "*Gevald!* I think I've swallowed one of the coins!"

"How could you put such a large coin in your mouth without noticing?" my mother shouted nervously, only slightly dubious.

"I'm sure I swallowed it," he shuddered. With this, he threw himself on the floor and writhed and coughed and groaned, and prepared to say the *Vidui*, the prayer said before dying, as we all stood around him and watched. When he didn't die, he got up and flung himself repeatedly across the back of his chair in a desperate effort to dislodge the coin. Eventually, his panic subsided when nothing untoward happened. He sat down to resume eating, muttering to himself that he was certain he had swallowed the coin. My brothers continued their conversation, and my mother resumed pecking at her plate. I stared at the pile of coins. It was possible that one was missing.

"Have some. Don't be ashamed," my father now said to me, his eyes laughing, his belly shaking, his words partly muffled by another bite of stale bread and crumbly cheese that he had cracked into his hungry mouth. His neediness seemed somehow primitive. I wondered how he has become this way. Unlike my mother, who told and retold her life like a prayer ritual, he rarely spoke about his past. When he did, I took it with a grain of salt. Even his birthday was suspect. For years, he had said he was born in 1905. Now he admitted to 1896. He had altered his birth year so that he would only be fifteen years older than my mother. Now it had become a statement of pride that he had a wife who was twenty-four years his junior. He claimed to have been born on May 29. He grew angry when we asked him how he was so sure.

Today, a window opened that linked his past to the present. "I've eaten hard bread and farmer cheese since I was a child," he said. His voice then became reverential. "My mother was an angel," he recollected. "You know that my father earned a good living, but her side of the family was very poor. My mother gave them the finest and best food we had, and she left for us only the scraps. You see what a great woman she was!"

◆ ◆ ◆

Who was this man Chaim Leib, my father? He was a gluttonous hedonist who lived in the moment of his senses. "Eat, don't be ashamed." I was fourteen and easily embarrassed. Yet, he was also in the moment when he wrote his fervent and sensuous poems. He was self-occupied, yet his eyes welled up and his lips trembled in remembrance of our martyred people. He spent little time focused on me when I was near him. Yet when I was in camp, he typed out postcards to their edges telling me how much he missed me and how much my letters meant to him.

I heard him on the phone, index cards nearby and pen in hand. "Hello, is this so and so? Speaking to you is a person named Chaim Leib Fox, you've heard of me? He then asked each listener, whom he had found through his detective work, about the particular Yiddish writer he was researching for his work at the *Lexicon*, the encyclopedic dictionary of all the Yiddish writers who ever lived, which was being prepared using German reparations funds. He was one of less than a dozen writers and historians working on this massive project.

After speaking to and asking questions of anonymous people on the phone and gathering notes about the authors in question, he sat at his portable typewriter, his brow furrowed as he banged away at the keys with the middle finger of his right hand until he had documented the work of yet another writer. I had never seen him show such urgency in his efforts—not when he was writing his poetry, not as he worked on his journalistic articles—as he showed when he was in pursuit of a nearly lost author.

"You know," he told me when he saw me staring at him, "I have the names of five thousand Yiddish writers in my head. I've already written the biographical entries for two thousand writers. Most of them are so obscure no one knows anything about them anymore. If I wouldn't write about them, their names and works would be lost forever."

I knew hardly anything about his life from my father, the biographer. I knew of my parents' early life together mainly because of my mother's stories, which were filled with so much pain. The only time I heard my father speaking about himself directly was when we came to America in September 1953, at a dinner reception that was held at the Atran House in his honor as a writer. Among the guests were figures from Yiddish organizations that supported displaced persons in Europe, as were artists and writers and others who were active in the Yiddish literary society of New York. These individuals greeted my family warmly, like long-lost friends. I realized that some of them were actually friends of my father from before the war and that they had kept in touch through copious letter writing, and they had communicated through articles in journals that transcended national boundaries.

My brothers and I were introduced to some of those in attendance in an interesting way. They had been in our lives from across the ocean without our having known it.

"Greet Sureh Jacklin," my father said to me, pushing me toward her. "Remember those fat crayons and the rhinestone belt and the clip-on ties you loved in Paris? This is the great writer who sent them to you."

I remembered the "Packages from America" that had come as exciting surprises from anonymous people far away. I had wondered how they knew to send things to us and how they knew what we would like. I smiled at Sureh Jacklin and others whose hands I shook. I marveled that these people, who looked like ordinary working folk, certainly not well-to-do, would go to the effort and expense for children they did not know.

These organizations and individuals were still welcoming artists, writers, and journalists who had survived the conflagration of Europe and who were now refugees who came to make a life in the *Goldene Medineh*, the Golden Land, all these years after the war. Some new arrivals got special honors when their ships docked in New York Harbor, even though many, like us, were destined to be spread around the country.

My father sat at the central table at the banquet, with my mother next to him. I noticed that his table manners were more careful than those he had at home. My brothers and I were at one end of the large horseshoe table. At various times during the meal, people got up to speak, and they talked about my father, his poetry, his journalism, and his survival. I couldn't help but feel he was a great celebrity and that I was a celebrity along with him.

When he was asked to speak, my father stood up at his seat. All eyes were on him. He gathered his thoughts for a moment, and with his right hand stretched out before him in a striking pose, he recited to the gathered writers and artists and luminaries the history of my parents' escape from Poland. He described the hardships in Siberia and Kazakhstan. Most striking to me was his description of the dangers they had encountered as they fled. I had heard from my mother about my parents' fleeing, but she had never told us the details of the dangers they had encountered.

"My young wife, Lea, my infant son, Mayer, and I were on a transport train filled with Polish Jews being taken east to a labor camp in Siberia, on Stalin's orders," my father began. "Not long after the train reached the countryside of Russia, German warplanes began strafing the train and bombing the rails. We fled the trains and spread ourselves out in the surrounding fields. Some of us who were running were killed immediately by the random strafing. I covered my wife and son with my body so that if we were strafed, they might survive. I dug in the hard winter ground till my hands bled. I took my passport that said I was a Jewish journalist and buried it there. If the Germans captured us, they would not select me for immediate death on seeing my papers. If the Russians where we were going asked for my papers, they would not send me to a 'rehabilitation' gulag, as I had heard they were doing to Yiddish writers.

"We were strafed and bombed several more times by the Germans until we were too far along the way toward the cold wasteland of Siberia for them to pursue us. We were housed in barracks in Siberia. Fortunately, other slaves like us had built them in years past, and we did not have to build them ourselves, as we had heard rumors we might have to do. There was much suffering and death, from the cold, from the starvation, and from the brutal work. The most suffering and wailing came from parents at the deaths of infants and young children. Most of these did not survive the cold. Lea and I worried about our infant son. We took turns wrapping him around our bodies as we worked in the woods around the camp. Our body heat and Lea's nursing kept him alive, until miraculously, when Hitler invaded the Russian side of Poland, our guards let us go wherever we wanted in Russia. Stalin needed our guards at the front.

"We managed to get on a freight train that was headed south to Kazakhstan, and we spent the rest of the war there. It was difficult. I got typhus and nearly died, and it left me weakened. Still, the Russians caught me and conscripted me into their slave labor army. I managed to escape, and they did not find me. Lea was the main one who kept us alive in Alma-Ata and the little village of Ili, where she carried fifty kilo sacks of wheat from barges to trains. She kept up that backbreaking work until we were allowed to return to Poland in 1946. Stalin had wanted to keep us as his slaves. But he was forced by the Americans to return all refugees. So he sent the following order: If you want to go back to your home country, you have to do so now. Otherwise you will have to stay and become a Russian resident and be unable to return. I worked desperately, and I found a way to get my wife and three sons on one train after another, going north and west, until we got to Lodz before the deadline, which was my youngest son Menachem's first birthday."

There was applause and appreciative murmurs when my father finished his account. Coffee and dessert were served. In the midst of clanking cups and spoons, one man got up and in a strong voice he said, *"Ich vil zugn a pur verter. (I want to say a few words.)"* The hall quieted down. He was an older man, with a completely bald head, dressed in a rumpled suit and a cravat over his plaid shirt.

"There is a story that Chaim Leib did not tell you that you should know about him," he began. "After Chaim Leib and his family came back to Lodz, they found the city desolate. The Jews who had lived there were almost completely gone. Of the three hundred fifty thousand Jews, few remained. Still, it was the only big city that was not destroyed by German bombing, and Polish Jews originally from Warsaw, Krakow, Lublin, and other big cities of Poland had begun to make their way there after the war from wherever they were, and they began to reestablish a Jewish communal life. They even founded a Yiddish school for the few children that there were.

"One of the cultural events the community eventually organized was a memorial program for the artists and writers who had been murdered by the Nazis. They published a lengthy pamphlet with the names of these martyrs. Hundreds and hundreds of people, including me, attended the event, which was held in a large hall. There were prominent members of the community who spoke about the Yiddish cultural life before the war and what the loss of our cultural creators meant.

"At one point, Chaim Leib asked to say a few words. He was a well-known personality in Lodz, and he was allowed to speak. This is what he said: 'In this pamphlet, with the long list of our martyrs, each of whose printed names is certainly stained with tears from all of us gathered here, there are two names that do not belong. Henryk Erlich and Victor Alter were not killed by the Nazis; they were Jewish members of the Polish government-in-exile in the Soviet Union, and their murder is attributable to Stalin directly. The intent to remember them in this publication is noble but misplaced. Let us not besmirch their memory by lying about their deaths. Let us honor them for who they were and what they tried to achieve.'

"The people gathered at the memorial gasped, and then they were completely silent. It was already a time when the Communists had taken control of Poland, and the government had their spies everywhere; and they were certain to have spies and informers at this large gathering. The organizers quickly ushered on another speaker, and the program continued. But Chaim Leib's point had been made. He had risked his life to honor the accurate memory of our heroes Erlich and Alter."

The man sat down, and the woman next to him clasped his arm, as he was obviously shaken by what he had just recalled. The gathered guests applauded and turned to my father, who bowed his head and remained silent.

These six years later, I stared at my father, bemused by his gluttony and his valor, as he now pounded on his typewriter at our dining room table, writing another biography, recalling yet another nearly forgotten writer. He looked up and saw me staring. *"Ni, vus kikste uf mir? (So, why are you staring at me?)"* he said with a little laugh through his preoccupation.

CHAPTER 10

◆ ◆ ◆ ◆ ◆ ◆

Jesus and Exegesis

The past was a member of our family, except for my father, who was usually rapt in his own current moment or in his own creative thoughts. Ironically, Jay liked to quote Omar Qyam: "The moving finger writes, and having writ moves on. Nor all your piety and wit can lure it back to cancel half a line, nor all your tears wash out a word of it."

Mayer said more than once that he would give up his life at its peak if his name and past deeds could be immortal in the memory of the world. "Everyone craves immortality," he said. Most people could only thrust their past into the future by the pedestrian means of having children. The past was immutable, and to us, memory was of ultimate importance. The past was unforgiving in dictating our present and our future. And, as a central member of our family, the past was always with us, stubborn and insistent on being reckoned with.

I was a child of just over a year when my parents returned from Kazakhstan to the city of Lodz after the war. Before I was three, I vaguely knew from my parents and from *pshetchkola*, nursery school, that we were Jewish. I did not know exactly what being Jewish meant, except that at the nursery school, Lererin Fiszman, our teacher, would take me in her lap, and I would rest my head against her enormous bosom as she told Yiddish stories and sang Yiddish songs to the little children gathered around her. Jewish people were those my parents stopped to talk to in Yiddish in the street, and Poles were other people they tried not to look at. Jewish people were scared of Polish people. Jewish and Polish people looked different, and I could tell them apart.

Jewish people had drooping eyes, even when they laughed. My under-standing had nothing to do with religion, a concept and a past I was completely unaware of.

My first experience with religion was overwhelming. One night, when I must have been two and a half, there was a knock on our door, and I waddled behind my mother to the dimly lit antechamber of our apartment to see who it was. When the door opened to the darkened hallway, I saw an apparition of six or seven older children and adoles-cents bathed in golden candlelight. The soft play of light and shadows around their eyes and cheeks seemed mysterious. Two members of the group stood in front and held a small, open wooden house, complete with miniature human and animal figures illuminated by the candles' glow. I wanted to enter this warm, tiny world with the baby at its center. When the children began to sing, I was completely awash with a won-derful but nameless feeling. The clear, lilting melodies were accented by sibilant Polish words that sounded like tiny bells. The exquisite harmonies did not seem to come from the round, open mouths of the singers. Rather, the music seemed to magically surround us all.

When the carolers were finished with their songs, my mother thanked them quietly and closed the door. When we turned around to go back to the other room, I saw that Mayer, who was seven at that time, had been listening in the background. He cheerfully sang part of one of the songs we had just heard, something about *"ponchke navide-les."* He laughed and waved his hand dismissively.

Did it seep in by osmosis that Jews did not believe in Jesus, or had I been told? Whatever the case, the sight of the carolers had been won-drous, and I wanted to like the little baby, even though I knew I wasn't supposed to.

I did not connect the baby Jesus in the crèche with the priests and nuns I saw walking along the streets of Lodz. I felt that these unsmiling figures, dressed in black cassocks and habits with crucifixes dangling from chains, could at any moment do some dark magic to hurt me. One particular experience always stayed with me.

One day, shortly before we left Poland, when I was three and Jay was six, we came upon a rotted-out tree stump on a small rise in a park.

It was a gray day, with a wind whipping and tossing dry leaves around the damp ground and the scattered tufts of grass that surrounded the stump. The stump had lost all its bark, and, with its roots desperately clinging to the ground, it looked particularly forlorn. The pale wood on the remaining trunk, which was severed about two feet above the ground, made it look like an oversized broken human bone. I watched Jay as he peered into the jagged top of the tree stump. Then I caught my breath as he reached his arm deep inside the stump and brought out a fistful of damp, marrowy earth.

Jay flashed one of his satisfied, dimpled smiles and said, "You try it."

I shook my head. I was afraid.

"You can reach the bottom. Look inside."

I braced myself and peered into the bereft tree trunk. I could see nothing. The hole in the stump appeared to lead deep, deep into the fathomless ground. I smelled the loamy earth from the unknown depths, and I recoiled from the bony stump.

"There's nothing to be afraid of," Jay said as he poked me on my shoulder. Still, he did not insist that I try to feel inside the tree.

We turned to descend the small hill, and that's when I saw them. The three nuns were walking slowly, almost solemnly along the path below. Their black habits swayed around them, their hems touching each other in silent communication as the women walked. Thankfully, they did not look at us. I sensed that, like the tree, they were connected with the vagueness of death.

Shortly thereafter, and periodically over many years, I had a recurring dream. It was both frightening and solemn. It revealed the constant proximity of death to me, a child who had just become aware that I was newly alive.

In the dream, I am on a small hill in a forest. Below me on a path is a carriage with two black horses. It is not really a carriage. Instead of the coach there is a large tree stump that is stripped of bark and that is suspended above the four wheels. Several nuns dressed in black habits approach this vehicle. As the horses stand in readiness, one by one, the nuns climb up a narrow ladder to reach the top of the stump. When each reaches the dark opening at the top, she slips in and disappears. When all the nuns have disappeared, the horses pull this eerie carriage off into the distance.

After we moved to France, I became more conscious of Catholicism. Jesus was suddenly everywhere. He was seeped inside the buildings and the faces around me. He hovered in the sweet scent of pastry shops and in the oily dirt that lay in the crevices between the cobblestones in the streets. He was a conscious presence at the movies. I saw him in his compassion for the lonely little boy on screen who came into church from the cold to see the packed pews and to hear the sacred choir music. His suffering was in the passion play, reenacted on film in various incarnations at every matinee at Easter time. As I understood it, Jesus was a Jew who was converted to Christianity. And although he had died so long ago, the nuns wore black dresses and white collars that circled their faces like the petals of daisies in an expression of mourning. Mostly, Jesus was the young man, naked against the elements, impaled on the crosses that loomed above church doors, proclaiming his suffering and his redemption.

The first time I actually remember seeing him that way was when I was five. My group at the Vladeck Heim was taken for an outing into the town of Brunoy. We marched two by two, dutifully following our leaders. And there he was. I had seen his image as a happy baby and now I finally saw him full-grown and in agony. I could not take my eyes off him, twisting my head backward as we walked past. He was hung on a cross on the facade of a church, so lifelike. His sinewy arms strained to hold on. His body gashed and his forehead tortured by a crown of thorns, his life force was helplessly draining away. His eyes rolled upward in unspeakable pain, beseeching heaven, as his gaunt face and his open mouth formed not a scream but a silent moan. I felt the cold, rusted nails in my hands and feet, and my body ached with fever. They had put him up there to make me guilty, somehow. *See what you have done! Yet, they must hate him. To put him there to suffer endlessly as they watched.* After seeing him like that, a sense of mourning gripped me whenever I heard the deep resonance of church bells.

And what was the message when the old woman concierge in our building on Clignancourt gave me the pink sugar baby Jesus nestled in its white sugar wooden shoe when my mother had given her a *pourboire* at Christmastime? I felt ambivalent and disloyal as I tried to figure out how to eat the little child. It was a violent feeling to bite off his head, tasting the sickening sweetness of the colored sugar. As a child, I dutifully ate the sugary head of Christ as I was supposed to, but I could not eat the rest.

Uncomfortable as it was, it was impossible for me not to love Jesus. They had lied when they said that the Jews had killed him, when everyone knew it was the Romans. And I knew that after this lie, they had kept killing Jews to take false vengeance on us. But that wasn't Jesus's fault. He had been wronged; he was tortured and left to die an excruciating death. And he still forgave. He understood. Like the rest of the Jews. When I played in the courtyard at the entrance to Vladeck Heim in Brunoy, I was no longer just D'Artagnan or Cochise, like Mayer had taught me. I was Jesus, with long, flowing blond hair, wearing a white robe, my sword glistening in my hand, galloping on my white steed, as I went out to fight for justice and the righting of wrongs.

Jay had been the first one to whisper the story of Jesus's death to me, and he taught me many more things about Christianity. When he was nine, after he had returned from Brunoy for good, Jay and I were crossing the boulevard near our school just before Christmas. The store windows on the boulevard were decorated with bright lights and filled with dazzling toys.

"Jews don't do Christmas," Jay said. "Christmas is to celebrate the birth of Jesus and the start of their Christian religion. I don't know what Père Noël and presents have to do with that. Anyway, they trick their little children into believing that Père Noël is real and that he comes to bring them presents on Christmas, when it's really the parents who buy the toys. They tell them that if they're bad, Père Noël won't bring them presents. They trick their children to get them to be good.

"Look. There's one of the fake Père Noëls in the toy store now. If you go in and sit on his knee and tell him you're a good boy and you want such and such a toy for Christmas, he'll pat you on the head and give you a candy," Jay said as he pushed me toward the door.

"Why don't *you* go sit on his knee," I answered, resisting.

"I'm too old. You're six. You can still do it."

"But I don't want to. We're Jewish. I don't want to lie!" I said, as he grabbed my arm, dragging me toward the entrance to the store.

"And what is that Père Noël but a big fat lie himself?! Go in there. It's alright," Jay prodded, urging me to do what he wanted to do himself.

Père Noël's lap was hard and bony, but he had a nice smile and a soft voice behind the fake white beard. "What would you like for Christmas?" he asked looking me in the eye.

I averted my gaze and caught a glance of the storeowners who stood nearby, beaming. *Good. They haven't recognized me as a Jew.* "I want a carpentry set," I whispered to Père Noël.

"Have you been a good boy?" Père Noël asked.

"Yes," I lied, topping off my fraud.

"Then maybe Père Noël will grant your wish. Here is a candy for you, and one for your older brother," he said, lifting me off his knee.

I felt enormously relieved when we left the store, although the whole event had lasted only a moment. Jay didn't usually like candy, but he liked mints. I liked candies, but I hated mints. So Jay got both mint candies.

"You know," Jay said while sucking on his candy, "eight days after Christmas is New Year. That's when Jesus was circumcised, just like other little Jewish boys—but not all, of course." We both knew he was referring to himself in the latter case. "The Catholics don't get circumcised at all," he added. As we walked toward home he turned to me and said, "Isn't it strange how they hate Jews, and yet they pray to one of us?"

I agreed that Christianity sounded peculiar. By this time, I knew something about the Jewish God. I knew from the Sabbath candles that my mother had started lighting on Friday evenings that God had given us a day of rest. I knew from the Passover Seder that we celebrated that he had rescued us, his people, through great miracles. I was loyal to our God long before I had ever attended a synagogue. That happened when I was seven and Mayer was preparing for his bar mitzvah. When the *melamed* my father had hired to teach Mayer what he needed to know told us that our God had created the whole world in just six days, I was proud. Our God was the best.

But at the age of six and seven, looking down from our apartment window on Rue de Clignancourt or on a chance encounter on the street, I was completely captivated by the children in their first communion outfits who were walking with their families to the Sacré-Cœur up on the hill. The boys wore top hats and cutaway coats, their sleek pants accented with a stripe down each leg. The girls wore dazzling white lace dresses and veils, a bouquet of white flowers in their hands. They all had large white ribbons in the shape of a cross on their left arms. The boys were stunningly handsome, and the girls were deliriously beautiful.

As they walked up the street, they looked solemn and serene, as if they were going toward some mysterious act of transformation. I had just learned the secret and awesome nature of sex, and watching this parade of children, who looked like brides and grooms, filled me with the same kind of momentous excitement. The French word *"noce,"* wedding, filled me with a strange sensual, pleasurable feeling that had not yet found its focus. At night, as I lay cramped in the crib that still served as my bed, I dreamed that I was one of those boys in coattails and white gloves. On my arm was my bride in her communion splendor. We stood within the crystal bubble of a helicopter that took us straight up in the air and to our connubial home.

How had I gone in my life from loving Jesus and girls in communion dresses to wearing a yarmulke? I was bewildered by my inconsistencies. Each day I now felt oppressed by the minutia of my faith, obediently tying my left shoelace before my right, anxious about cutting my fingernails in precise order, compelled to flush them down the toilet as prescribed by the *Shulchan Aruch*. I loved my Jewish God, but I was repelled by praying from the *siddur,* and I consistently desecrated the Sabbath. How I wished we had remained in Pittsburgh, beyond the power of either Jesus or yarmulkes.

◆ ◆ ◆

I slouched uncomfortably in my desk chair in the back of my fifth-grade Chumash class. Mr. Wolf stood in front of the board, cleaning his pipe, which looked so small in his large, thick hands. With his ruddy jowls, his stubbly goatee, and his wide girth, he looked grandfatherly. Some of the boys fidgeted, their ten-year-old bodies cramped in their seats. Stray prayer fringes jerked about them, making random patterns along the aisles. Other boys defied their confinement by propping their hands on their desktops and rocking back and forth in the rhythmic cadence of study, bowing toward their open Pentateuchs.

We all waited for Mr. Wolf to put his pipe in his jacket pocket, the signal that he was about to begin the explication of the verses we had just learned, the coda to the lesson. His head bent in thought, he began to pace slowly, his bulbous old men's shoes creaking with each step. All other movement and sound in the class ceased as he started to speak softly in his deep and resonant voice, and we hung on his words.

"When God spoke the Ten Commandments, the Children of Israel trembled in fear at the terrible power of God's voice. 'Let not God speak to us or we will die,' they wept to Moses. We are told that they cried out '*Na-aseh venishma.*'" He took a small piece of chalk and turned to write the two words on the board. "'We will do and we will listen,'" he translated. "What did they mean by that?" Mr. Wolf ignored the scattered hands that went up. Punctuating his words, he continued, "It means, even before we understand, we will leap at the opportunity to follow God's commandments, without doubt, with *emunah sh'laymoh*—complete faith. It is said that the souls of all the Jews who will ever live were present in witness of the granting of the Ten Commandments at Mount Sinai, and they all cried out, '*Na-aseh venishma.*'"

Mr. Wolf paused. Some boys rested their heads on their arms, which were folded on their desks. Others sat erect, looking at the black letters on the white pages of their Pentateuchs. Most seemed deep in thought, as if renewing the vow of *na-aseh venishma* that their souls once proclaimed at Mount Sinai.

"Today, we will talk about the Fourth Commandment: Remember the Sabbath day, to keep it holy. What does it mean, the word 'remember'? The commentary tells us that when this Commandment was spoken, two words sounded at the same time, '*shomer*' and '*zocher*'—to observe and to remember." Mr. Wolf carefully wrote these two words on the board. "What does it mean to observe the Sabbath?"

Many hands shot up. Mine stayed in my pockets, as usual.

"Fox, you answer," said Mr. Wolf quietly, giving me an easy question.

"To do no work," I answered.

"That is correct. On the Sabbath, on Shabbos, we are not allowed any of the thirty-nine categories of work described in the Mishnah or any activities that might lead to them. Fox, what does it mean to remember the Sabbath?"

I remained silent. This I could not answer. I had not prepared the lesson with my father, as many of the other boys had with theirs. The hands shot up again. Mr. Wolf called on another boy.

Wurtzberger got up from his seat. His blond head was slightly stooped in humility, belying his confidence as he recited what he knew. "To remember means to honor. We honor Shabbos with special prayer services. We also light candles for Shabbos. We dress in special clothes. Every meal is special. We eat special bread, challah, and we make kiddush with wine." Wurtzberger sat down, his eyes averted, but a thin, satisfied smile rested on his lips.

"Very good," said Mr. Wolf, resuming his measured pacing in front of the class. "And why do we do these things?" he asked rhetorically. "To separate the Sabbath from the weekday, to keep it holy. We are told that if we do everything that is commanded us on the Sabbath, our spirit is nourished, and we get an extra soul on Shabbos." Mr. Wolf's face softened into a warm smile. "You can feel this extra soul in the peace in the house, in the joy when the family is together."

I squirmed in my seat, while the other boys nodded in agreement.

In hushed tones, our teacher continued, "The Rabbis tell us that it is the observance of the Sabbath that has kept the Jews alive as a people. If we stopped keeping Shabbos, the Jewish people would eventually disappear."

I sat up. I felt chastened in my chair.

"One more thing before we end our lesson." Mr. Wolf turned and scanned our faces. "We are told that if all the Jews around the world observe even one Sabbath at the same time, it would bring Moshiach." He took out his pipe from his pocket. "So, what we have learned today," he said, pointing the mouthpiece of his pipe around the room, "is that each of us assures the continuity of the Jewish people by keeping Shabbos. And each of us has the power to help bring the Messiah."

I slumped back in my seat, defeated.

The next day, when Mr. Wolf entered the class, I still felt chastened. My thoughts wandered off to fields and helicopters and another classroom. "I like you. Do you like me?"

Thunk! Thunk! Thunk! My chest resounded like a barrel, the breath knocked out of me, as Mr. Wolf's large, beefy hand came down hard on my back repeatedly. "Fox, you must pay attention!" he screamed, his neck and face engorged and crimson, his old men's shoes prancing urgently by my desk.

I felt the stinging welts rise on my back.

"He cries so loud," I heard someone whisper.

I felt ashamed in front of my classmates, although a number of them had experienced the effects of Mr. Wolf's explosions. Tears and mucus stained the black letters and yellowed pages as I sat hunched over my Pentateuch, locked into the wood and iron prison of my school desk.

◆ ◆ ◆

I sat pressed into the soft armchair in my parents' bedroom, my fourteen-year-old body hunched over. My memory was physical as I felt yet again the stings and welts caused by Mr. Wolf's rageful hand. *Was it from the time I entered the yeshiva that I started looking from behind my eyes?* I asked myself. *Was it then that I started peering out from behind the edges of the mask of a placid and calm demeanor, never committing myself in the open, not even to myself, lest I give myself away, lest I scream in confusion?* I wanted to leap from the chair, but all I could manage to do was shift my body. My scalp beneath my yarmulke started to itch. I did not scratch. The itching would stop in time. I listened to the stillness.

My parents were settled into their penny-a-point game of rummy in the kitchen, their form of quiet communication across the gray Formica table. I stared out the window. It had gotten completely dark on this Saturday evening. Outside, my classmates must have been heading home from evening services, dressed in their Sabbath suits, walking beside their shining fathers. At home, over sweet wine, with braided candle and silver spice box, they would perform the *Havdalah* ceremony, separating the Sabbath from the weekday, the holy from the profane, while I was enclosed in this darkened room, trapped in this Harlem apartment, wondering what it would take to escape.

The exegesis of my life began again.

Mayer broke out of his boundaries. Can I, too, be what I once was? Can I reclaim what was lost?

When you contemplate what is lost, you are longing for the fleshpots of Egypt, Menachem.

Is that all it is, do you think?

Remember the commentary that translated the word Egypt, Mitzrayim, as boundaries. When we left Mitzrayim we left our boundaries. Think of all you know now that you wouldn't have known had you stayed in your provincial Pittsburgh. You would have been an **am ho'oretz***, an ignoramus, in the ways of the sacred. You've broken out of your ignorance.*

Oh, but what a relief it would be not to know, to act on impulse for a change, to respond to a feeling without embarrassment, without having to double-think its meaning before deciding what to do.

An animal responds on impulse. A righteous human being curbs his desires.

So, should I put fences around my feelings?

You should separate the holy from the profane.

More boundaries?

There are two sides to a fence, and both sides are bound by it. If you straddle both sides, you are doubly bound. Either wear your yarmulke or take it off.

CHAPTER 11

◆ ◆ ◆ ◆ ◆ ◆

Lubavitch Summer

The summer when I turned eleven had been a difficult one. My mother had heard about murderous gangs in the neighborhood, and she was frightened. She started pestering my father early in the spring that he should find a way to get her children out of the city for the whole summer. The previous summer, Mayer, Jay, and I had spent many days walking to High Bridge Park to swim in its huge city pools. We had been among the many poor kids, black and white, who went there to splash around and cool off the only way we had on hot summer days. It was either that or being cooped up in the apartment, watching reruns of the *Gail Storm Show*, *Amos and Andy*, and the constantly repeating films on *Million Dollar Movie*. The following year, Michael Farmer, a boy who had suffered from polio, would be brutally stabbed to death at High Bridge by a teen gang called the Egyptian Kings.

My father used his connections in the Yiddish-speaking world to get Mayer a summer job as a counselor-in-training managing the sports equipment shack at Camp Kinder Ring, a large facility on Sylvan Lake, run by the Workmen's Circle. Jay and I were sent to camp—three different ones. The first two weeks of July, Jay and I enjoyed the nondenominational Camp Vacamas in Butler, New Jersey. Then we spent the next three weeks in the drudgery of Camp Agudah, an ultra-Orthodox, non-Hasidic camp in Fleischman, New York. This was topped off by three weeks at Camp Gan Yisroel in Ellenville, New York, the Lubavitch camp that had just been organized. Vacamas had been a wonderful, freeing experience, and Camp Agudah was a place we endured. But Gan Yisroel presented a different reality altogether.

◆ ◆ ◆

Lights were out. Only outlines of the rafters and the window spaces were visible in the faint light that came from the light pole in the playing field nearby. There were only screens in the window frames, and it was cold. I was to spend three weeks in Camp Gan Yisroel in this its first year of existence. I wrapped my blankets tightly around my shoulders as I lay in my narrow and uncomfortable cot. Sunk into the middle of its unsupportive springs and mattress, I was barely able to turn to my side. I had learned that a faithful Jew must sleep on his side. To sleep on one's back meant facing God directly, an act lacking in humility. But what was I to do? I could lie on my stomach. But that would be symbolic of turning my back to the Creator.

My bed was next to the sink at the end of the clapboard bunk building. In some ways this was the least desirable spot, being next to the bathroom. On the other hand, it was a coveted place. In the morning, one was technically not supposed to take more than three steps before *neygl vasser*, the ritual of hand purification. The first thing any fervent Jew of any stripe must do upon waking is to say the *Modeh Ani*, what I thought to be one of the most lyrically beautiful prayers ever expressed: *Modeh ani lefonekha melekh khai vekayom shehezarti binishmosi behemlo rabo emunosekha.* I am thankful before You, living and eternal king, who restores my soul with Your bountiful love and Your faith.

God must be the first thing in one's thoughts upon awaking. And the first thing on one's lips must be the expression of thanks that one has survived the deathlike state of sleep. This prayer of thanks does not contain God's name. That is because one cannot utter it in a physically or spiritually unclean state. One certainly must have touched one's private parts in the night, so one cannot utter God's name with unclean hands. Also, one's soul has left the body in the night to report to the Almighty. And it has left through the fingernails, leaving behind the residue of the spiritual degradation that the body to which it was entrusted soiled it with on the previous day. The fingernails must be purified with water. Hence the name *neygl vasser*, literally "nail water."

Each morning when my eyes opened, I whispered the *Modeh Ani*. Staring at the rafters and beyond them to God, I was filled with fervor as I recited it. I was the first in my bunk to purify my fingernails. And I did not have to tread three steps to the sink in the cold morning air in order to pour three cupfuls of water over each hand to do it. Only after I performed this ritual did I utter God's name in the *al netilas yadayim* prayer for the spiritual cleansing of the hands. The other thirteen members of my group followed suit, but only three of the others could make it to the sink in three steps.

When *neygl vasser* was completed by all, the typical morning ablutions of face washing and toothbrushing took place. Then the campers hurriedly dressed and rushed off to the *beys medresh* hall for the formal morning prayers, which on weekdays lasted from a half hour to an hour, depending on whether the Torah was read on that particular day. On the Sabbath, the praying, the Torah reading, and its attendant ceremonies lasted all morning and into the early afternoon.

One of the counselors, his black hat balanced precariously on the back of his head, led the morning services that were shared by the entire community of about one hundred or so male campers and staff. A large wool *tallis*, or prayer shawl, decorated with stripes and dangling its *tsitsis*, was draped over the leader's shoulders. On weekdays, *tefillin*, or phylacteries, completed his ritual garb. The *tallis* and its dangling fringes bounced jerkily as the leader chanted and swayed in prayer. His role was to maintain the pacing of the group prayer, not to be the representative of the group before God. It was only if someone did not know how to read or to say the prayers, that the *bal tefilah*, the leader, represented him. But it was the illiterate's "Amen" that counted then, not the reading itself. Everyone prayed individually. The lack of unison, the murmuring of prayers, and the occasional shouting out of liturgical phrases by any given supplicant during services were intentional and reaffirmed that everyone stands alone before God.

All those over the age of thirteen wore tefillin on their left arms and on their heads. These little leather boxes and straps held the tenets of the faith: You shall keep the word of God between your eyes, in your arm, and over the doorposts of your house; *Shema Yisroel, Adonai eloheynu, Adonai ehad.* Hear oh Israel, God is our Lord, God is one. Most of the assembled did not wear talleisim. Their *arbah kanfos*, those smock-like garments that dangled their essential *tsitsis*, more humbly served for the same rites. And everyone swayed to the cadence of his own prayers. This swaying back and forth, with heads bobbing and bowing, was symbolic of trembling, which is the prayer of the body.

Only when morning prayers were over was breakfast allowed. On Saturdays, the younger campers who were not yet bar mitzvah were allowed a bit of cake and milk before the services. Understandably, everyone was ravenous when services were over on the Sabbath. But few left in a hurry. Most lingered in or around the prayer hall, where they felt closer to what was holy.

Most weekday mornings after breakfast, we had clean-up, Talmud studies, and a sports activity. The afternoons were geared to swimming and sports, but there was a lot of slack time, which I liked. I was free to wander, as I had been in Brunoy and Les Andelys in France. I spent some time with Jay and his new friend.

Ira was an unusual character in the camp. Whereas most of the boys wore subdued clothes and leather shoes, he wore tight dungarees, a black leather jacket, and motorcycle boots. Perched on top of his long, black rebel hair that fell in front of his face, he wore a small yarmulke that was held on with a bobby pin. He was twelve years old.

No one paid Ira any adverse attention. He prayed and studied Talmud like everyone else, although he tended to stay off by himself. Jay, who was fourteen, had befriended him and treated him with respect. He had always liked unusual people. Ira rarely smiled. His face stayed mostly neutral, and he answered questions with as few words as possible. The one thing that animated him was singing popular songs he had learned from the radio. He had a pure and soaring voice that was a mixture of sweetness and sadness.

Jay and I asked Ira to sing one particular song over and over. Ira would begin by closing his eyes. Then, shaking back his hair, he would raise his shining eyelids to the sky. When he opened his round, full mouth to sing, there arose from somewhere within him the sound of an angel. "Everybody's got a home but me," he sang.

Each morning, I rushed to the *beys medresh* for prayers with everyone else. I looked for Jay to come out the bunkhouse next to mine to get the chance to walk with him. We usually walked in silence in the chill morning air, our heads bowed in thought. Somehow, we both used this short journey as a time of reflection. The only sounds around us were the soft murmurings of the other campers and the swish of the dew-laden grass that flecked our shoes. This was certainly different from the walks we took in the woods and fields of France. Those seemed a lifetime away.

Inside the prayer hall, some of the boys and men had already started in their preparations and prayers. Most had favorite places in the room. Some liked to be in front, near the *bal tefilleh*, where they could follow along more closely and join in more loudly in the communal singing. Some found places in the back, where there was more room for the vehement rocking and swaying that helped their *kavoneh*, or spiritual devotion. Jay and I found inconspicuous places at one of the benches toward the middle of the hall.

Amid the murmur of praying that began to rise about him, Jay carefully took out one of his tefillin from its velvet pouch and kissed it. He uttered the requisite prayer and placed the phylactery over the biceps of his left arm, the black box pointing toward his heart, as required. He slowly wound the strap onto his arm. I could see him exercising the same care and precision in creating the requisite pattern as he had when he had carved designs on his walking sticks at Les Andelys. His concentration was complete, and he believed in what he was doing. When he had finished with his arm, he wound the excess strap temporarily onto the palm of his hand. He took out the other phylactery, kissed it, and placed it on his head like a crown, guiding its long straps over his chest so that they dangled and flowed like graceful ribbons. He then completed the process by winding the strap around his hand that ends in the pattern that spells the first letter of one of God's names, *Shaddai*.

Jay then picked up a *siddur* and opened the prayer book to the start of morning prayers, and I followed suit. And I knew that we both had the same conflicts and frustrations about what we were doing. We wanted to participate and belong, but we couldn't fully do so. Neither of us had adequately learned how to read or recite the prayers. We had no more ability than six- or seven-year-olds. We stumbled along as best we could. Those prayers we knew how to recite, we whispered or sang wholeheartedly. Whether we understood the Hebrew words or not did not matter, as long as we knew how to say them. It was the ritual of articulating the words that counted. The many prayers we didn't know, we faked, swaying to-and-fro and mumbling in chagrin, hoping no one would notice. We were the illiterates whose prayers were mostly transmitted in our "Amens."

For my part, I felt like a fraud. After all, the sage Rabbi Akiva had been an illiterate farmer when at the age of forty he began studying how to read along with little children. He had no shame about it. I had had the opportunity at yeshiva from a young age to admit that I didn't know, to get help and start from the beginning, but I hid instead. True, I was conflicted about belief itself, but that was my biggest failure. My hope was that God, the all-knowing, would have compassion and understanding because he had made me this way.

At night, I lay in my bed among strangers who were supposed to be my people, other boys for whom there was no schism between what they practiced at home and outside in public. Images of my father frying up pork-saturated Spam and gathering up the drippings for himself in Paris alternated in my mind with pictures of him swaying, his head covered by a *tallis*, his eyes brimming with tears, as he said the Kaddish at the memorial service on Yom Kippur. Perhaps, like my father, my purpose was to know more of the larger world than these boys. And perhaps God would accept what was in my tormented heart as well as in the few prayers I was able to read to Him.

◆ ◆ ◆

One night early in the first week, as we settled into our beds in the darkness, springs creaking as we tried to find comfortable positions in the merciless cots, Lazar, the thin, pale, wraithlike firebrand who had started the camp with the Rebbe's blessing, came in and nodded to each boy as he walked slowly and silently down the wide aisle between the two rows of beds. His eyes fixed on mine in the near darkness, and he smiled. As he leaned against the wall that was closest to me, in his plaintive voice he said, "*Chevreh*, boys, let me tell you a story." Then his voice began to float into the air as he declaimed the tale. "In a Jewish village in Eastern Europe, not too long ago, there was a pious couple who were blessed with many children."

I could picture a small village with crooked little houses and mud streets, with a wooden synagogue in its central square.

"But," Lazar continued with a sad shrug, "one of their sons was born mute. He was a cheerful and pleasant boy, but he could not say one word. He heard well enough, and that helped him in a way. He learned how to whistle. His father was not particularly happy with this because whistling was considered unbecoming and rude. Still, this was the way the boy expressed himself, and he was grateful for that. The boy's happy times and his sad times could be heard in the songs he whistled.

"On most mornings, the boy accompanied his father to the synagogue for prayer services. They took their usual place in the back of the *shul*. The boy held the prayer book open like everyone else, and he seemed to follow along, but no one knew for sure if he recognized the words in front of him or what he understood. He turned the pages and stared out in front of him in silence. One Yom Kippur, the whole community had spent all day gathered in prayer at the synagogue. The boy stood next to his father as the sun was beginning to set. The congregants were all anxiously awaiting the time for *N'ileh*, the concluding service. 'Rabbi, can we start it now?' they asked. But the rabbi said, 'No. We have to wait.'

"'But why, rabbi?' the congregants asked. And the knowing rabbi answered, 'Our prayers are gathered in front of the gates of heaven, waiting to be let in, but the gates will not open. We cannot conclude until our prayers are admitted.'

"The members of the community were bewildered. This had never happened before. They milled around the *shul*, some praying and contemplating how they could be better Jews in the next year, some hoping that their special prayers for their loved ones would be answered, some thinking about whether they would be written into the Book of Life or not. All of them were thinking of the breaking of the fast with their families after *N'ileh* was concluded.

"'Rabbi,' they asked after some time had passed. 'Is it time?'

"'Not yet,' answered the rabbi. 'The gates of heaven have not yet opened to let in our prayers.' And so, the people waited and waited for the rabbi to give the word. But it did not come. People became anxious. Some paced the hall. All of them were praying either silently or out loud. And they were all worried: *What if our prayers are not accepted?*

"And that's when it happened. In the back of the *shul*, the mute boy, who had been waiting like everyone else, looked preoccupied. He didn't look at his prayer book. He did not notice the agitation around him. Instead, after the long day of fasting, he felt something stir deep inside of him. He wanted to express his love for *Hakodesh Boruch Hu*, the Holy One, Blessed is He.

"'*Reboynu Shel Oylem*, Master of the Universe,' he thought with all his heart. 'I cannot speak my words of prayer. Please accept the only prayer that I can voice.' And that's when the most beautiful, soulful whistling rose above the sounds of the loud and frantic praying of the rest of the people.

"Suddenly, there was shocked silence in the room. People were furious. 'Whistling in the synagogue? Defiling the holiest day of the year? It's not only a sin but an outrage!' They knew who had done it. They turned to the boy with fury in their eyes. The boy suddenly looked frightened. He didn't know what he had done wrong. He turned to his father, whose eyes were downturned with shame. Members of the congregation suddenly walked toward the boy with menace in their eyes, ready to throw him out, when they heard the rabbi shout. 'Stop!' he ordered.

"The people stopped and turned to face the rabbi. Looking into all of their eyes, the rabbi began. 'We have all been waiting for the gates of heaven to open and accept our prayers,' he said. 'But all of our pleas to God could not pry open the gates of mercy. They did not have sufficient devotion and piety. The boy's whistling was the prayer that was so pure of heart that it provided the extra push that helped the rest of our prayers open the gates. Now we can conclude with *N'ileh*.'

"The people looked humbled as they concluded *N'ileh* and envisioned their prayers flying toward the throne of the Creator."

With that, Lazar's shadow looked around the still bunkhouse. Then he lowered his head. "Good night, boys," he said, and he silently walked out.

The story served as a balm to me. My inability did not have to be an impediment. The Bal Shem Tov, the first Chasid, had said, "Even if I am completely ignorant, if I believe, that is enough!" My belief and my wordless mumbling, murmuring, and swaying would be my whistling until I learned more of the prayers.

The second Saturday morning of camp was particularly glorious. The morning air was crisp and sweet as Jay and I walked to the prayer hall, wearing our Sabbath suits. My mood was light as I picked up my siddur. The singing of the *bal tefilleh* and the murmurings of those gathered around me had a surprising softness. I could almost see the sounds hovering above our bowed heads. Looking at my prayer book roused no tension in me for the first time. My body was light and insulated. Whatever I could read and offer would be enough.

When I left the prayer hall after services were concluded, the midday sun shone so brightly that the trees and grass, the buildings, and the young men and boys clustered in small groups were nearly lost in the glare. And it even seemed that the dazzling light almost entirely blocked out the sounds around me. I waited for Jay to come out so that we could walk to the dining hall together. He was inside, talking to Ira. I saw Lazar walking slowly toward me. His wiry hair and his scraggly beard were brilliant red in the sunlight. Frail-looking though he was, he radiated an enormous confidence and strength of will. Smiling with his whole body, he caught my gaze with his fiery eyes.

"So? How *are* you?" he asked slowly and quietly, and his voice was the only thing I heard. He bent his head forward slightly. His eyebrows were raised in indication of the import of the question. Although it did provide room to be interpreted as a simple greeting, I knew what he meant. He wanted to know if I had caught the spirit. He did not want to press too far. I was embarrassed by the respectful concern he was showing about my faith. He knew that its flame was barely kindled, if at all. After all, Lazar had known me in Pittsburgh, when I did not wear a yarmulke or *tsitsis*. And maybe he had intended the story of the mute boy solely for me.

"Alright," I said, only slightly less ambiguous in my answer than he had been in his question.

"Good," he said, nodding. "Good." He nodded again, and he walked away.

I was good at vagueness. Some of my favorite words had become "maybe," "could be," "perhaps," and "possibly." Most of the time, my use of these words of doubt had become a way to cloud my own mind and feelings against recognizing the irreconcilable fragments my life had become. I had to hide so much. I had developed an external life and an internal life, and neither was adequately real. They were both "as if."

In the yeshiva and in camp, we studied tractates of the Talmud that expounded laws and practices for a nonexistent land governed by religious Jewish law: When does someone get punished with lashes of a whip? When is one to flee to a city of refuge? In my external life, I practiced a studied ease and casual posture. I held in my pouting lower lip, and I opened wide my puffy eyes so they would not look as if I were always on the verge of crying. In my internal life, I began to spend a good deal of time in fantasy. I dreamed mostly of being spontaneous.

I was ashamed of both my external facade and my internal urges, the former because of its deceit and the latter because they expressed my base instincts. But in all circumstances, I was cautious, worried that I would be tripped up and exposed. Maybe. Perhaps. Possibly. These were good words to hide behind.

However, this time, when I answered Lazar in the warm, midday sunshine, I was not trying to hide. I was trying to assess what I was truly experiencing. I did not need to lie to him. This time my vagueness reflected some stirrings of faith without inadequacy. I recognized that unlike the people in the yeshiva I attended, the people here, even those with austere clothing, close-cropped heads, and long *payos*, were somehow more like me. And they did not judge me. I felt it might be possible to find a way to be, if not as part of them, then certainly among them.

Jay came up to me a few moments later, and we walked the short distance to the dining hall, his arm around my shoulder. The noise level of the dining hall was almost deafening. Finally released from the intensity of serious ritual, the campers were hungry for food and whatever else was mundane. Jokes and baseball arguments flew along the benches and across the oilcloth-covered tables. The traditional meal of cholent was served, as it was every Saturday. It was a stew of vegetables, potatoes, and rolled meat that was slow-cooked overnight. Boys traded parts of their meals. Some preferred the vegetables to the meat, which was gray and heavy and lay in the stomach like a weight.

When the meal was over, the *benchers* were passed out, and one of the counselors led the thanksgiving blessing after the meal, saying, *"Raboysai nevoreych! (Gentlemen, let us pray!)"* to which the assembled responded, "Blessed be the name of God forever, and ever!"

An enthusiastic roar of responsive singing followed, accompanied by the pounding of fists and the stomping of feet to the beat of the melody. The sound was electric. Surrounded by these boys and men in ecstatic song, I was swept up by the fever pitch. Along with everyone, I recited and sang this benediction after the meal, which I knew well:"- *Veochalto, vesovotoh, uverachto.* (You shall eat, you shall be satisfied, and then you shall be thankful.)"

Only when you are satisfied, then shall you praise God, I thought. I sang loudly without fear of being caught in error, without fear of being heard at all.

On that Saturday night, as on all others after sunset, the boys and men gathered in the dining hall for *Havdalah.* With eyes closed in deep concentration, and swaying fervently, one of the scraggly bearded young men recited the prayers. He passed around the silver goblet of wine and the silver filigree box of cloves and spices with the wish that the sweetness of the Sabbath that was symbolized by them would linger with us for the rest of the week. When the cup was returned to him, he held the braided candle aloft and doused its multiple flames headlong into the wine. A loud cheer rang out in the hall when the candle sputtered and sizzled. The separation between the holy Sabbath that was leaving and the mundane weekdays that were to begin had been effected.

It was now time for the *melaveh malkah* the escorting of the Queen Sabbath, to say goodbye to her for another week. The long dining tables were quickly pushed together into the center of the hall or piled onto the outside porches. Many of the men and boys gathered around the perimeter of the hall, their faces brightening and their bodies catching a rhythm. With one hand on the shoulder of the person in front of him, each began a lively two-step swaying and marching dance, moving forward to the cadence of a song that sprang spontaneously from the group. The floorboards of the old dining hall began to creak and groan under the shuffling feet. The dancing grew more vehement, and every song became more emphatic. As the line snaked around the room, bystanders were yanked in to join the swaying and swerving of the reveling leviathan. As hours passed, the energy only grew higher. The room thundered with the rhythm of stomping feet, and the walls vibrated with the blissful songs that rose up to heaven and no doubt to any neighbor who happened to live nearby.

In a space in the middle of the room two men crossed their arms and locked their hands together. To the rhythm of the sounds of singing, hand clapping, and foot stomping around them, they began to whip each other around faster and faster. They squatted and bounced up like springs, as they did a flying *kazatske*. Their grinning faces grew flushed as their heads arched back and their legs flailed about them. *"Moshiach kimt shoyn bald!"* the words of the song rang out. Two boys got on the shoulders of two other young men and all four linked arms and twirled around with gusto. "The Messiah is on his way!" they sang with every ounce of fervor that was in them.

Jay and I were watching the spectacle from the sidelines when, suddenly, some hands grabbed us and swept us into the frenzy. We had no choice but to throw ourselves into it. Our bodies rocking, heads swaying to-and-fro, we stomped our feet and joined in the song. *"Zol shoyn kimen di geuleh! (Let our redemption come now!)"* I let myself be carried along by the throng, my eyes closed. In the swirl of devotion around me, I was beginning to sense what it was like to give one's self over, to lose one's self completely, and to fold into the arms of God.

Give me a sign, oh Lord, and I will follow you blindly, I cried silently. *Bring* my *redemption now! Zol shoyn kimen* mayn *geuleh!*

After some time, Jay broke from the line, and I followed him out of the building and into the cool night. We walked silently across the lawn and then across the road and past a scruffy thicket to the small lake. In the distance, we could still see the glowing lights and hear the booming of voices and feet that emanated from the dining hall. But the lake was still and dark. Jay picked up some stones to skip. I looked up to the canopy of stars.

Reboynu Shel Oylem, why is this so difficult for me? I asked silently. *Do I need more will, or do I have to give up my will entirely to be close to You?*

We straggled back to our bunks well past midnight. As I walked into my cabin, I could see that some of the other campers my age were already sleeping. Some of the others were still out among the revelers whose dancing and singing I could hear in the distance. The next day, they would stagger half asleep to morning prayers.

In the nights that followed, in the stillness, among the other eleven-year-olds in my bunk, none of whom I had actually become friends with, I continued my dialogue with God. *I need to stop being a fake. I want to shed my double life. Help me live in one world.* The rafters of the bunkhouse seemed ghostly and as high as heaven above my narrow bed. I shivered beneath my blankets, waiting for sleep.

◆ ◆ ◆

During the week, Lazar again came to tell us another story. In the dark and the stillness of the night, he created yet another world for us to consider. He began in his soft, unobtrusive voice: "One Friday afternoon, before the Sabbath was to begin at sundown, a porter, who lived in a port city, was looking for work. Anything would do, so long as he could earn a *gilden* to buy fish to honor the Sabbath meal. But no customers appeared. When he was about to give up hope and go home to his wife to tell her that they would have to honor the Sabbath as best they could, suddenly he saw a man dressed in odd green clothing, with a green feather in his cap.

"The man beckoned him with his finger. 'I have all these bundles,' he said, pointing to a stack of boxes. 'If you carry them for me, I will reward you well.'

"'Where to?' asked our porter, eager for the work.

"'Just follow me,' said the man.

"The porter picked up the heavy boxes and followed. The man in green led him through winding city streets and though the outlying village beyond it. The porter followed him through fields and into a dark forest, the boxes on his back becoming heavier and heavier. Our porter was nervous. 'Where is he leading me?' he worried.

"Suddenly, in the middle of a clearing, the man in green stopped. 'You may put the boxes down here,' he said.

"'You want them here, in the middle of the forest?' asked our porter.

"'Yes, exactly,' said the man in green.

"The porter put down his load. He expected a good tip for having carried his burden all this way. That is when the man in green turned to him and said, 'I have no money to give you, my good man. But I have something better. Here is a map to a land where you will find gold and jewels waiting for you to pick them up in the streets.'

"The porter, who had always been a patient man, could not control his anger. 'You brought me out here to give me a map?!' he shouted.

"'Yes,' the man in green simply said. And with this he placed the map in the porter's hand. Then he and his packages suddenly disappeared in a puff of smoke.

"The porter was stunned by the disappearance of the man. He was certain that this magic was something he must pay attention to. He went home to his wife with nothing but his map in his hand.

"'I know that if I follow this map, I will find my fortune,' he told his wife after she had lit the Sabbath candles and he had said the Kiddush over water and the crust of bread they had. After their meal of bread and water, he went off to a restless sleep.

"The next evening, when the Sabbath was coming to an end, the porter's wife spoke to her husband. She said to him, 'Through the years, I have scraped together whatever I could for the day when all hope was gone. But now I know that I was saving this for you.' She thrust a small sack that contained some coins into her husband's hand. 'Take all we have and buy the boat and the supplies you need to get you to the land where gold and jewels are found in the street,' she said. 'And bring some back!'

"The porter wept as he gratefully took the small pouch. He knew he had to try to find the land of gold and jewels. He outfitted a small sailboat with as much food and water as he could afford. He said good-bye to his wife and sailed off into the unknown, following the map of the man in green.

"His first days at sea were beautiful. The winds were steady, the waves were gentle, and he made steady progress toward the land he sought. At night, he dreamed of returning home with his fortune.

"But soon, the winds stopped completely, the sea became smooth as glass, and the sun began to beat down on him fiercely. It was not long before he drank his last drops of fresh water. He became delirious from the heat and the thirst. 'I am going to die out here in the middle of the sea,' he cried.

"At that moment, a powerful wind came, and storm clouds gathered above him. Thunder and lightning exploded all around him. The clouds burst open, and rain poured out in torrents. The howling wind began to toss about the little boat as if it was a toy. It cracked the mast of the little boat, and the sail flew off and disappeared into the sheets of rain. The boat bounced on the crests of waves one moment, and the next it dove into the angry foam below. For a full day and a never-ending night, the storm raged as the porter held on for his life. Finally, having spent all his strength, he passed out in his shattered boat.

"When he awoke, all was quiet. He was surprised to be alive. The sun was rising in the distance, and gentle waves were moving his boat along a direction. 'Which way am I going?' he thought when he got his wits about him. He searched around for his map, and he found it stuck in a crack of the boards. Miraculously, it had not been swept away by the storm. As he studied the map, he suddenly noticed something glowing on the horizon. It glowed brightly even in the light of the sun. 'My boat is heading right toward it,' he thought fearfully. 'Who knows what other trials await me there?' he worried, clutching his map.

"As his boat moved closer and closer to the glowing spot, it became brighter and brighter. The boat got closer still, and he saw that he was nearing land. When the boat finally scraped to a halt on the beach, the porter jumped out and pulled it in to secure it. That's when he discovered that his feet were not standing in sand—but in gold dust!

"He fell down to his knees, laughing with joy. He picked up handfuls of gold dust and threw them up in the air, watching the specks glitter as they rained down on him and his tattered clothes. Instead of seashells, he found rubies and pearls. He laughed in disbelief as he stuffed diamonds and emeralds in his pockets and threw other gems into the waves.

"He soon realized that he was starving. All his remaining provisions had been lost in the storm. He looked around to see if there might be edible plants. That's when he saw a road. 'This road must lead somewhere,' he thought, and he began to follow it. He soon saw signs that people lived in the land. He passed fields and fences. All along the road he found bracelets and necklaces laden with precious jewels. He laughed in amazement as he stuffed his pockets.

"Finally, he reached a town. He walked down the main street, and everywhere in the gutters along the sidewalks there were jewels and golden adornments. He came to an inn and walked through the door.

"'Innkeeper!' he shouted as he sat down at a table. 'I want your finest meal!'

"The innkeeper looked at the man dressed in rags and asked, 'With what are you going to pay for this meal?'

"The porter reached into his pockets and pulled out a fistful of jewels and proudly answered, 'With this!'

"The innkeeper looked at him in puzzlement. 'You want to pay with that dust? You can pick that up in the street. It's worthless!'

"The porter realized that the man was right, that in this land he had nothing. He held his head in his hands and began to cry. The innkeeper took pity on him.

"'Look,' said the innkeeper. 'I can see that you're a poor man. I'll feed you, and then I'll give you work.'

"After giving him a simple meal, the innkeeper handed the porter a broom. 'Here,' he said. 'You can sweep out the place.'

"The porter understood his plight. He had no way to get back home. He took the broom, and he began to sweep. He swept out the same gold dust and jewels that he had picked up so happily just a short while before.

"'But what do you use here for money?' asked the porter as he swept.

"'Why, fats, of course!' answered the innkeeper. 'Any kind: chicken fat, cow fat, duck fat. You'll get paid at the end of the week.'

"The porter accepted his fate and worked for the innkeeper. He forgot about the gold and jewels. They were foolishness here. But he soon discovered that there was much opportunity in this strange land. He started his own business, and after a number of years of hard work, he was a rich man. He had amassed seven warehouses of fat!

"Although much time had passed, he never forgot his dream of returning home and bringing with him his fortune. He had kept the map for the return journey. One day, he hired some large ships equipped with sturdy sailors, and he had them load up the holds of the large vessels with the contents of his seven warehouses. And the sailors followed the map to bring our porter back home. This time it was a smooth crossing.

"When the boats were approaching the port city where the porter had lived, the people there began to smell an awful stench. They soon realized that the terrible smell was coming from ships that were nearing. They all fled the horrible smell of rancid fats as the boats tied up to the docks.

"When the porter stepped onto shore, he saw that no one was there. 'No matter,' he said to the crew. 'Just carry my fats up to that hill. I'll pay for the land later. That's where I'll build my warehouses.' The men did as they were told. Then they set sail with the map back to their own land.

"People began to stream down to the port. 'What are you doing to our hill?' they shouted.

"'I'm storing my wealth there,' said the porter.

"'Wealth?!' someone screamed. 'That rotting fat is less than worthless!'

"That's when the porter realized his mistake. Again, he fell on his knees and began to cry. The people left him in disgust. Only one person remained behind. It was his loyal wife, who had waited for his return for all these years.

"'We have always been poor in our life together, so things will be no different now,' she said to console him, as she led him back to their hovel.

"The porter was exhausted with grief. He took off his clothes and went to sleep to forget his misfortune. As his good wife folded his clothes, a few small things fell out of the pockets. Yes, she found a few tiny diamonds and rubies that would have been mistaken for dust in that other land.

"The porter and his wife sold the jewels, and they managed to live out the rest of their lives on the proceeds of these few precious things that the porter had accidentally brought back with him."

Lazar sighed. "What does the story tell us, *chevreh*?" he asked into the night. He let the question sink in. "The story tells us that the *Reboynu Shel Oylem* sends us out from his kingdom in heaven with a map to a land where we can pick up gold and jewels in the street. What are these precious things? They are *maasim toyvim*, good deeds. They are *lernen*, studying Torah. They are *tsedokeh*, acts of charity and righteousness. The opportunities are everywhere. It is so simple to do them, as simple as picking them up off the street." Lazar paused.

Quietly he continued, "But what do we do? We run after fats instead. These fats are money, pride, speaking badly of others. We chase after these things so much that when we return to the Kingdom of God from which we came, we only have a few jewels that we've picked up almost by accident. Hopefully, they will be enough to see us through. Good night, *chevreh*," he said and silently slipped out of the cabin.

What are my jewels? I thought. *Should I throw away the life I've led, that my family has led? Are you saying that my parents are only pursuing fats because they don't follow all the rules you find sacred? No, I don't believe it. There must be jewels in our lives. We are better people than you can understand. Still, my parents sent me to you to tell me what a Jew is and what God wants from me.*

◆ ◆ ◆

And Lazar came on yet another night. "*Chevreh*, I have another midrash for you." And we listened in the stillness and the dark.

"In the time of the Czars, the Russian army would take Jewish boys, as young as nine years old, to train them for a twenty-five-year tour in the military. They commanded the *Kahal* to provide these children. And when the leaders of the community fell short in the number of children they had taken, the soldiers kidnapped the rest to fill up the quota. This is the story of one nine-year-old boy who was captured as he cowered in his hiding place one winter. They grabbed him and marched him at gunpoint to the assembly place, where he stood in the snow with twenty-odd other boys, most of whom were under twelve. From this forlorn place, the boys were marched to a soldiers' camp, and they were trained as soldiers. They were marched through the cold of winter and through the heat of summer. They were marched until they forgot who they had been and only knew that they were soldiers in the Czar's army.

"But our young boy did not want to forget. He struggled to keep the faces of his family before his eyes. He struggled to remember that he was a Jew even after several years marching in his ill-fitting uniform and carrying his heavy load.

"One winter, in a driving snow, he decided to make his escape. He thought that if he fled into the blinding white snow no one would notice until he was far away. And then, maybe they would think that he had died of the cold along the way, as so many other young boys had.

"As they marched out of a forest one night, he dropped back and hid behind a tree. He hoped no one had noticed as he ran headlong into the woods. He ran as fast as he could, shedding his heavy pack as he went. He did not know where he was going. He only knew that he had to flee. He ran through heavy forest, became soaked through as he crossed ice-laden streams. He ran desperately through the night and the entire next day. As night fell again, he could run no further, and he fell onto the bitter-cold, snow-covered ground. 'I will die here,' he said to himself. 'It is better than the living torture of the army.'

"He was just about to close his eyes to enter the sleep that would lead him to his death when he thought he saw a glimmer of light through the distant trees. He wasn't sure he had seen it, but he decided that he would use the little strength he had to reach the light. He crawled and stumbled and gained energy as the light grew stronger and closer. With almost his last breath, he reached what turned out to be the entrance of a cave. He entered it, but he saw only dim light. The cave was warm, and his need for sleep was so great that he huddled in a corner and passed out immediately.

"When he woke up, he didn't know how long he had slept. But he now had his strength back. He looked around him and realized that the cave was quite large. He turned to find the source of the light, and he saw that the light was brightest in one corner. He got up to explore the light and discovered that there was another cave behind the one he had been in. And this was where the light was coming from. He walked into this cave and found that it was brightly lit, as if by the sun. And he became frightened by what he saw next.

"There, in front of him, he saw a table covered with a velvet cloth. On the table was a golden bowl filled with water. Next to this was a two-handled cup, also made of gold. But even more frightening to him was what was on the other side of the table. There he saw a marble platform with a magnificently adorned throne. Sitting on the throne he saw a man with a long beard who wore the crown of a king. The king's eyes were closed. His arms were stretched out before him, and his hands were formed into fists.

"The boy was so terrified by this man with his closed eyes and his outstretched arms that he ran out of the cave into the woods. He ran and ran in blind fear into the darkness of yet another night. And again, the cold sucked out his strength until he could almost go no further. And again, he saw a light in the distance. He ran to this light, which turned out to be coming from the synagogue of a small village. The boy reached the door, opened it, and collapsed in front of the holy ark.

"The members of the community were conducting evening services when this boy dressed in a soldier's uniform fell before them. The rabbi saw that he was flushed with fever, and he had some of the men carry him to his house, where his wife cared for him through two days of tortured sleep. He woke on the third day in time to walk to the synagogue where the members of the community were again conducting evening prayers. When he entered, the rabbi stopped the service. He asked the boy what had happened to him. And the boy told the community about the cave and the table and the king sleeping on his thrown with his fisted hands outstretched.

"The rabbi's face turned white. 'Do you know who you saw?' he asked the boy in a trembling voice. 'It was *Moshiach*, the Messiah. He was waiting for someone to pour the *neygl vasser*, the water from the bowl over his hands to wake him, so that he could bring peace and redemption to the world. You could have wakened the Messiah. If you had only known what to do!'"

With this, Lazar became silent for a while. Then he said, "Good night, *chevreh*. When you have the opportunity, be sure you know what to do."

I pulled the blankets tight over my shivering body.

◆ ◆ ◆

My group's table and benches were at the far end of the dining hall. I sat in the corner, near a window that led out to the screened porch that wrapped around the building. Next to the window on the porch side was a payphone. The third Thursday in camp, the phone rang during breakfast.

"Someone answer the phone," the counselor ordered.

I was closest, so I jumped up to the window ledge, reached around, and picked up the receiver. Before I could say hello, I was barraged by a loud, growling man's voice yelling from the other end. I couldn't understand a word of what it said, but it sounded very threatening. Then the person hung up. Later that morning, I heard of another similar call during a Talmud study group on the porch. At lunch the phone rang again. This time it was answered by a counselor. "What? Who is this?" Then a hang up.

That day and the next, the rumor was whispered around camp that the *shvartsers* down the road were threatening to "get us" if we didn't stop making so much noise with our loud singing and dancing late into the night on Saturdays. A quiet but general anxiety spread among the campers in my bunk. Many of them lived in Crown Heights in tense proximity to the black community that had grown up around them. I was nervous too, given the increased reports of violent crimes in my upper Harlem neighborhood that I heard about almost nightly on the television news at home.

When I mentioned it to Jay, his face was serious. He raised his eyebrows and shrugged his shoulders in a gesture that meant, "What can we do? We'll just have to face this." I wondered what my mother would feel if she knew she had sent us away from the dangers of our neighborhood to the dangers here.

On Saturday morning, I met Jay on the path, and, dressed in our Sabbath suits, we walked in silence to the *beys medresh*. It was another brilliant morning, and there was a slight chill and the scent of wet fallen leaves in the air. I felt the melancholy of the fall creeping in. It meant that I would soon be imprisoned indoors, yet again destined to wear the yoke and harness of my yeshiva. Although to some extent I was a fraud here at Gan Yisroel as well, at least here the expression of warmth and joy and fervor were valued, especially as we sang our prayers and danced with wild abandon at *melaveh malkah* on Saturday nights. And Lazar knew who I was, and he accepted me.

As Jay and I approached, several boys were already milling about outside the prayer house before services were formally begun. Sudden bursts of laughter broke out from among them and just as quickly faded. A boy my age giggled as he suddenly ran awkwardly after his friend. Then just as suddenly he slowed to a stop. The other boy called to him, "*Zay moykhl! Forgive me!*" And they huddled next to each other, speaking softly. Honey cake and poppy seed strudel and cartons of milk were laid out at the usual table outside the entrance of the hall for the younger boys, but few partook. I certainly didn't. I thought the others must all be as scared as I was.

The *bal tefilleh* began the service with the same intense devotion as usual, and the older members of our community fell in with the fervent swaying and chanting that seemed to allow them to commune directly with God. And the younger children, with their soft supplications, joined in, carried along by the elation. I looked around me at the bobbing fringes of the *taleysim*, with their borders of black-and-white stripes and ached to have the same faith. Black-and-white stripes. The threat to "get us" would not let me be. Long ago, the German madman had threatened to "get us," and so many of us were no more. I wondered if my parents were braver than I was when they first heard the threat.

The afternoon passed as the other Sabbaths had—rest period after lunch, a session of Talmud study, quiet walking and milling about the grounds. The writing of letters and physical sports were not allowed. The playing of board or card games was also eschewed. Jay and I walked around together, for a time joined by Ira. He looked small and uncomfortable in his Sabbath suit as he came up behind us suddenly. His mop of hair swayed before him as he looked toward the ground and walked quietly with us. Just as suddenly, he departed with a "See ya." When we were by ourselves again, I asked Jay how he felt about going to George Washington High School in the fall. He said it would be a relief. There was no need to say more about it, although both our thoughts churned about how he would change come the fall.

We walked along the edge of the ball field. The scraggly sumac and scrub oak trees that bordered it and the mysteries of the woods behind them did not beckon as they had when we were in France. Now our explorations were internal. Our self-definitions were devoid of the resonance of the natural world or musketeers or Indian braves. And we said nothing about the rumor that weighed on us and also served to define us.

In the evening during *Havdalah*, the silver wine goblet and silver filigree spice box were passed around to eager hands in the crowded dining hall. Sip the wine. Breathe in the sweet spices. May all who are gathered here have a joyous and sweet new week! *Just let it be calm tonight*, I said to myself. Then the tables were pushed into the middle and the singing and dancing began. If anything, it sounded louder and more ecstatic than usual to me.

The entire assembly erupted in a *nigun*, and the voices resounded as two hundred feet pounded out the rhythm of the song. I consciously stayed on the sidelines next to Jay, my protector. But a pair of hands suddenly pulled me into the dancing throng. With my hands on the shoulders of the person in front of me, I sang softly and slid my feet quietly along the quaking floorboards. I looked for Jay, but I could not find him on the sidelines. He must have been pulled into the din as well. I ripped myself out of the winding line and looked for Jay. When he came around, I grabbed his arm and pulled him out of the heaving procession. We needed to stay together.

We remained next to each other the rest of the evening. When one of us was pulled into the line, we both joined in. And we left the line together as well. We did not venture outside the building, as we had before, to escape the almost deafening noise, to be just with ourselves under the canopy of stars. We stayed indoors. There may not be strength in these numbers, but at least there was anonymity, and there were better odds.

Before midnight, Jay and I left with a group of campers who were returning to the bunks. We parted ways when we reached mine. "It'll be OK," Jay said, patting my shoulder. "Good night."

I bounded up the steps and was relieved to find that most of my bunkmates were already in their beds. I huddled under my blankets in the chill night air. There was no lock on the door, and the windows were just screens. It felt as cold as a winter night in our drafty Harlem apartment. I pulled my pillow over my head and hoped to wake in the morning.

I awoke with an anxious start. No one was in the bunk. I jumped out of bed, fearing the worst. Then Jay walked in. "Hey, sleepyhead, everyone's already in *shul*. I came to get you. Come on." Then he added with a superior smirk, as if he had known all along it would end like this, "Nothing happened."

I dressed quickly and bounded out of the bunkhouse relieved. "Nothing happened!" I laughed as I walked brightly next to Jay. Our black neighbors down the road had only made empty threats. When the time of our thunderous Sabbath celebration came, they weren't outraged enough to act.

At the end of morning prayers that Sunday, as had happened on several other recent days, one of the camp leaders got up to remind us of our religious obligations. "Remember, it's after *Tisha B'Av*, and we are in the month of *Elul*. Between now and Rosh Hashanah, then Yom Kippur, we have to reflect on our behavior, especially our *aveyros*, our sins, and we have to commit ourselves to be better. To help us in this, tomorrow night we will have a light show at the lake. Some of the counselors will be enacting the story of Jonah, which is the *haftorah* for Yom Kippur, as you all know. The story of Jonah tells us that everyone is capable of *teshuvah*, repentance, that God is merciful to all his creations.

"So, between now and tomorrow night, we should think especially hard about how each of us can be a better person and a better Jew. And since God cannot forgive us for the sins we have committed against other people, we have to ask those whom we have injured to forgive us. And we have to forgive those who have injured us. Since it isn't always possible for people to know whom they have injured, we must ourselves grant forgiveness to anyone, known or unknown, who knowingly or unknowingly might have sinned against us. And it's not enough to just toss off 'Sorry' or to lightly say 'I forgive you' without thinking about it. We have to do this with all our hearts and with all our souls."

On the way to the dining hall, I forgave the people who had threatened us, and I asked forgiveness in my heart for expecting the worst of them. "What's a light show?" I asked one of my bunkmates as we walked.

"Oh, it's very nice. It's lights on the water," he said, but he couldn't elaborate. "It's nice. You'll like it."

The following evening, free activity lasted longer than usual. When it grew dark, our counselor gathered us up in a group, something he didn't usually insist upon, and our procession to the lake was more formal than usual. Other groups also streamed along the path and lawn at the same time. This was a special event. We were dressed in light jackets against the cool night air. We crossed the road and joined the others who were already sitting on the inclined ground that bordered the lake, facing the dark, shimmering water.

There was a festive murmuring among the campers. But it grew immediately silent when one of the counselors stepped in front of the gathering and began to declaim. His form was silhouetted against the silver seams of the water as he trumpeted the words:

"The Lord said to Jonah, 'Rise up! Go to the great city of Nineveh and proclaim to its inhabitants that their wickedness is known to me.'" Another counselor, as Jonah, raised his arms and hid his face. "No!" he shouted. He ran about in panic, looking for a hiding place, as Jonah would have. He crouched in fear as he could find none. Then he continued in an anguished voice, "No, my Lord. Do not send me to the evil city of Nineveh. Those that dwell there do not deserve Your love. They will not repent." And the narrator continued, "But the Lord again bade Jonah do as He commanded. 'No. I must flee,' cried Jonah. And he ran to the port of Joppa where he paid passage for a ship going to Tarshish."

At this point, several counselors near the shore lit candles that were affixed onto paper plates, and they sent them floating onto the placid surface of the lake. As more and more candles drifted along, they looked like golden water lilies bobbing on the water. The surface of the water became a shiny fabric that covered the opaque depths as unfathomable as those of the Great Sea. The counselors surrounded Jonah, close to the water's edge, and rocked with him as if they were in a boat.

The narrator continued, "Then the Almighty caused a fierce wind to blow upon the sea, and there arose such a storm that tossed the ship about so furiously that it was in danger of breaking apart. Each passenger and sailor cried out to his own god to save them from disaster."

At this point, the counselors surrounding "Jonah" put him down and began to wring their hands and raise them to the skies. One of them used his arms to make waves on the water, and soon all the candles and plates began to heave and rock and gutter, and some of them tipped over and sputtered into darkness.

"Only Jonah calmly went down into the innermost part of the ship and lay there fast asleep," the narrator said, as Jonah crouched into a sleeping position on the ground. Another counselor came near and stood over him. The narrator then continued, "The captain of the ship said to Jonah, 'How can you sleep? Rise up and call upon your God. Perhaps your God will save us.'

"Soon the doomed men on the ship decided that perhaps the gods must be angry with someone on the ship, and that is why it was being punished so. They drew lots to see who it might be. The lot fell upon Jonah, and the men asked him who he was. 'I am a Jew and I worship the Master of the Dry Land and the Sea.' The men became even more frightened as the sea grew even stormier."

"It is you who have done this by your fleeing from the presence of the Lord!" one of the counselors proclaimed.

In unison the rest shouted, "What shall we do with you that the sea might be calm again?"

A silence of seconds followed, as we on the shore, absorbed in the story we knew so well, awaited the response.

"Toss me into the sea!" said Jonah with a shrill, piercing cry.

We all gasped. And that was when the crack of rifle shots thundered out of the nearby bushes. Men with dark faces and white eyes and teeth shouted and growled and yelled incomprehensibly as they waved their guns in the air and fired off several more rounds. The boys around me screamed and began running in all directions. I could see fire come out of the rifle barrels as more volleys were fired. I looked around desperately for Jay, but I could not find him in the darkness. I was blinded and deafened in the chaos. I panicked as I realized that the threat I had dreaded had not disappeared. It had returned on its own timetable, after I had let down my guard.

"Run to the *beys medresh*!" I heard a voice shout out. Most of us did exactly that, following its command. I spotted Jay in the prayer house and ran over to him.

"I was looking for you!" Jay shouted, almost angrily, at me.

We could hear more shooting from outside. All the boys inside the synagogue were on the floor. Some were quaking in fear. Many more were shaking in prayer, holding on to large religious tomes for security. Then a counselor's voice rang out. "Pray! Pray with all your hearts and souls! Beg forgiveness from God. Forgive those who have sinned against you. None of us knows when our last day on earth will be. Any day could be our last. We must always walk in the paths of righteousness."

The boys around us prayed even louder, and Jay and I joined in. We picked up large tractates of the Talmud and wrapped our arms around them. I prayed that this was not my last night alive and that some Maker would show me mercy.

Then, the counselor shouted once again. "They're coming this way! Everybody out of the *beys medresh!* Run to the field outside!"

There was more panicked screaming, as boys with Talmuds and prayer books in their arms ran to the field. We heard the repeated sharp cracking sounds of more rifle fire, and all of us fell to the ground. I lay there with my face close to the cold, damp ground, pressed as close to the grassy earth as I could to avoid getting hit by a bullet. I turned my head to see Jay, who was right behind me, in the same posture.

My mind flashed to my parents. *Was this what it was like when you were taken from Bialystok to Siberia, when the Germans strafed your train?* The freight train stopped, and all the passengers ran out to the sur-rounding field. My father had told the story at the reception dinner in his honor when we first had come to New York less than three years before. He said that he covered his wife and infant son, Mayer, with his body to protect them. He buried his passport in the ground. I would have to ask him about all that if I ever got out of this predicament.

Suddenly, there was more shooting behind us, accompanied by familiar laughter. "It's alright, *chevreh!*" Lazar's voice boomed. "It's Color War!"

I turned around to see Lazar surrounded by some of the counselors as well as the men who shot off their rifles. All of them were now shouting, "Color War! Color War!"

The boys closest to them got up first. Then the rest of us followed, seeing that it was safe. Jay and I walked up to the men and saw familiar grinning faces under the blackening makeup.

"Now, boys, return the *s'forim* to the *beys medresh* and come to the dining hall where we'll divide all of you into the Blue and Red teams!"

Jay and I returned our books to the prayer house. We walked silently, but we could each see the disgust and bitterness in each other's eyes. As we walked toward the dining hall, Jay broke the silence. "Color War!" he said and spit on the ground.

We were divided into two teams for a three-day sports competition that most of the campers were excited about. Some of the campers who did not shine in religious studies were able to make their mark in these physical events. I could not get emotionally into it. The events that had led up to it reverberated in me at almost every moment.

I was disillusioned, hurt, and disappointed. They had maligned a group of people in the same way they complained that Jews were always maligned. They had tricked us, those whom they were supposed to protect. In the shadow of a greater horror, they had created a make-believe scenario to horrify us into observance and faith. They were so good at symbolic worlds, parables to translate into our lives. What else was make-believe about what I had learned from them? Was I really starting to commune with God in my prayers and my walks under the stars? Or was that also an illusion carefully planted and nurtured by their acceptance of me? My head swam.

Activities were much more structured now, and Jay was not on my team. I didn't see him as often as I wanted to. I think he made himself scarce, along with Ira. No one missed them in the hoopla and manufactured excitement

I sat with the Red team at meals now, each team occupying separate sides of the dining room. Special events were planned for mealtimes, intended to rally the campers even more. It was lunchtime on the second day, and we were going to be treated to some piano mastery from two of the people in camp. The first one was a tall, olive-skinned counselor, who usually wore a suit every day. He had a scraggly beard but very delicate facial features, and he walked with calm dignity. I had heard that his family was originally either from Yemen or India, that he had become a Hasid when the family moved to Brooklyn. It was announced that he would play a Chopin étude.

The dining hall was quiet and respectful as he played the upright in the corner of the hall. He played exquisitely, with lilting trills and sweeping melodies throughout. When he finished, I applauded with full force, but I found myself to be the only one who did so. The rest of the crowd gave him only tepid applause.

The second person to play was a redheaded boy of about eleven. The whole dining room was quiet in anticipation. He also played Chopin. He played well—for an eleven-year-old. There was no subtlety of feeling. The focus was on his mechanics, which were coming along but not yet smooth. When he finished, the entire dining room broke out in thunderous applause, cheering, and foot stomping that did not subside for several minutes. Shouts of "Encore! Encore!" reverberated in the room.

I asked my neighbor at my table why the wild cheering, and he gave me an answer that stunned me. The redheaded boy was the son of the secretary of the Lubavitcher Rebbe, and as such, he had *yikhus*, special status. He was like the son of the king's prime minister to the kinsmen who surrounded me.

I cringed inwardly. I wondered if my beginning faith and the sense of belonging that I had begun to experience in camp had been a manipulation that would ultimately seduce me to mindlessly follow a new form of Jewish king.

The last night of camp was marked by "The Banquet," a lovely meal with brightly decorated tables and splendid food. There were several self-congratulatory speeches about the success of the first year of camp, and there was dancing well into the night.

The next day, we packed our duffel bags, suitcases, and trunks into the busses that took us back to 770 Eastern Parkway, in Brooklyn, where we were welcomed by the Lubavitcher Rebbe himself. He waved slowly to us as we danced wildly before him. Jay and I danced too. I was happy to see the Rebbe. He was an important man, a famous celebrity to me. He stood erect, looking distinguished but austere in his dark suit, dark beard, and black fedora. His face was inscrutable to me as he looked out at us, not kindly as I heard it was, and he would not be my source of faith and belonging.

CHAPTER 12

◆ ◆ ◆ ◆ ◆ ◆

Light and Heat

In my Harlem and yeshiva seclusion since the age of nine, my only genuine social life had been with my family. Outside its confines, I was dependent on my parents to bring me to parties or gatherings where there were other children from their social circles. From the time I was eleven, my mother especially liked to take me to events where there was a girl my age.

In early spring, when I was not quite twelve, at a dinner party at the Bronx home of my mother's friends from her hometown of Konin, I was introduced to Marissa, who was my age. I was besotted. She was the most beautiful girl I had ever seen. She had the blackest locks of hair and the deepest, widest black eyes. She had full, beige-pink lips that were hypnotic. She and her parents had just returned from a car trip to Miami Beach, and Marissa had an exquisite bronze tan. The silky white dress she wore, with its delicate line at the neck and short sleeves, enhanced the soft brownness of her smooth skin. In truth, I had never seen anyone with a tan before, and it only added to her mystery and glamor and to my intoxication.

Marissa had such feminine ways. She sat next to me, erect and poised, at the dinner table, which was set for fourteen people with a damask tablecloth, Czech crystal, Rosenthal china, and German silver. When she saw that I needed help, she leaned close to me, and I breathed in her delicate scent as she quietly pointed out which utensil I should use for each course, from the outside in. She first showed me the serrated teaspoon to be used with the Indian River red grapefruit her parents had brought back from Florida.

"You don't need to add sugar to these, they are so sweet by themselves," she said as I scooped out a section.

For her own part, Marissa held her soupspoon delicately, with her pinky in the air, as she soundlessly took a mouthful of her golden soup. I noted that she held her knife and fork in the European manner as she cut small morsels of chicken. She neatly dipped them in the fragrant sauce before lifting them to her mouth, and she ate close-mouthed, shutting her eyes with apparent pleasure.

As the meal wound down, her parents suggested Marissa entertain me in her room. Her room may have previously been a dining room because it had French doors covered in lace curtains. She showed me her blue and yellow parakeet, taking it out of its cage and placing it on my finger. She explained the scratching board it used to file down its beak and claws. She showed me how she cleaned the cage every night to make sure the bird stayed healthy.

"You sometimes have to do dirty things. It's part of living, my mother said." She chuckled as she returned the budgie to its cage. "I'm going to let it go to sleep," she said, as she placed a cover over the domed cage.

"It goes to sleep when you cover it?" I asked with incredulity.

"The light would keep it up. It's dark under the cover, so it knows it's night." She laughed, rearing her head back, and I saw the two rows of her lovely white teeth and the pink of her throat.

Marissa was a wonderful hostess. She gaily asked me about myself, if I liked yeshiva, what I liked to do when I was not in school. I answered politely, not knowing how to be open or if that would be welcome. Then, she went out into the living room and came back with a crystal decanter and two delicate small crystal glasses. She put the glasses down on her bureau and poured chocolate liqueur into them. Taking one glass for herself, she offered me the other. She looked at me through lowered eyelids, and she smiled as she put her glass to her lips and took a sip. I followed suit. Her eyes, her smile, the glass to her lips, the silken liqueur—I had never before experienced such a sweet caressing of my senses in my life. Then she asked me a question that caused my body to twitch in the most pleasant way. "Why do you wear your pants so high? It's now the style to wear them below the belly button."

Marissa would have to stay only in my dreams and fantasies, as I did not see her again until the following year, in the early summer. The Charoffs, an elderly couple who had a summerhouse and swimming pool at Greenwood Lake, had invited all their fellow members of the Koniner Society up for a day of picnicking and fun. The Koniner were Jewish remnants of the small city of Konin, Poland, who had survived and were now living in New York. Marissa was there among the other children of these survivors, most of whom, including her parents, had numbers on their arms. Among them were Marissa, and another girl, Anna, whom my parents had introduced me to at other Koniner functions, such as the paddle wheeler trip up the Hudson to Bear Mountain. But alas, after a day of swimming, laughing, and boating on the choppy lake, Marissa and her seductive smile would again have to exist only in the solace of my fantasies for a long time after that day.

◆ ◆ ◆

From age eleven through age fourteen, I had two weeks' respite from my typical existence in the summer. My father had enrolled me in Camp Vacamas, a Jewish Federation camp for poor New York children. It was wonderful. Set on a lake and many acres in Butler, New Jersey, it brought me back to the fields and woods I had roamed with freedom in Les Andelys. Beautiful cabins were set among the trees, and there was a large decked waterfront for swimming and a dock with rowboats. I passed the test for the deep water somehow, but most days I took the option of boating and exploring the lake and its shores. The lake was teeming with life—sunnies, perch, minnows, frogs, tadpoles, turtles, and the occasional swimming snake. I had loved boats from the beginning and now even more. As the boat rocked gently with each stroke of my rowing and I breathed in the living water-scented air, I listened to the rippling currents against the skiff as it glided under the open sky. I felt alive.

The dining hall was massive. The entire camp of several hundred campers and counselors gathered outside it, waiting for the doors to open for every meal. It was always so festive and loud as the children from all the bunks gathered. The campers came from all backgrounds. It was a nondenominational camp, with Jewish, Irish, Italian, African American, and Hispanic children. There was always an undercurrent of excitement as boys' and girls' bunks intermingled. The girls most frequently teased the boys to get their attention. I did not need such teasing. I had picked out the girl whose face and bearing caused frissons of pleasant feelings to ripple over my body. She did not notice me, but I got to touch her hand the few times we had square dancing in an open section of the dining hall.

Each bunk had its own large square table, where we could all face each other and talk. At lunch and dinner, along with a variety of vegetables, some of which I had never seen or tasted before, there was usually a meat dish. For drinks there was a choice of water, "bug juice," or milk. I did not like milk, but it was nice to have the option of having it with meat. It did not seem like such a sin.

At the age of thirteen, my body was developing and robust, and I became a good softball player at camp. I was a home-run hitter, but I had a terrible throwing arm. I played the outfield, and I either had to make a mad dash to catch the fly balls or I had to run in balls I had caught on a bounce because my throws were likely to go off in random directions. At the gatherings before meals, girls wearing pink lipstick were actually interested in me. I was embarrassed and did not know how to respond except with shyness. Underneath, I was still the yeshiva boy in a boys-only class and had little experience in talking to girls.

But the rest of that summer provided a crack in the door to my freedom. My parents had rented a room in a big, old house in Edgemere, Far Rockaway. The rent went down after Fourth of July, and they got it at half price. Our room was on the second floor, and there was a bathroom down the hall that was shared with the other three sets of residents on the floor. The room was quite bright and airy. It served as kitchen, dining room, and bedroom. The refrigerator was from a bygone era and whirred. The wooden table had mismatched chairs, but we could sit comfortably around it, and there was a big oak dresser on one side. My parents' bed sat against the windows. At night, my brothers and I set up our narrow cots. The sea air was cool and made for good sleeping.

I was always the first one up. As my family breathed heavily in their sleep, I dressed quietly and, summer book in hand, tiptoed down the stairs and out the porch door. The yard was large and private, with its tall privet hedge. I lay down on the aluminum and plastic-webbed lounge under the huge mulberry tree. All was quiet and serene. This was a far cry from the confines of the armchair in my parents' bedroom or the stocks of a school desk.

In the afternoons of my first days in Far Rockaway, Jay, who had been there for almost two weeks before me, showed me the lay of the land. Jay always wore white shirts, chinos, and loafers, except when we went to the beach. Rolled towel in hand, he wore a tight bathing suit then, and he pumped up his muscles as he walked resplendently along the crowded beach, packed with people and blankets and beach umbrellas even on weekdays. The black curls of his pompadour tumbled down his face as he introduced me to members of his "crowd," a gaggle of fifteen- and sixteen-year-old boys and girls, parked on their blankets near the 32nd Street boardwalk stairs. They looked so grown-up to me, and they seemed so comfortable with themselves. Jay had been there only a short time, and he had already made a wealth of acquaintances. But he did not abandon me for them. He showed me how to dig for sand crabs, and we spent hours diving into the crashing surf. In the evenings Jay was off, sporting his white shirt with rolled-up sleeves, sometimes accompanied by Mayer in his Como sweater. Mayer was awkward, and he welcomed Jay's ease with people. Mayer often stayed behind, however, reading his science fiction books by the lamp near his cot. He was more comfortable that way.

During days on my own, I wandered about the ball field at the end of my street. It had been part of the air-defense station whose decommissioned mortars were still located behind chain-link protection at one end. The field was now used by the PAL for Little League games, and I watched many games from behind home plate. I wondered how I could join a team and wear a real uniform. Often, I walked through the field and into a thicket of brush and trees and sat on the slope beneath which a finger of the bay had made its home. I pulled out long, thick strands of black mussels, reeking with a musty, rotting smell. I wondered how people could eat such things.

I rode the Schwinn that my brothers had given me along the boardwalk from Beach 35th Street to Playland at Beach 98th Street and back, the pounding and sizzle of the high surf on the beach in my ears, the bright sun beaming down, and the damp wind chilling me and feeling so good under my shirt.

In an empty parking lot by Beach 28th Street, I met a group of boys trying to organize a softball game. "Wanna play?" one asked, and I now had my own crowd. I played ball with them almost every day. We rode our bikes like a swarm of flies throughout Far Rockaway and Bayswater, looking for empty school playgrounds and ball fields to play on in the mornings.

They all lived in bungalows by the beach between Beach 27th and Beach 28th Street. There was a long courtyard down the center where families mingled and barbequed and young children played. It was a world of its own, with middle-class people from the Bronx. The wives and children spent their days here instead of in hot apartments in the city, and the working husbands came in the evenings and on weekends.

Totally unexpectedly, Henri, who had been Jay's younger friend in Les Andelys and whose sister, Elvira, had been Jay's "girlfriend" when he was eleven in that children's home, was now in New York, and his family was spending the summer in a basement apartment in a year-round house in the warren of streets around Collier Avenue. He now became my friend, Jay having moved on to an older crowd. Henri introduced me to the boys and girls who lived around his house. We all started going to the beach together in the afternoons. In the evening, we gathered in the lingering light on someone's porch and told jokes or talked about playing seven minutes in heaven. Once, we played spin the bottle, and I had my first kiss on the lips from pretty Debbie.

CHAPTER 13

◆ ◆ ◆ ◆ ◆ ◆

My Friend

From my first day at Breuer's in fifth grade, Aaron always made a beeline to talk to me, to ask me things, to get me to answer him, and I didn't want to be rude. For as long as we were friends, I was uncomfortable with him.

"Hi. Do you like playing punchball?" he asked, as we played the game in the playground with the other boys during recess. He was not wearing his fancy outfit anymore, but he was still nicely dressed, and he wore very sturdy, heavy shoes that made him exert so much effort when he ran the bases. "What do you like better, punchball or slug? Can you roof a Spalding?" We pronounced it *Spaldeen*. "I can roof one five stories and sometimes six on 186th Street. I bet if we can get into one of the buildings on the block, we'd find plenty of Spaldings on the roof."

I made the mistake of answering him. "You're probably right," I said, trying to end the discussion. Instead, it emboldened him.

"All you have to do is ring all the intercom bells and someone will let you in without asking who it is," he said excitedly.

"So, do it," I retorted.

"I don't have the nerve, but I know you can do it. Please, please. Come on. I'll share my Potato Stix with you. I'll buy you a cherry Coke," he pressed on. "Oh please, please."

I walked away from him without another word. He ran after me and caught my arm.

"Alright, alright. I'm sorry," he said. He trailed next to me as I tried to get to another part of the playground. "Maybe another time? I'll do it with you," he added, hoping that would make a difference to me.

I turned to him and answered with as much conviction as I could, "I'm not interested in getting any Spaldings. Now stop!"

"Alright, alright," Aaron laughed. "I really had you going there, didn't I? Sorry. I just want to be friends."

I looked at him again. "Stop sticking to me, you creep," I wanted to say. But I didn't want to be rude, so I remained silent.

I tried my best to avoid Aaron in class and outside, but by the next week, he had seen me take the subway home. I tried to get to the train fast, but by the second week of school, he finally caught up to me on the downtown side of the A train at 181st Street.

"Hi," he said casually, as he positioned himself next to me. "Do you get a subway pass? I saw you get one from the secretary. I get one too. You have to live more than a mile from the school to get a free pass, you know. What stop do you get off?"

I couldn't see the use of not telling him since we took the same trains.

"You're at 145th Street? No kidding. I get off one stop before you, at 157th. That means we both change from the A to the IRT at 168th Street. We'll be going together."

In time, while I did not like his constant intrusiveness, he became my only friend at school.

◆ ◆ ◆

Aaron always pleaded with me to come to his house when we had off from school on Sunday afternoons and holidays. He always wheedled his way out of coming to my house. He lived at 153rd Street and Riverside, and I lived at 146th and Broadway, the same eight blocks in either direction. I couldn't decide if he wanted to win some kind of finagling game or if his parents didn't like him going to someone else's house. Aaron lived in a three-room apartment with his parents, little brother, and grandmother. Its windows faced the Trinity Church Cemetery, and that seemed spooky to me, but not to Aaron, who was used to it. At least it provided an open view north for a few blocks and a partial view of the river.

Aaron always had some pressing scheme he wanted to carry out. "We need a clubhouse," he urgently said when we were in seventh grade.

"Alright, alright!" I finally capitulated. I had experience in building huts in the woods of Les Andleys with my brothers. I found an isolated spot hidden by wild grasses and bushes close to the abutment and chain-link fence above the railroad tracks. I showed it to Aaron.

"Naw! Naw!" he shrieked. He had a fixed idea about what his clubhouse should be like. "We have to dig it out of the hill, like a cave."

He would have it no other way. He dragged me to a slope close to the promenade on Riverside Drive. "Here! We can hide our clubhouse under these bushes, and no one will find it. We can get plenty of wood scraps for the walls from the building going up next to the yeshiva."

It made no sense to me. I wondered what he wanted to do in this earthen hovel, even if we did succeed in digging it out and keeping it from the squirrels and rats. Since he expected me to take the lead in making this clubhouse, it didn't happen.

One Sunday after school, not long after his clubhouse scheme had evaporated, I went to Aaron's house. We were in the room he shared with his parents. His bed was in a corner of the large room. His parents' bed occupied the middle of one wall, and a highboy dresser stood on the opposite wall. Next to it sat the small desk Aaron's parents had just gotten him so he could do his homework in peace and quiet. He was very proud of it. It made him feel like a real student. And maybe it would help him; he was smart and knew a lot of things, but he was always struggling with his grades.

I stood in front of his bed, and he stood by the window to have a catch with a Spalding. I had planned to tell him something today that I had been thinking of telling him for a long time. If he is my friend, I reasoned, I should at least be honest about this and trust him.

I said to Aaron, "I want to tell you something important."

Aaron was silent. He listened as he threw the ball to me.

I caught the ball and held it. "My family is not religious, and I'm not religious. I think you are not religious too. I want you to tell me the truth." I threw the ball back to him.

"Aw, naw!" Aaron protested. "You're just saying you're not religious to trick me into saying I'm not religious, and then you're gonna say you were fooling, that you are religious and then I'll have said I'm not religious."

"No, I just want you to know about me," I said. "I don't want to hide this anymore. You can do what you want."

"You're just trying to trick me! I am religious!" he said forcefully as he threw the ball wildly.

The ball rolled under Aaron's bed. I reached down for it on my hands and knees, and that's when I found the can of shaving cream Aaron had hidden there. I pulled it out and presented it to Aaron. I was silent, but I smirked. Religious people used electric shavers. It was against religious law to use razors or shaving cream. Aaron hung his head and shook my hand.

"Don't tell anyone. I'll get kicked out!" he said.

"Why would I tell anyone? I'm in the same position," I said, reassuring him.

From that day on, we were able to meet on Saturdays without pretense, with each other at least.

◆ ◆ ◆

Aaron's parents hired a special rabbi to teach him the Torah and *haftorah* portions for his bar mitzvah. "You see this," he said, showing me a plain album cover. "This is a record of my bar mitzvah portions. I only study with the rabbi once a week, because it's expensive. With this record, I can practice on my own. Do you know what *trop* is? It's the musical marks you *leyn* the Torah with. There are these little marks above all the words that tell you how to sing them. It's hard to learn these notes, but with the rabbi and the record, I can learn to sing my portion by heart without learning *trop*."

Aaron's bar mitzvah took place in the Conservative B'nai Israel Synagogue on 149th Street between Broadway and Riverside. It was a huge, impressive building with a stately granite facade. The sanctuary was magnificent, with its lofty domed ceiling, brilliant chandeliers, delicately carved altar, and massive Torah ark. There was a rabbi who sat on the bimah, holding a siddur, and a cantor with a high, crownlike yarmulke who chanted the morning service.

I sat with Aaron and his family. He was wearing a beautiful, brushed-wool brown suit and his own new *tallis*, and he looked excited and happy. He looked at me with a warm smile and held my glance. I knew he was glad that I was there with him. Besides his family, Aaron's uncle and aunt and cousins, and the friends of his parents, there seemed to be few regulars who attended the services. Most of the former members of the synagogue had moved away. Mainly older people occupied the sparsely filled pews. I liked the fact that men and women sat together, though. This would have been a scandal in an Orthodox shul.

Aaron recited the blessings and chanted his portion in a quavering voice, without any errors. In school, the boys who had had their bar mitzvahs all talked about the number of errors they made—one, two, or at worst, three. Neither of us had been invited to any of our classmates bar mitzvahs and didn't expect to be invited to those that had not yet happened. I was the only one of our classmates who attended Aaron's celebration, and I knew that Aaron would be the only one of my classmates who would attend mine eight months later.

Aaron recited the speech his rabbi had prepared for him, "I will keep the *mitzvos* . . . I will wear my tefillin . . . I will bind God's commandments to my arm and keep them always before my eyes . . ."

Aaron's parents looked proud, his little brother grinned, and his grandmother cried with joy.

Aaron's party was an open house. This meant that people could come anytime during the afternoon to celebrate and join in for food and drink. One of Aaron's old Austrian relatives had made the smoothest, most delectable homemade eggnog, as well as a light and delicate seven-layer cake and other wonderful pastries. Aaron went to greet each new arriving guest. In between, he and I indulged in the eggnog and cake. I was pleased for Aaron. He had done well that day. I was his only friend, but his family seemed to have an active life that Aaron participated in. I had never known this about him. Our relationship had not broadened out beyond school.

Mayer had had his bar mitzvah in a large Sephardic synagogue in Paris. I remember a loud and bustling event in that *shul* in the round. Jay had had his bar mitzvah in Rabbi Berger's small jewel of a synagogue on 148th Street. It had always charmed me, with its faux marble columns, colorful walls, jeweled Torah ark curtain and altar coverlet, and women's balcony with its painted ivy decoration. The *shul* had a high ceiling, and soft light filtered in from its high windows, but it felt cozy and intimate. I would have loved to have my bar mitzvah there. But it closed about two years after Jay's bar mitzvah. There was simply no community to either support it or even form a minyan anymore. Old Rabbi Berger, with his gaunt, kindly face and short gray beard, had lived alone above the *shul*, in a sparsely furnished apartment. His wife had died years earlier. I wondered where he went after the *shul* closed.

My bar mitzvah service was to take place in a *shtibl*, a prayer room, on Broadway and 158th Street. It was a large, double-sized room with storefront-type windows and half curtains on the second floor of a two-story building that had stores on street level and offices and our *shtibl* on the second. The space had a holy ark, an altar, and long tables with benches and chairs for the men in the front section. There were benches for about twenty women in the back section, which was separated from the men's by a knee wall and a gauzy *mechitzah* curtain. There were rarely more than one or two women on a regular Saturday. The services were led by one of the laymen who had a not-unpleasant, booming voice. There was no rabbi in this *landsmanshaft* prayer room. Most of the congregants were from the same city in Hungary, and they knew each other before the war. A few Polish Jews, like my father and me, were warmly accepted as well.

My father and I attended services there every Saturday morning for a year. I was pleased that my father was doing this for me. In fact, he got to the services punctually, while I arrived at least a half hour late every Saturday. He knew how to daven, and he prayed the liturgy with fervor. In between his prayers, he took time to turn the pages of my *siddur* to the beginning of the service when I arrived. He pointed with his finger, indicating that I could not join the congregation where it was, but I had to begin at the beginning. He was not aware that I could not read the prayers well and that I mumbled through many of them. He obviously thought, without evidence, that I was as competent in this as he was as a boy in Poland a half century earlier.

The services lasted until well after one o'clock. Starving, I shared in the Kiddush, usually herring and schnapps. The thimble-sized amount of hard liquor mellowed me a little, but not enough. I left before the seated adult celebrants, including my father, who discussed the week's Torah reading as it related to politics.

I headed back down Broadway toward home. I always stopped at the regal quadrangle at 155th Street and the National Museum of the American Indian, whose entrance was marked by a huge totem pole. I usually looked in on my favorite artifacts and searched for new favorites among the never-changing exhibits. There were so many low glass cases to explore, and I had hardly examined more than a few of them.

On one particular day, I walked past the American Indian museum, down the stately plaza to the Hispanic Society Museum & Library, with its bold statue of El Cid in the courtyard and its centuries-old artifacts exhibited in the hacienda-like main hall. I always felt I was in the Spain of a bygone era in this grand space. As always, I was eager to go to the large gallery that was just for the Sorolla murals. They were a panorama that filled all the walls of the room and depicted everyday Spanish life from an earlier time. *Did Sorolla paint them in this room?* I wondered. *It looks like he must have.* Regardless, the paintings washed over me in their breadth of vision, and I wanted to go inside them. When I left to go home, I had finally let go of the tension that had built up in me during the time I had spent in synagogue.

When April came, I realized that I must start studying. On a Saturday afternoon after shul, I went to my father, who was writing a letter at the kitchen table. *"Tateh, ch'miz hubn a rebbe zich tsitzegraytn. (I need a rabbi to help me prepare.)"*

My father looked up at me in disbelief. *"Di gayst doch in yeshiva, zay lerner dus nisht os? (You go to yeshiva, don't they teach you that?)"*

"Nayn Tateh. Yeder yingl hot zan aygner rebbe far deym. Mayer hot gehat a melamed. Un Yankel hot gehat Reb' Berger. (No, Dad. Every boy has his own rabbi for this. Mayer had a special teacher. And Jay had Rabbi Berger.)"

"Ober zay zenen nisht gegangn in yeshiva yurn lang. Di mist zich alayn oslernen. (But they did not go to yeshiva for years like you. You have to teach yourself.)"

I was confused. *He goes to Sabbath services for a year for my bar mitzvah, but he won't get me someone to teach me to chant my Torah and Haftorah portions?* *"Chozhbe koif mir a pliteh. S'iz du azelche far yede parshe. (At least buy me a record. They're available for every Torah portion.)"*

"Vifl cost aza pliteh? (How much does such a record cost?)" he asked.

"Tseyn doller (Ten dollars)," I replied, thinking this was not too much.

"Kenst zich alayn oslernen, (You can teach yourself,)" he said as he returned to his letter.

At that moment, I wished I were Mayer. Mayer would have said, "Then I won't have a bar mitzvah!" But I was not Mayer.

It was a warm Saturday afternoon, so I went up to the roof, where bedsheets were drying on the clotheslines. I took a blanket and my Chumash, and I began to read and reread my *maftir*, my Torah portion, trying to say it smoothly. Over the next few weeks, I got it right, and I began reading my Haftorah. When that was smooth, I tried to add the melody to the *maftir*. But I didn't know *trop*. So I made up a melody that sounded like *trop*. People who knew *trop* would realize it was wrong. But what was I to do?

The Haftorah melody was easier for me to make up. The actual parts of the melody were so beautiful that I had learned them just from having heard them so often, and it was not hard for me to make up my own progression that sounded authentic. I already knew the prayers over the Torah and Haftorah and their melodies, so I didn't have to learn or practice those.

The day of my bar mitzvah, on May 31, I put on my new black suit, an embossed white shirt, my silver tie with its red speckles, and my new black wingtips. My cousin, Arthur, who had come in from Toronto for the occasion, helped me knot my tie and put on the Swank cufflinks and tie clip Mayer had lent me for the occasion. The small *shtibl* was packed with friends of my parents in both the men's and women's sections. If any of them knew I was faking the melodies, they didn't show it. They all congratulated me. I guess only the regulars at the *shul* knew, but they were kind to me, patting me on the back and shaking my hand. *"Sh'koyach!"* they said. "Congratulations!"

I read the speech my father had written for me. He had no trouble doing that for me. *"Ich bin shtoltz tsu zayn a Yid vi mayne eltern un mayne ovos,* (I am proud to be a Jew like my parents and my forebears,)" it started.

I read the same speech at my party in the reception hall of the Atran House of Jewish Culture, on East 78th Street, where my father worked. A hundred and twenty people gathered at long banquet tables in the elegant room adorned throughout with the dramatic paintings of Isaac Lichtenstein. Aaron sat on the raised dais next to me. He was surprised that there were eight other boys and girls there, children of my parents' friends, whom I knew and whom he'd had no awareness of. My brothers, who'd had their bar mitzvah parties at home, sat at a back table and were quite content to be there with a few friends in suits and some girls their age in party dresses. They danced to records on the hi-fi they set up.

My parents, laughing happily, embraced their friends from the Koniner Society and their cultural friends. There were celebrities from the Yiddish artistic world here. Accompanied on the piano by her husband, a well-known singer performed a Yiddish art song to rousing applause. A Yiddish comedian belted out his routine to peals of laughter. Several luminaries of the Yiddish literary world, authors and poets, offered remarks, and they all included their wonderment that a boy my age could speak Yiddish so well and make a Yiddish speech. One writer gave me a gift of a Mané-Katz watercolor. The painting by the renowned artist was the first work of art I was to own. This was my parents' Jewish world. This was where they felt at home. How did yeshiva fit into this world? And where did I belong?

I said goodbye to the guests, my jacket pockets filled with their gift envelopes. Aaron had come with his grandmother. He handed me an envelope and shook my hand. "It was a nice party," he said. I could see from his eyes that he felt a little betrayed. He did not know that I had other friends, another life I hadn't told him about. Impressed, no doubt, by this party and all the people, he did not know how impoverished my other social life actually was.

I was dazzled by the amount of money gifts I receive. The next day, my father took charge of the checks and cash and paid for the caterer with most of it.

◆ ◆ ◆

After the summer, Aaron was still trying to make friends with our classmates, or at least to talk to them. They had always shunned him. Now in ninth grade, he had a new gimmick he wanted to try to talk to them. He gave our classmates nicknames we could call them to get their attention. He called Benny "Beano" and Solomon "Salty." When that just led to their annoyance, he came up with another scheme.

One Sunday at his house, he said exuberantly, "Let's make phony phone calls to them. We'll act as if we're doing a survey."

I looked at him with a dubious expression. "It makes no sense."

"Oh please, please!" he pleaded.

Of course, he would not call them himself, but he cajoled me to do it. I would do the talking in a husky voice as Aaron pranced around and made strange noises with a grinding machine his father kept on their kitchen table.

One day, Aaron looked up the teachers' phone numbers in the phone book, and his eyes lit up. "Let's call the teachers to a teachers' meeting Monday night, right after the Chanukah evening services at school," he said, cracking up.

"I don't think that's a good idea," I answered.

Again, he badgered me. "You're so much better at it than I am. You can change your voice and I can't. Oh please, please."

So I did it.

"Hello, this is Miss Mitchell," I say in heavy, German-accented English. "Is Rabbi Krieger at home? No? Well, would you tell him there is a teachers' meeting this coming Monday at seven thirty? Thank you, Mrs. Krieger. Goodbye."

After the phone call, I was a little nervous. I hoped Rabbi Krieger would ask about the meeting at school. In the least, he would be at the Chanukah service on Monday and he'd find out then that there was no meeting after it. But Rabbi Krieger asked no one about the meeting his wife told him about. And he did not attend the Chanukah services. He went to the meeting. When I found out, I imagined him leaving his comfortable home, taking the subway, and arriving at the dark and locked school building.

Mr. Breuer immediately suspected Aaron of this prank because he had been caught doing other untoward things before. Once in the principal's office, Aaron confessed immediately and told him I had been in on it.

"I cried and fell to my knees in front of my mother, and I begged Breuer not to throw me out this time. I won't do it again, I said," Aaron reported. He looked at me sheepishly. "I'm sorry I snitched on you. Breuer didn't believe me that I was the one who faked Miss Mitchell's voice. Krieger was there. He said he wouldn't have been fooled, but his wife didn't know the secretary's voice." Aaron laughed hysterically as he told me this. "I'm sorry. I'm sorry," he cried out while laughing.

I don't know why I was such an easy mark. How did he get me to do things I had no interest in doing? His whining ultimately got to me. I could have told him I wouldn't be his friend anymore. But then I would be alone in school.

Aaron was suspended for three days. My father was summoned to the principal. I knew that other boys were afraid of their fathers' punishments over even small infractions. I never worried about that with my father. I was not afraid of my father's punishment because I knew how my father would react. I sat next to my father in Mr. Breuer's office. With apologetic eyes and wrinkled brow, my father spoke, defending me, "Menachem is a good child. Sometimes he can be too playful and unthinking, but he is basically honest."

Mr. Breuer looked at my father and then at me. The principal had a slight smile on his face. I wondered how he felt about Rabbi Krieger. "I won't discipline him," he said to my father, "but I want you to."

"Of course!" my father vowed. "Thank you, Mr. Breuer, for your understanding. I will certainly teach him a lesson."

My father and I left the office. I accompanied him to the subway. Neither of us said a word. "*A gitn, (So long,)*" he said as he entered the train station. No word was mentioned when I got home. Indeed, we would never speak of the matter again.

I looked at my father as he sat at the kitchen table, beating out beautiful words on his Hermes Yiddish typewriter. I looked at his serious expression and weighed his nonreaction to me against the depth of feeling that burst forth from his poems. I felt the empty space between us that I had long known, and I thought to myself, *Would I prefer to have my classmates' anxiety about their fathers' disapproval, or the blur of emotion that hangs suspended between the independence and neglect I feel?*

◆ ◆ ◆

In the nearly four years I knew him, Aaron always tried to persuade me to get off at the 157th Street subway station and walk him home. He lived at 153rd and Riverside Drive. We often took the shortcut through the Riverside oval, which had elegant buildings surrounding a landscaped patch of green. When I dropped Aaron off at his building, I had to climb the hill to Broadway by myself. Only sometimes did Aaron compromise, and he grudgingly agreed to walk along Broadway, up the incline to the top of 153rd Street to the southern edge of the cemetery, where we would go our separate ways, he down the hill to Riverside and I straight down Broadway. He never offered to take the train to my stop, but then again, I never asked him to.

Aaron was generous with his things, though. He shared his afterschool snacks with me when I didn't have one. One Saturday, his parents once snuck me in to an Amateur Athletic Union meet, although I was not a member. Aaron's father, in his forties, participated as a gymnast. And Aaron shared with me lots of knowledge he had of things that stunned me and that I couldn't believe.

"Do you know that at AAU meets, a glass of Coke costs a dollar?"

This was incredible to me. You could get a fountain Coke for a nickel and a seven-ounce bottle for a dime anywhere. I just shook my head.

"I've heard that in some hotels, a Coke can cost two dollars," Aaron shouted.

I just waved him away with his preposterous tale.

One day, as we walked along Broadway, Aaron became very animated. "Look! You see that guy walking over there?" He pointed at a tall, slender man wearing sharply creased and very smooth forest-green and black plaid pants paired with a coffee-brown, cowl-neck sweater. "Look how well he's dressed. Those pants are so well cut. They cost at least twenty dollars, I bet. Maybe as much as forty!"

"Get outta here," I responded. This was implausible to me. After all, at Robert Hall, you could get an entire suit for nineteen dollars. My mother bought me my once-a-year dress-up suit at Barney's, the expensive store, for forty dollars. And this included alterations.

"You never believe me, but I know it's true," Aaron responded, pained that I doubted him.

Aaron was always frustrated by my skepticism and my half-hearted responses to what he said with great conviction. And he was right to be. I held myself back from him. He often said things that I didn't want to admit to myself, things that glaringly showed how little I had and how little I really knew about things. More than anything else, I held back because I was so uncomfortable with his emotional cravings and his enormous envy about the things he talked about. He always seemed agitated and unsatisfied.

At his house one Sunday afternoon, his father went out to get cold cuts for a sandwich dinner for the family. *"Tsunge, Papa. Tsunge! Tsunge!"* Aaron cried out in German, the language of his home. The veins on his wide forehead popped out and throbbed, and his eyes pleaded desperately as he trailed his father to the apartment door and practically cried for his father to get beef tongue for dinner.

It made me cringe that Aaron so openly expressed his enormous cravings, even over such a petty thing as food. It reminded me too much of my father, whose sighing and grunting and leering over food repulsed me. Stooped over the table, my father was totally engrossed when he ate, and his moist eyes, greasy fingers, and open maw as he chomped gave me inward shudders.

◆ ◆ ◆

Aaron turned fourteen at the start of ninth grade. He was obsessed with the girls in our school, who were the only girls he seemed to know even a little. We had had afternoon secular classes with them through the eighth grade, and he was always whispering to me, pointing out which ones were growing breasts when he saw them around the school building. He pestered me about which ones I liked. I was completely uncomfortable with his leering and his urges, and I would not join him in them.

One Saturday afternoon in the fall, Aaron called me to meet him on Riverside Drive near his house. I told him that I could meet him at 149th Street. Surprisingly, he agreed to this compromise. He was waiting for me, pacing in front of the benches. We both wore our Sabbath suits in case we were seen. He saw me coming and ran toward me. We sat down on a bench. Aaron looked around to make sure we were alone and that no one would see that he was carrying something on the Sabbath. From his jacket pocket, he took out a small address book.

"Look what I found! I was at the triangle near Fort Tryon Park, and I saw this on the ground," he practically whispered. "It's an address book filled with all these Irish girls' names and phone numbers."

I looked at him and shook my head. Another one of his desperate schemes.

"Please! Call some of them for me," he pleaded, and he added an old familiar line. "I'll never ask you for anything again."

But this time, I flatly refused.

On the following Monday, Aaron met me in the schoolyard. "I called some of them," he whispered. "Most of them hung up. A couple talked to me for a few minutes! One said she would meet me at the Inwood Triangle next Saturday at three o'clock. I told her I had a friend, so she said she would bring another girl with her."

"I am definitely not going!" I said with conviction.

"Please, oh please. I can't go alone. I won't know what to say. You know some girls. You know how to talk to them."

I was extremely doubtful, but curious, and I let him persuade me.

"I didn't give her my real name," Aaron said. "She thinks I'm Tom Mahoney. Your name is Johnny Ahearn, by the way." He cracked up.

Again wearing our Sabbath suits in case our schoolmates who lived nearby saw us, we waited a half a block away from the Inwood Triangle, spying to see if the girls would show up and what they looked like before we made a move. I was relieved when no one came.

CHAPTER 14

◆ ◆ ◆ ◆ ◆ ◆

Forgery

I knew I should have left the yeshiva before ninth grade, but I was afraid to. The world outside my Harlem apartment was bleak, and I did not trust myself in it. I decided to remain and be part of the first high school class in my expanding yeshiva.

Aaron greeted me as I walked down Bennett Avenue toward school on the first day. I had not seen him since early in the summer, and he looked good and surprisingly confident. He had combed his hair in a different way since then, with a black curl hanging down his forehead, and he looked more self-assured somehow, and stronger. Maybe he had been doing gymnastics with his father.

We'd spent the first two weeks of the summer together, but I did not tell him much about the rest of my summer, and he did not share what he had done either. It had felt good to be away from Aaron and school. And now, somehow it sort of felt good to start the new school year. I felt good about myself in general. My summer in Rockaway had been revelatory and exciting. I'd ridden my bike, and I'd owned my Rockaway neighborhood. I'd played softball with a team, I'd had a crowd that hung out at the beach like Jay's did, and I had gotten to know girls better. I'd hoped Aaron would be more satisfied, too, and easier to be with.

I was just thirteen and my body was changing in ways that surprised, perplexed, and pleased me. I felt like a regular teen when I walked up to school wearing chinos and loafers and a brand-new, bright crimson V-neck Banlon sweater over my Izod white knit shirt. Of course, I wore a yarmulke, but I had a nice pompadour that could not be subdued by it.

Weeks into the fall term, Aaron sprung his cockamamie scheme to meet some Irish girls he didn't know! He was still so needy. There were secrets I kept from Aaron, and it bothered me. Would I have to tell him about my happy times away from him, with a new set of friends who were not as desperate and demanding? I dreaded that this would have to happen. But I was spared in a way that gave me mixed feelings. I would not have to talk to Aaron about my experiences in the summer in Far Rockaway. I would not have to fend off his barrage of questions and endless pestering over details so he could get heated up through my experiences. At the same time, I would face the sadness, along with relief, that I would soon lose him as my friend.

We had just received our first-quarter report cards. My Hebrew grades were passing, although I didn't know how. It was likely just an attempt by Rabbi Krieger to encourage me. Failing me would have been futile, after all. My rabbis, like Krieger, had always told me that I was smart. If only I applied myself in Chumash and Talmud I would do so well, they always said. I knew that wasn't true.

I just could not read the texts or understand the Hebrew and Aramaic languages. I don't know why they didn't notice that. By this point, I had given up on Chumash and Talmud, and I didn't care what I got in these Jewish studies. All I cared about were my grades in my afternoon studies in English, math, history, French, and science, which were clumped together and called "English" in our school. I did relatively well in these. My grades were always in the mid-eighties, as they were in this report card. That was good in my school, where nineties were rare and were usually granted only to budding geniuses of whom there were a few.

At the end of the school day, I placed my blue report card in my briefcase to bring to my mother to sign. I always pointed out to her where to sign because she did not know on her own. No matter what my grades were, she always said, "You could do better." Her crinkled eyes and the hint of a repressed grin would reveal that that was what she thought she needed to say. She did not know what these grades meant in my school. I never tried to explain them to her.

On our way home, after evening prayers, Aaron looked completely agitated and distraught. He paced on the 181st Street A train subway station platform. "I don't know what I'll do. I am in so much trouble!" he whimpered, his shoulders stooped. He was nearly crying. At one point, he yelped. "I promised my parents this time I would pass my English subjects. I can't face them. It's not the punishment; it's their disappointment. They will look at me with such hurt eyes. I can't take it. And they'll pull me out of this school and send me to public high school."

I had known Aaron was not doing well, but I had not realized he was failing. Aaron seemed to be a smart kid. I didn't know why he was doing so poorly. I looked at him with sadness. I patted his back and did not know what to say.

"Listen, I know how you can help me," Aaron said, desperately taking hold of my arm, his eyes pleading. "We have to give my mother a fake report card to sign."

I looked at him in disbelief.

He continued, "We have to break into Weldler's office and steal a few blank forms. You'll fill in the fake report card in Dr. Spier's handwriting. I know you can do it. Remember how last year you practiced signing his name like he does, in that fancy script? You showed it to him, and he was very disturbed by it because it looked just like his? You have to fill out the report card like he does."

I pulled back. "No, this time, I can't do this favor for you. If you want to do it, you should do it yourself. Remember, you are the artist who drew the outline of Abraham Lincoln's face for the school newspaper. You can do this, if that's what you want."

"No! I haven't drawn since the fifth grade. I can't do it. Anyway, my hand will tremble too much. Please, you have to do this for me. It's the last thing I'll ever ask you to do. If you don't do it, I'll just die!"

The next night, with everyone gone for the night, Aaron crawled through the pass-through window of the principal's office and opened the door for me. Rummaging through a tall cabinet, we found the empty report card forms. We went into one of the empty classrooms. I looked at Aaron's pathetic report card, with all the red-circled grades, and I felt sorry for him. He looked embarrassed. His failings were a secret he had not shared with me before. I used my best Dr. Spier handwriting and gave Aaron 70s and 75s. Then I signed Arthur Spier's name in a flourished hand that was indistinguishable from the legendary math and science teacher's. I did not make any mistakes, and I did not have to use any spare report card blanks.

The next morning, Aaron told me what happened at home when he presented this forgery to his mother. "She was so happy," he said, looking glad that he had pleased her even in this way. "'I'm proud to sign this,' my mother said."

"Now there is one thing left to do' Aaron said. "Sign the real report card in my mother's handwriting. You have to do this for me," he said bluntly. "You can copy her signature from the fake report card."

I shook my head. "You know her handwriting, and I don't," I responded. "You have to do it yourself."

"No! No!" Aaron nearly screamed, then lowered his voice and looked around. But no one paid him any mind on the loud playground. "I'm so nervous I'll mess it up, and there are no do-overs to this one," he said.

In an empty classroom that evening, after everyone had left the building, with the model of his mother's signature on the fake report card, I practiced on blank pieces of paper until I was confident I could forge it.

"It's perfect," Aaron sighed. "I'll make it up to you, I promise."

"There's one problem," I told Aaron. "What are you going to do next report card? I'm not doing this again. This is too big a risk already."

"We won't do this again. I'll work harder and improve, I swear. And I'll confess to my mother, showing her the real report card with the fake signature and the bad grades and then the better ones. I'll leave you out of it. I'll tell her I did it," Aaron said. And I think Aaron believed he *would* do better next time and that he'd nobly confess his crime and be forgiven and made clean.

The next day, after Aaron handed in the real report card with the fake signature, I saw that he felt better. He was not tense, and he actually seemed to be listening more and taking notes. Then the following day, he was called out of the middle of morning Hebrew classes, and he did not return until lunchtime. He looked completely distraught. "They found out," he told me.

I waited for his explanation, completely panicked.

"Don't worry," he said. "I left you out of it. I confessed that I did it."

"How did they find out? What's going to happen now?" I asked, not sure Aaron had told me the whole story.

"I did tell them you helped me break into the office," Aaron admitted. "But they don't know about you and the forgery. They believe me that I did it," he protested. Sensing my anger and my dread, Aaron told me the rest. "Yesterday they called my mother to come in to discuss my 'situation.' She came in this morning to the meeting with Weldler and Krieger. She said, 'I don't understand. Aaron came home with a passing report card.' Then they pulled out the real report card. 'You call this passing?' Weldler asks her. My mother did a double take. 'This is my signature,' she said, 'but I did not sign this report card.'" At this, Aaron chuckled. "You did a real good job, Fox."

"So what's going to happen now?" I anxiously asked Aaron.

"They're kicking me out. This is my last day. I have to take all my things with me at the end of the day. It's too bad. I think I could have done better this quarter if I had the chance."

"I'm sorry," I said, with a mixture of sadness and relief.

"I guess we'll have to see each other more outside of school," Aaron said.

Neither of us had a real sense of what this change was going to cause between us.

I was not called in to the principal that day, and neither were my parents called. The following day, Rabbi Weldler called me to his office. I was in panic and terror that I would be kicked out, too. I didn't know how I would face my family with my failure and shame. But all Weldler asked me were the details of the office break-in. He clearly completely believed that Aaron was the one who persuaded me to help him. I was allowed to return to class without even a reprimand.

"Maybe you'll do better without your friend around," the principal said as he sent me back to class.

In gratitude, I did try harder in my Talmud class, but it was really no use. I couldn't read the text. The Rashi commentary was in a completely different manuscript. I didn't even recognize the letters. Somehow the other students knew it, but I had never been taught it. I always tried my best in "English" studies, so nothing changed there.

I only saw Aaron on a Saturday several weeks later. He had to sneak out to see me. His parents blamed me for corrupting him all these years. I walked with him to the seedy yeshiva his parents had enrolled him in, Heichel HaTorah. It was housed in a dilapidated, gothic-looking building at Riverside Drive and 140th Street. It looked like an abandoned castle on the outside. Inside was a drab and decrepit grand staircase and large and small rooms with yellowed walls. Some had broken-down tables and beds, mainly used as dormitories for residential students, high school boys who were living away from home. Aaron introduced me to a few of the guys, boys in white shirts, black suits, and wide-brimmed black hats. He seemed to have made some friends in this short time. But he wouldn't be staying long. He was biding his time there, in this place where they had no secular studies at all, until he could enroll in the spring term at George Washington High School.

I met up with Aaron again on a Saturday several months later. He'd been in George Washington for a couple of months by then. "You can't believe what it's like," he told me. "We study the same subjects as at Breuer's, but somehow I'm pulling eighties and sometimes a ninety on tests. I knew it was something about that place. And I'm taking music. The first time I went into the music room, the teacher asked me, 'Would you like to blow or bow?' I didn't know what he was talking about. He said I could be in brass or woodwinds or stringed instruments that use bows. I chose 'bow,' and now I'm learning the bass."

It's uncanny how disaster turned into something good for Aaron, and for me, too.

"And I met up with this Spanish guy, Raymond, who lives on 152nd Street. He says he's part of the Egyptian Kings. You should see the switchblade he has. But he's OK if he likes you and you're not part of a rival gang. I don't really spend time with him. I got to know this

Israeli kid, David, at school, and we eat lunch together and take the subway home together too."

Rabbi Weldler was right that I would change in positive ways at school once Aaron was gone. But it may not have been in a way he would have predicted. I began to talk to Solomon, who told me I should call him Sam. He was a tall, blond guy who wore button-down shirts, crew neck sweaters, tweed slacks, and expensive shoes. He'd been in my English class since fifth grade. He was a clever guy with a good sense of humor and a nice way of seeing things. He read a lot and knew about things like stocks and cameras and the government. More important, there was an outwardness and lightness in our banter and conversation, even about important things—nothing like the almost painful inward intensity that was Aaron. We became good friends by the end of the school year on the class trip to Washington.

But what did this mean, being friends with Sam? We did not spend time together in each other's homes. I had been to his house for only a moment when Sam had to get something. It was clearly a religious home. Sam had been in the doorway of my apartment just once, when he'd returned my bike that I had lent him. I'd felt awkward about not inviting him in. He would have seen milk and meat on the dining room table where my parents had been entertaining the recruiting officer who had just signed Mayer up into the army. There were many things I could talk to Sam about, but I did not trust him to know my family's lack of religious practice.

CHAPTER 15

◆ ◆ ◆ ◆ ◆ ◆

At the Beach

To my delight, my parents decided to return to Rockaway that summer, when I was fourteen, and I looked forward to it after what would be my last two-week summer session at Camp Vacamas. One afternoon, I rode my bike home down Ocean Crest Boulevard to find we had company in our one-room summer home. A Koniner couple with their daughter, Anna, whom I knew, had also rented for the summer.

Anna was a very pretty girl. She had fine blond hair, which she wore in bangs and a ponytail. Wide lids and almost invisible eyelashes shielded her hazel-blue eyes. There was a hint of freckles on her upturned nose and high cheekbones. She had delicate ears and thin pink lips. When she looked up at me and said, "Hi," her voice was dull, showing little emotion, and her face had a barely perceptible smile. She had the same birthday as I had, but she was a year younger. It would have been hard to guess had I not been told that she was just thirteen. She had a teen body that was pleasing to my eyes. My eyes ran along her curves, her thin legs, and down to her dainty sandaled toes.

My mother turned to me and said, "Anna's parents work in the city during the day. She will be alone. Why don't you spend some time with her? Introduce her to your friends at the beach."

I warily agreed. I was not sure how it would work out. My bunch of friends was getting along fine. In fact, I had introduced my ballplayers to the kids on Henri's block, and things were going well. It did not seem to me that Anna would fit in, judging from her despondent manner.

The following day, I went by Anna's house, which was only a

few blocks from Henri's, and we went to the beach. My friends were already sitting on blankets or riding waves when we arrived.

"This is Anna," I said.

All the boys looked at her with interest. Some of the girls looked at her and clearly wondered if she was my girlfriend that I had not told them about. Nonetheless, one of them said, "Hi. Join us!"

"Thanks," Anna said, but she remained standing.

One of the boys ran up soaking wet from the waves and splattered water on everyone else, and the girls yelled at him. "You should see the man-o'-war jellyfish floating around. Don't go in the water!"

The kids then all seemed to start talking at once, jittery and debating the dangers of the man-o'-war. Anna did not join in or even sit down. She looked out at the waves. I took her home only a little while later.

During the next few weeks, I visited Anna every few days. It was not out of obligation. She was very pleasant to be next to, and she smelled so nice. We went for walks, mostly errands she had, going to the small local grocery store, mainly. There was a placid air about her most of the time. She took in her surroundings without visible reaction. She was sometimes playful in a childlike fashion, and that warmed me to her. When she was upbeat, I noticed even grown men staring at her. When she was in a passive state, she seemed to recede into the sidewalk.

I sat with her on the beach and watched out for her in the waves. She did not know how to swim. She wore a shapeless knit yellow bathing suit that was oh-so-suggestive of the form beneath. I swelled with pride that such a pretty girl was with me. Teenage boys always craned their necks to look at her as they cruised the beach. Some of them clowned to get her attention. She either giggled a little or did not react.

Anna's parents asked me to tutor her in reading and math. She was very far behind in school. We sat at her kitchen table as I explained some number problems to her. She did not seem to pay attention. She rested her head on her hand and only looked at me and not at the work. Occasionally, I could get her to try some simple number problems. I waited as she worked slowly on multiplication. I looked at a picture of her from kindergarten that her parents had placed on a nearby shelf. She was very pretty then, but she was bigger and a head taller than the other children in the class. Odd, I thought. She was rather petite now.

Nothing more serious happened between Anna and me that summer. Mostly, I spent my time with my more animated crowd. As the mulberries began to drop profusely from the old tree, annoying me as I read under it, and as solitary leaves curled their way down to the ground from the maple in the yard, I began to dread the end of summer. It would soon be back to the drudgery of my isolated life. I would revert from the open-faced, active boy in the sunlight to the miserable, hunched-over, gray-faced youth trapped in a living lie.

CHAPTER 16

◆ ◆ ◆ ◆ ◆ ◆

Cataclysms

Once back in the city, my life outside of school was again solely dependent on events of the Koniner Society. One Saturday evening that winter, my parents hosted a card party, and Anna came with her parents. We were sent to the room I shared with Jay to entertain each other. Jay was working late as usual at the supermarket. Anna and I sat next to each other on the high-riser in the room. I showed her some poems I had written, hoping to get her interested in some of the things I liked.

She seemed to ignore what I said. She just looked at me with doe eyes. Then she suddenly kissed me on the cheek. I turned to her and saw her feigned bashful smile. Then I kissed her softly on the lips. She suddenly jumped up on her knees, grabbed my cheeks in her soft, sure hands, and kissed me forcefully and long on my mouth. My entire body radiated as we kissed and kissed with a soft furor. She placed my hand on her checkered pinafore dress, and I felt her firm breast. I don't know how long we kissed and petted. It was the most exhilarating and anxious time I had ever experienced. I kept an ear cocked to sounds of a possible opening door, but that, thankfully, did not happen.

"We should go back out now and show our faces," Anna said with an impish smile. Before I opened the door, she added a kooky little rhyme I would hear from her every once in a while, and she chuckled the same about it every time. "Don't make love by the garden gate. Love is blind, but the neighbors ain't."

I visited Anna at her Inwood apartment on some Saturdays when her parents were at work. After very few words, we petted lightly but for a long time, as we had done before. We did not have much to tell each other. I wanted her as a real girlfriend, the kind I had seen on television, who goes to the movies or out for a soda with her guy, with an understanding between them. We did go for a few walks in Fort Tryon Park, but mostly we stayed inside. I took her to the movies one Saturday. We saw the lush and ethereal *Green Mansions*, with Audrey Hepburn and Anthony Perkins. It was a hard film to understand, all mood and no real story. It seemed to be about the girl, Rima, who was of the forest and who had a way of thinking unlike that of other people; she was infused with a wordless sensuality. I tried to see Anna as Rima, in her silences, and I held her hand.

During that same spring, something else cataclysmic happened to me. I had been having nocturnal emissions for a while, and I knew what they were. There was no sensation associated with them. I woke up in the morning with some sticky fluid on the underpants I' slept in, and I tried to hide them from my mother by throwing them into the hamper and putting on a clean pair.

It was in Mr. Kaufman's geometry class. He announced a pop quiz. These lasted exactly ten minutes, and they consisted of finding two proofs. Your grade was either zero, fifty, or one hundred percent. The problems were on the board, and all the members of the small class scrambled to write down the first one and get to work. I huddled over my paper. I solved the first proof fairly quickly. But as I started to solve the second one, I began to feel a strange throbbing sensation in my groin. My penis was pressed against the side of my pants leg. Suddenly I felt a swoon as my penis erupted with ecstatic, sweet, joyful electric force that spread over my entire body.

I heaved in my seat, and I could hardly breathe. I hoped no one had seen this, but of course the others were sharply focused on their papers. How would I finish the second problem of the quiz in such a state? I forced myself to be lucid. I realized at that moment that the so-called theorems and proofs we were taught were just statements of obvious observations. Just in time, I made up supportive statements and a theorem that sounded plausible, and I got a hundred on the quiz. Two amazing wins in ten minutes.

Now I knew the secret of the body that no one had talked to me about. Just as quickly, I intuitively understood the word "masturbation," and I knew how to do it without being taught. I was sure no one in my family noticed how much time I was now spending in the locked bathroom. Within the span of a few short months, my body had rescued me from the dreariness of my existence. I was still cooped up, but some good things had happened to me.

CHAPTER 17

◆ ◆ ◆ ◆ ◆ ◆

Catharsis

I always did well in my secular subjects. My religious studies were a completely different matter. From the first day that year, I had faced the prospect of my failure in Judaica with as much serenity as I could. Having been left behind yet again, I had to tolerate the humiliation of now being three grades behind in Talmud class.

At least our teacher was going to be Rabbi Nitzlich, a tall, easygoing, young Hasidic man with a wispy beard. As September and October paced onward, he always wore cheerful, light-colored suits and looked comfortable with himself. He had recently gotten married and moved from Brooklyn to Monsey, and, wherever relevant to class discussions, he shared personal stories that revealed a warm and human side of him. What we were studying, Tractate *Pesochim*, about the rules and practices of Passover, was exciting to him. I could see him almost taste the ideas he was explicating to us.

I liked him. I wanted to do well for him, even though it was difficult for me. I struggled, being neither able to read nor translate the text or its commentaries adequately. But I listened intensely to this kindly man. He did not make me feel bad as other rabbis had about my lack of ability. He did not scowl as if I were failing him and myself. I tried to ask some questions that seemed germane when I could. But, mostly, the ideas and the practices he taught us were not relevant to me. They were not burning issues for me as they were for Nitzlich and most of the boys in the class.

I loved the Passover Seder celebration at our home, although it was not like the one we studied in such minute detail in class. When

Passover came to my house, it meant that it was finally spring. It meant that we were gathered at a festive table as a family, dressed in our new holiday clothes. My wonderful adult cousin, Arthur, would drive in from Toronto for the week. He always brought such fun and adventure with him. My brothers, Arthur, and I would always kibitz as my father tried to get through the text of the Haggadah. We ate matzoh, dipped our eggs and parsley in salt water, made Hillel sandwiches with horse-radish and *charosis*, and ate my mother's sweet gefilte fish, *kneidlach* soup, and roast chicken and beef. At our Passover Seder table, we could feel whole, like any other real family at least for several hours. Of course, this coming Passover, Mayer would not be there.

During our Passovers, we did not worry that some crumb of dust in the house might be leavened or that there was a forbidden bottle of hard liquor made of grain spirits in the credenza. Some of the boys in my class worried they would literally be excommunicated and not go to heaven with the rest of their family after death if they accidentally ate a piece of leavening on Passover. One of the boys, without thinking, had nearly eaten a piece of popcorn at the circus last year, and he needed reassurance. I didn't have the pressure to perform all the details my classmates found immensely important. I was not worried about what a vengeful God would do to me. Still, somehow, the boy's popcorn story roused my superstitious side, just like my anxiety was always evoked as I cut my fingernails and I was driven to flush the clippings down the toilet, as the rabbinic law dictated. Rabbi Lowenthal had told us a few years before that a person he had known had forgotten to do so, and he had died.

Mostly, as the details were discussed in their minutia in class, I spent my time challenging God.

Is this what You want from me, to be concerned about small details? The ancient Hebrews smeared the blood of the Pascal lamb on their doorposts so that the angel of death would pass over their houses.

We no longer eat a Pascal lamb. Nor do we smear blood of any type. What happened to those details? How were they explained away? In the book of Vayikro, *Leviticus, You forbid the eating of blood, without explanation. Do you really want me to understand? Some of Your laws have no explanation.*

Is it that we humans are not made enough in Your image to understand their reasons? Are not our souls little pieces of Your being?

But I would rather talk to You about Your names, Elohim *and* Adonai. *I have been taught that* Elohim *connotes the God of Justice and that* Adonai *stands for the God of Mercy. I do not understand either. You smote the Egyptians with ten plagues. All of ancient Egypt suffered. Were ordinary Egyptians guilty for the suffering of the Hebrew slaves? I doubt it. So why were they all punished? And the plague of the firstborn, where all the firstborn males of Egypt died, was that not mainly to punish Pharaoh for his wickedness? But it says in the Chumash that You hardened Pharaoh's heart that he rendered suffering unto the Hebrews. He was your instrument, so why was he punished and not rewarded for doing as you bade him do? And what of the innocent firstborns? What had those innocents done that they should die?*

Every year, my brothers and I put aside our joking and clowning at one moment toward the end of each Seder. It was a part added by some families in most recent times, the remembrance of those who had died at the hands of the Nazi beasts. We remembered this on Passover especially because it was on the first night of Passover, April 19, 1943, that the remaining Jews of the Warsaw Ghetto rose up against the Nazi murderers, knowing of their certain deaths in doing so.

They rose up for Kidush Ha'am *and* Kiddush Hashem, *the sanctification of our people and of You, our God. But where were You during that time? In the fourth cup of wine at the Seder that precedes this honoring of our fallen martyrs we say,* "Shfoch Hamoscho, *pour out Your wrath against the nations of the world who do not acknowledge You . . . who have devoured Jacob and laid waste his habitations." Where were You when a million children were ripped from their parents' arms and murdered?*

My religious schoolmates and their families at their Seder commemorations did not acknowledge those we all had lost so recently. The Holocaust commemoration of our family was not part of the ritual described in Talmud *Pesochim*, and they knew nothing of it. We never talked about the war in yeshiva, and I never asked why. It was as if the members of the religious community were from a different people than we were, although they were supposed to be the real Jews.

As he recited the words of loss and lamentation at our Seder each year, my father's lips would tremble and his eyes would well up with tears. Mayer, Jay, and I would be solemn. I would look over at my mother, hanging her head while seeing the faces of her lost family before her. We would be relieved that she could keep her composure. Arthur always appeared to accept our acknowledgment of those who had perished; he looked at us tolerantly as we honored our six million dead. I don't really know what was in his mind at such moments every year. From the age of nine, he had survived the Lodz Ghetto and several concentration camps, witnessed so many who died, including his mother, sister, and grandmother. *He did not want to remember.* He tolerated our remembrance out of respect for my parents.

Numerous times had I pestered Arthur to tell me of his experiences in the *lager*—the concentration camps—and he always rebuffed me, except for one time. Fed up with me, he said, "Alright, I will tell you one story, and then I want you never to ask me about these things again, OK?"

I nodded.

Arthur began, "You are sitting on the floor of your barracks in the *lager*, cold and hungry. You share a crumb of bread with the man who is sitting next to you. You both fall asleep, and the next morning you discover that the man beside you is dead. What do you do?" Arthur paused. I did not know what to say. "Well, Michael, what do you do?"

I shook my head. I had no idea.

"You check to see if his shoes are better than yours." Arthur looked at me to see if I had understood. "No more questions, Michael."

"Shfoch Hamoscho!" says the prayer. "Pour out Your wrath!" Why didn't You pour out Your wrath, I ask You? Maybe it is because You love blood. No Jew is allowed to eat blood. It all belongs to You, and You crave it. I reject You! I reject You with such blinding rage that You can no longer exist! Yet I still talk to You, and You are still in my heart. But I will not succumb to be under Your yoke. I will hold on to the fire in me that is You, but You will not swallow me up like Nadav and Avihu. You see, You do not exist.

CHAPTER 18

♦ ♦ ♦ ♦ ♦ ♦

Secrets and Lies

My family returned to Far Rockaway that following summer, when I was fifteen, and so did Anna. I met up with my friends, and we played ball, hung out at the beach, and had parties. I became infatuated with Francine, a pretty, dark-haired girl with a golden tan, who sported a pageboy hairdo and wore bright blouses and white shorts. Not only was she pretty, but she read books. Her favorite was the 700-page *Vanity Fair*. She knew all the popular rock and roll songs and could talk about movie stars. She danced the Lindy with the other girls because the boys didn't know how, but she slow danced close to me, with her head on my chest. Sometimes I got to kiss her goodnight.

I still saw Anna. We would lie on the soft quilt of her large bed, petting. She let me take off her top and her bra and kiss her firm pink nipples. My hand often crept to her shorts and to her tuft of blond pubic hair, but she always stopped me from going further. She laughed a lot in those moments, and then she looked even more beautiful. But she was not my girlfriend. Besides necking and collecting small shells and stones on the beach, there was little else she seemed interested in. I gave up trying to teach her any math or talking to her about the things I had on my mind. I had Francine for that. I was living a double standard, and I knew it. But Anna told me that she kissed other boys on the block where she lived, so I thought it was alright.

As the summer wore on, Anna began saying something odd. As we lay resting after the heat of our touching, she placed her head in the crook of my arm and said in the most serious tone, "What if we have a baby?"

"That's impossible!" I responded. "It can't happen."

But over time, she kept repeating this question, and I began to realize that she *wanted* a baby, and she thought that petting would give her one.

Anna often came to our one-room home on Ocean Crest Boulevard. My mother adored her. She fed her, brushed her hair, and bought her pretty clothes. She was the daughter of one of her closest friends. My mother had always wanted a little girl of her own, and I had been her third boy instead. Anna loved being held by my mother as much as my mother loved holding her. I thought I would likely wind up marrying her one day, or maybe not.

One afternoon Anna was particularly fun to be with when she came over. She giggled a lot, and she wanted to dance the cha-cha to the B-side of a hit single. She always wanted to play it and dance to it whenever she came over, and this time even more so. We put "Rio Maiori" on the turntable of my brothers' component hi-fi that stood on the dresser, and we danced to it over and over. As we moved back and forth to the song, I looked into Anna's beautiful face and her large blue eyes, and she smiled a secret smile at me. I held her soft fingers in mine and watched the smooth movements of her feminine body in rhythm with mine, and something changed in me. We were more than dancing. I felt suddenly so close to her, and I was sure that she shared the feeling.

As Anna and I danced, I saw my mother looking on with amusement and pleasure and, as usual, a touch of sadness in her eyes.

As the afternoon wore on, Anna said she would be going home. Would I walk her? And could she borrow the book she saw next to the turntable? It was *Mutiny on the Bounty*, which I had just finished.

"Of course," I said, pleased that she might want to read it.

As we left my house, she suggested we cut across the ball field, which was not in the direction of her house. We went behind the brush and trees where we would not be seen. Anna put the book on the ground and sat on it so she would not get her shorts dirty. We began to kiss. She unbuttoned part of her blouse, and I cupped my hand around her breast inside her bra.

The summer was coming to an end, and I was bracing myself for another difficult school year. Well, at least I would be different now, I consoled myself.

One afternoon, I came home from Anna's house. I was spending most of my afternoons with her. We didn't say much, but I felt a sense of calm. I found my mother musing to herself at the table. She greeted me with an ambiguous smile. "Michael, I have something to tell you. It's a secret."

My mother loved secrets. They were the scenarios of her life when she huddled with her women friends. She had also shared secrets with me since I was young, and it was not an easy thing for me. They entrapped me in the web of her vivid, painful world, and all I could do was try to escape. I usually listened silently, or I tried to comfort her with my words, knowing the futility of that.

She took a deep breath and said, "Sit down here."

I sat down and waited for her to speak. This time it was different. The secret involved me.

"I never told you, but I think you know that Anna's parents, Shloime and Malke, each had families before the war. The children were ripped away from them before their eyes. Nazi beasts! They should burn in hell! Anna's parents survived the concentration camps, and they came separately to a DP camp in Germany. Shloime had a relationship with a young German girl. It happened a lot then. The Germans were starving, and the girl went with him. She became pregnant and had a little girl. That is how Anna came into this world. This German girl, she was young. She had nothing. You can understand, she did not want the baby, and she left in the night when Anna was maybe a year old. Shloime soon met Malke in the DP camp, and they decided to get married. Malke could not have any more children. Anna would be their child, the only one that they could have. They registered Anna as Malke's child, born at home. Anna does not know that Malke is not her real mother."

I held my head in my hands. I wanted to scream out, "Why are you telling me this?!" But I remained silent. I got up from the table and headed for the door. "Malke *is* Anna's real mother," I whispered as I left.

I crossed the playing field and sat on the bank of my secluded finger of the bay. The late-afternoon air was growing cool. For a long time, I sat without any thoughts at all. Numb. Then, a moan came out of me, and I began to wail and yelp and snivel. My body shook and swayed back and forth as I screamed, "Secrets and lies! I don't want my life to be secrets and lies! I finally have something for myself, and I feel good, at least good enough! But you pull me back into the harness of sadness and loss. I want to be a full person! I want to live in the now! I know you want that for me, too. So why did you spoil it for me, Mother? You pulled me down. I know you try to live in this world, but the war is your real world. And I tried, Mom, to be in that world for you. Maybe you didn't want to, but you sucked me into your pain. I am your Menachem, your consolation, your little cavalier, your comfort, but that's not all I am, and you know that. I thought I could comfort you and make you happy by being with you in your painful world. But I can't continue. And I can't believe the whole world is evil and cruel. I don't want to leave you alone wallowing in the past. But I have to, and I feel so ashamed."

I visited Anna the next day. She was in an especially cheerful mood. She was making herself boiled frankfurters for lunch, and she placed one wiener at her crotch and pranced around with it, laughing hysterically. I laughed with her. I turned to her kindergarten picture on the shelf and wondered if she was actually older than she was said to be. We petted on her bed. I felt tenderly toward her. I held her close and rocked her and kissed her on the forehead. She sighed and stayed in my arms.

On my way home, I thought about her lack of interest in anything. Her mind was closed. *Does a one-year-old child remember being held and nursed by one woman and then held by another woman who is substituted? Could a child's wish to close off such knowledge to such an extent that she also shuts down her openness toward so much else in her life?*

I knew that somewhere inside her heart and mind, Anna longed for her birth mother. And I knew that she wanted to redo her life by wishing for her own baby and, in that way, taking care of her lost self. Oh Anna, Anna, the box you live in is even more closed than mine.

CHAPTER 19

◆ ◆ ◆ ◆ ◆ ◆

A Chance at Freedom

"Y ou'll be a number," said Rabbi Weldler, the English principal. He was a man with a round face and a small rectangular mustache over his curved and sensuous mouth. But it was his large oval eyes and his sad eyebrows, and his past kindnesses, that made him convincing.

I had wanted to leave yeshiva when we graduated from eighth grade and again after ninth, but I did not want to go to a rough public school. We weren't told we could apply to specialized high schools, like the Bronx High School of Science or Music and Art. It wasn't a secret plan to keep us for themselves, to fill the first class of the high school they were starting; it was understood that yeshiva boys needed to further their education in a yeshiva. A Jewish young man continues with his religious studies, which are of equal or greater value than his secular studies, all his life.

"If you switch to public high school, even if it's a good one, your Jewish education will definitely come to an end," Weldler said with a most sincere expression. It was an ironic worry with regard to me, one of the failures of this religious instructional program.

◆ ◆ ◆

At the beginning of my eleventh-grade school year, I was moved up with the same Talmud group. We had Rabbi Krieger again that year. I could see the discouraged look in his eyes as he glanced at me sitting in a middle row near the back and then at Sam sitting across the aisle from me. He saw the futility of changing our seats. Bernie sat in the front, in the row all the way to the right, leaning against the wall near the door. We all passed each other smirks and looks and made faces during the morning sessions. Sam and I passed each other notes. Sometimes we had quiet contests, timing ourselves to see how long we could hold our breaths.

One day, I stopped at Rabbi Krieger's desk on my way to lunch. I told him I had a question. Rabbi Kreiger told me that I should meet him after my lunch at the *Mesiftah*, the advanced study hall, where he was now heading to teach a class. When he saw me coming through the classroom window, he eagerly rushed out to greet me. I could see the disappointment in his eyes when he heard what I wanted to ask him. He thought I had figured out the Gemara question. He thought he had made a breakthrough with me, and I had come up with the supreme question in the section we were studying.

"The Torah does not condone slavery," he said. He could not talk about it more now. We would talk about it again another time.

The next day after lunch, Rabbi Kreiger met me in the hall outside his *Mesiftah* class. He said, "The word '*oved*' in the Chumash can mean slave or servant. Jews in olden times had indentured servants. They worked for a period of time to pay off debts or as retribution for a crime against the person. The Talmud tells us that the indentured servant must be treated with dignity. For example, the master is not allowed to shame the man by having him carry his towel on the way to his bath. When the servant's debt was repaid, and his term was up, his obligation was over and he was free to go his way. If the servant refused to leave when his term was up, the master was told to knock out one of his front teeth to show that this man had no shame and preferred servitude to freedom."

"Thank you, Rabbi Krieger," I said and smiled genuinely at him when I left.

He smiled back and rushed off. It was the only personal exchange I had had with him throughout the several years I had known him.

Sam and I spent some time together outside of school. We went ice-skating at Wollman Memorial Rink in Central Park where, by chance, we would occasionally run into one or two of his friends from outside our school. They were cheerful, funny guys who resembled some of the more burly youths of George Washington, except that they wore fifty-cent-piece-sized yarmulkes. Sam and I attended a *Melaveh Malkah* party at Yeshiva University on a Saturday night, where klezmer sounds wailed frenetically from a clarinet band and young men milled about, and joked and sang and danced and said goodbye to the Sabbath for yet another week. We didn't spend any time with Bernie outside of school, somehow. He lived on the Upper West Side, which seemed like a completely different kind of place, and we got the sense he had another life there.

One December afternoon, after our brown bag lunches and afternoon recess, as the three of us were about to walk toward the *shul* for *mincha*, afternoon prayers, Sam announced to Bernie and me, "I'm planning to leave Breuer's. It is no longer for me. I thought you should know."

This was totally out of the blue. Bernie and I looked at each other wide-eyed and taken aback. Sam and I had been real friends for two years, but we had never talked of his conflicts about being at yeshiva.

"Where will you go?" I asked.

"George Washington," Sam answered. "I know some girls there. They say it's a pretty good school, especially in the alpha classes. Also, there are real opportunities in other areas. They have a real newspaper, not a mimeographed sheet like we have. Maybe I can join it, write or be a photographer for it."

I looked at Sam in disbelief and relief. I thought, *If Sam, who is religious, can leave, I can, too.* His words and his decision gave me strength. "If you leave, I'll leave too," I said to Sam with conviction.

"Me too!" Bernie chimed in in his cheerful, devil-may-care way. "Hell, I've had enough of this penny-ante school myself."

"If you guys leave, it's your own decision, not because I'm doing it," responded Sam.

We went to *mincha* in the sanctuary with all the members of the high school and our teachers. Stanley, our classmate, led the service in his rapid, staccato Hebrew chanting. All together there were about sixty to seventy students, grades nine to eleven, in the entire boys' school. When Sam, Bernie and I left, there would be only eight boys left in the eleventh-grade class, the highest grade so far in the school. In the solemnity of the *amidah*, I watched Sam praying softly and swaying with apparent great sincerity. He would soon no longer engage in this afternoon practice, at least not in a minyan. Tall and quietly strong, he had evoked a call in me to independence. In this moment, he was my George Washington, leading me to another George Washington.

When I got home in the evening, my mother was sitting in her usual place, at the kitchen table, a piece of bread in her hand, reliving something in her memory. "I'm going to leave yeshiva, and go to GW," I told her, taking her out of her reverie. "I'll start in the January term."

"You know best," she responded quietly, knowing that it was true. "Jay has a class tonight, so we ate supper already. I'll get yours now," she said as she heaved herself up from her chair.

She took a plate out of the oven where *kotletn*—small, oval-shaped, fried meatloaves—and French fries were keeping warm. She brought me the salad left in the large salad bowl for me to finish, too. I was ravenous, and I ate quickly. I put my dishes in the sink when I was finished.

"Go tell your father," my mother said. She hummed a quiet tune to herself as she began to wash my dishes.

I found my father in the living room, sitting in an easy chair with one eye closed, reading a Yiddish journal by the light of the standing lamp. I told him. He looked at me with both eyes cocked wide open and with sad eyebrows. "*Ni, zol zahn azoy, (Well, let it be so,)*" he responded and returned to his journal.

As I left, I saw him rub his eyes with one hand. I wondered whether he was thinking about the end of the Jewish education of his youngest son or harking back so many years ago to when he ended his own in order to join the secular world.

◆ ◆ ◆

"Here everybody knows you; you're an individual," Weldler continued.

I wanted to believe him. I had been at the yeshiva so long I could not really see myself in any other school, even George Washington High School, with which I was vaguely familiar. Aaron had gone there, but I no longer kept up with what he was doing. Jay and Mayer had gone there. I didn't get a sense they had felt they really belonged. I didn't get a sense of them there at all, except that it seemed impersonal to them.

Mayer had had two friends there, Yves and Victor, and Jay had had none, except that he hung around with Mayer and Victor. And after GW, what had happed to them? Mayer had not finished a year of college, and Jay had not gotten in at CCNY, where he wanted to go, and he was in night classes there. College was a kind of frontier I knew I had to conquer. It seemed harder to me, knowing that Mayer and Jay had not succeeded there.

I have to leave yeshiva, I thought without an ounce of doubt, as I listened to Weldler and nodded respectfully. But George Washington was so big and impersonal. More than two thousand students went there. My entire school had less than four hundred students from kindergarten through eleventh grade. I knew every boy and teacher from the seventh grade up that inhabited our squat little annex building.

I pictured hordes of broad-shouldered young men and feminine young women walking through the large iron gates that led to that massive Federalist building, with its neat lawns and plantings, its curved walkway up to its colonnaded marble stairs, and its tympanum like that of the Parthenon, or at least it seemed so to me. Whenever I saw some of the students on the subway, I felt intimidated. They seemed older, more adult, and they seemed to know what they were doing. It was disconcerting but exciting at the same time to think I could be among them. I also had to acknowledge to myself that the students in that massive school were "other," alien and dangerous to me from my vantage point in yeshiva. Despite my summers in Vacamas and Rockaway, I was afraid of the outside world.

And I had to confess to myself that I had become a religious Jew of sorts, admittedly one who dabbled on the outside, one who sinned and did not follow the prescribed practices, one who questioned every arbitrary-seeming rule and *midrash*. One who did not believe in God. I did not believe, yet I had been cradled in the arms of God. I would be a stranger among strangers when I entered this new world on my own and stripped of God's embrace.

◆ ◆ ◆

I paced the floor in my parents' bedroom, arguing with myself. When I left, I would be giving up all those things that in the constructed reality of my yeshiva and religious life had become real and part of me as much as they had enraged me and as much as I had wanted to cast them off as make-believe—all those "as ifs" that the Talmud discusses as real. Did the cities of refuge of the Talmud ever exist? And what were we doing, discussing their uses and rules now? Were we to think that the world will soon have them again, if they ever did?

I had listened closely, believed, and doubted. Perhaps, possibly, probably, partly. Vagueness is the way I had lived, somewhere between the fervor of faith and the bluntness of the greater world. I believed irrationally that in the stories of God speaking to mere mortals, God was speaking to me. "Take off your shoes, Moses-Menachem, for you are on hallowed ground." And when God spoke to Abraham, he was speaking to me, his infinitesimal creation, who can nonetheless fathom the breadth and depth of the universe and still feel myself at its center.

After all, even though He had recently failed my people so miserably, God's covenant with Abraham and me was as binding on God as it was on Abraham and me. I could not shake the idea in me that it was real. Yet, I knew that the universe was indifferent. I wanted to be part of a society in which it was understood that, despite its apparent order, life is just chance and we make the best of it. We were all really no different from the society that knowingly lives beneath an active volcano and remains there nonetheless.

I paced back and forth in the room until I crumpled to the floor and into a ball. I cried softly to myself and cradled myself in my arms. *When*

I leave the cloister of yeshiva, will I be giving up part of who I have become, part of who I am in this created world of "as if"?

I finally stood up and felt stronger, like someone who first gets up from his sickbed after a prolonged illness. "What is a Jew?" I asked myself, stretching tall. I answered, "A Jew is someone who argues with God whether he believes in Him or not. And God will still argue back, at least in my heart and mind, no matter where I am."

◆ ◆ ◆

"If I thought you would be missing out on any important academics by being here at Breuer's, I wouldn't be here as your principal," said Rabbi Weldler, and I did not doubt his sincerity, although by now I knew there were choices for me that yeshiva could not offer. "We have a proposal for you three boys," he said to us as he gathered Sam, Bernie, and me in his office. "Mr. Breuer and I and some of the faculty have decided that you boys have been frustrated in Gemara. It hasn't been for you. We are prepared to offer you a course in Jewish philosophy. It would be readings in English and discussions between yourselves and the teacher, who would be someone you trust. Maybe Rabbi Nitzlich. Maybe Rabbi Schick; he has a wealth of knowledge. I believe you like and respect them both."

Sam, Bernie, and I discussed this last-ditch proposal among ourselves and decided it was too little too late. "Why didn't they offer this to us before?" said Sam. "Anyway, I have my reasons for leaving that have nothing to do with any difficulties with Talmud. There's a bigger world out there I need to be more part of."

"I'm ready to go," added Bernie.

I just nodded my head in agreement. But I said to myself, *You guys come from Orthodox families. You can hold on to the religious part of yourselves just by being at home. I will have to struggle on my own to maintain my crumb of connection.*

As I sat in Gemara class in the mornings over the weeks that followed, waiting for January and my exit from this school, I no longer worried about avoiding the thwacks from Rabbi Krieger's chair slats.

He wouldn't use them. He could no longer say, "Spare the rod and spoil the child" when looking at me.

My own path emerged for me. I had lived with my contradictions for so many years, on my own, without anyone else being a part of them or even knowing about them. Seeing Mayer shot in Lodz. Jay interminably imprisoned in the infirmary in Vladeck Heim. My brief idyllic life in Pittsburgh. My father's Yiddish books and his lofty speeches at cultural banquets in New York. My mother's memory movies and her pain-filled sighs as she sat at the kitchen table, a piece of bread in her hand. Color War at the Lubavitch camp. Years of my incompetence and hiding at Breuer's. Far Rockaway and Anna. The regular kid and the distorted Jew in me.

I can live with a new set of contradictions with less pain. I can still talk to God, without believing in him. I can be the contorted Jew inside and still be part of the world.

I straightened up in my desk, raised my hand, and answered the difficult Gemara question posed by Rabbi Krieger, to his shock and to his hopeful and disappointed eyes.

CHAPTER 20

◆ ◆ ◆ ◆ ◆ ◆

Becoming Ordinary

I registered for school in the small cubicle of a grade adviser. She was friendly and asked me my interests. It was probably too late to start a musical instrument, she said, so she scheduled me for mixed chorus along with my academic subjects. My day would run from 8:05 to 2:15 every day, approximately half the time I spent daily in yeshiva. Two days later, I joined the throngs of students who streamed through the iron gates of George Washington High School for the first day of classes of the spring term.

Mr. Abramson, a soft-spoken, well-dressed man with wavy salt-and-pepper hair, was my homeroom teacher. He helped me fill out the forms that the other students were already familiar with. Then he asked one of the girls to walk me to my first class, since she was also in it.

Her name was Lillian, and she was a pretty girl with a round face and soft pink lips. She wore a pleated skirt, a yellow sweater, bobby socks, and saddle shoes. Her fine brown hair was done up in a flip and bounced as she walked. I sat next to Lillian in Mr. Prendergast's English class and petite, freckled Linda in Mr. Davis's math class. It reminded me of when I'd sat next to Sandra in third grade in Pittsburgh.

Linda pointed me the way to my third period physical education class. I was swept along the crowded down staircase to the basement locker room. It was a catacomb of alcoves and hallways filled with row after row of beat-up dark green metal lockers and narrow wooden benches. As scores of other students rushed by me to get to their lockers, I paused to savor the moment. In the dim light from the caged-in incandescent light bulbs, my eyes took in the cracked and dingy walls and the scuffed and grimy concrete floor. My nose took in the musty odors of sweat and dust. My ears perked to the sounds of blustering banter and cursing, and the banging of metal doors. I absorbed the image of multiple legs and arms scrambling into gym uniforms. I studied my classmates. Some were tall, muscular, and physically imposing young men who looked too old to be in high school. Others were no more than young boys just beginning to show signs of future manhood. There were freckled and square-jawed youths, sporting blond crew cuts; boys with creamy, café-au-lait skin and silken curls; and there were older-looking young men with rich brown faces and tightly kinked or processed wavy hair. On the whole, I didn't feel noticeably out of place.

I sped to find my assigned locker. Jay, ever protective, had taught me to cover the numbers when I worked my combination lock to avoid spying eyes and theft. I rushed to get out of my clothes, and I frenetically put on my orange gym shorts, white T-shirt, and sneakers, afraid of being late. A few students were just sauntering to their lockers. They puzzled me as they moved with slow and measured pace, showing calculated disdain for most of the others, who were already running up the stairs to get to class. No one was going to hurry these latecomers. They made me more anxious, and I bounded up the stairs two at a time to get to the gym.

On the landing, I stood at the end of a line of boys, as a student monitor checked their names on Delaney cards and assigned them their spots. The bored-looking monitor sitting on his stool checked my name. Without looking up he said, "Remember your spot number. That's how your attendance will be marked."

I entered the cavernous gym, which seemed bigger than my entire yeshiva high school building had been. Some two-hundred-odd boys in identical white T-shirts and orange shorts milled about in small clusters, waiting for the class to start. I looked for my spot. Letters spaced on the front wall of the gym marked the rows. My spot would be the third place in row J.

Three teachers, dressed in khaki pants, sneakers, and T-shirts stood on the raised wooden platform up front. One blew his shrill whistle and boomed, "Line up!" through his cardboard megaphone. Everyone casually found his place. The stragglers who had dawdled to their lockers walked in and took their spots just in time.

"Attention!" bellowed the teacher in charge, and two hundred boys stood silently erect.

I imitated the student in front of me. He was a bit shorter than I was, but he had muscular shoulders and legs, a short neck, and bristly black hair. He looked like he could be an Army recruit, like Mayer.

"At ease," said the teacher more calmly.

I quickly glanced around me to see all two hundred bodies gracefully spread their legs slightly apart and hold their hands behind their backs. It was a powerful sight to see this unity of motion.

I must remember this always, I said to myself as I consciously took in the teachers on their wooden platform, the students around me, and the warm, musty smell of the gym. I burnished into my memory the brick wall in front of me that was painted olive drab to eye level, where it gave way to light green with the black letter J on it. *I'm finally a number*, I thought to myself. *It's almost anonymous, except that it's mine.*

I could feel both relief and excitement in my body. This was a new beginning. No one would take America away from me again.

◆ ◆ ◆ ◆ ◆ ◆

Epilogue

I enter my old apartment at 3569 Broadway. Which one is it, 9C or 9A? It must be 9A; it has a dining room.

Jay is at his drafting board as I walk into the dining room. "I don't know where you got your fanciful ideas, Michael," he says. "That's not how I remember it." He smiles dreamily as he returns to his drafting board and adds some interesting pencil lines to the sketch that is materializing on it.

Mayer doesn't look up when he hears me enter his room. He just smirks as he lies sprawled on the high-riser and continues reading his science fiction book. "You made up a lot of stuff. That's not how it happened at all," he says as he keeps looking at his book.

In the kitchen, Mom looks up as if wounded by the words I'd written. "I haven't suffered enough that you have to say these things? What did you know, you were only a child." Her bosom heaves with a big sobbing sigh. She holds her head in her hand at the kitchen table and resumes watching the mind pictures that flicker in front of her eyes.

My father looks up from his newspaper in the living room, cocks his eyebrows, shakes his head, and chuckles. "*Chozhbe shayne verter,* (At least they're nice words,)" he says. Then he gets up from the living room couch, folds the paper and says, "I think I'll go rest for a while."

I turn to them all and say, "Now that you live only in the movie of my mind, I offered the only version I know—my own. It has to be the official version."

◆ ◆ ◆ ◆ ◆ ◆

Author's Note

In the summer of 1961, one school term after I left yeshiva, I got a job as a junior counselor at a camp run by survivors and partisans from Poland and Lithuania, who were the remnants of the Jewish Labor Bund (Alliance). Despite all the loss they had suffered during the war, they had reestablished their organization devoted to social justice, cultural pluralism, and Yiddish culture around the world. Indeed, Vladeck Heim, where I resided as a child of four and five, was created by them. It was one of a number of sanatoriums and orphanages they reestablished immediately after the war to show that Jewish culture and institutions had survived and could not be snuffed out. In New York, in 1959, they had created Camp Hemshekh (Continuation) as a summer home for their children to learn and live and celebrate their secular Jewish heritage of Yiddish and social justice.

Being at Hemshekh was a revelation and a freeing experience for me. Here were children and youth, ages five through twenty, most of whom came from Yiddish-speaking homes and spoke Yiddish, and many of whom had or continued to have Yiddish cultural education that was not religious and that reflected closely the lives lived in their homes and that mirrored mine in that way.

The camp celebrated Yiddish language, literature, theater, and music, as well as our shared history. We commemorated the uprising of the Warsaw Ghetto as a symbol of Jewish resistance during the war. Even the five-year-olds understood the meaning of our commemoration. Jews did not go as sheep. It was not something that had to be introduced to them; they understood from their parents' experience. It was not hidden in shame and bewilderment as it had been in yeshiva. I was grateful, and I participated with all my heart.

Most important to me, I found a group of youths there whom I could model myself after. They were American, "ordinary," in most of their daily behavior and values. Yet they revered and smoothly and easily integrated their secular Jewish heritage as part of who they were. Through them, I learned where I belonged.

The friends I made in Hemshekh that summer and some of the subsequent years have remained among my closest companions for the past sixty years. When we get together at reunions and other gatherings, the old spark and sense of community remains and is nourished. What is even more wonderful for me, there is a group of about a dozen of us who share our lives through phone calls, Zoom sessions, get-togethers, and travels. We don't have to explain what we mean when we see or talk with one another. In the absence of my birth family, long gone and long mourned, they have become my close family of choice.

◆ ◆ ◆ ◆ ◆ ◆

About the Author

Michael (Menachem) Fox, Ph.D., is a licensed psychologist in New York. In past years, Michael taught psychology in the School of Education at the City College of New York and at the Pratt Institute. He worked as a psychologist in the public schools of Yonkers and Mamaroneck, New York.

A native Yiddish speaker, for the past fifteen years he has worked with the Yiddish-speaking children and families of the Hasidic communities of Brooklyn. Remaining close to his roots in younger days, Menachem taught Yiddish and Yiddish singing to children in the secular after-school programs of the Worker's Circle and the Sholem Aleichem Institute. For a number of years, he led the Yiddish singing class at the Columbia University/YIVO summer Yiddish program.

Along with Miriam Hoffman and Rena Berkowicz Borow, he co-led the Yiddish theater workshop at the Oxford University summer Yiddish program. In collaboration with Zalmen Mlotek and Joanne Borts, Menachem co-created and performed in *Kids & Yiddish*, a musical show for families, at the National Yiddish Theater/Folksbiene. *Kids & Yiddish* ran for eleven holiday seasons.

Menachem also co-wrote and performed in *Children Of . . .* at the American Jewish Theater and was a principal performer in *Two by*

Wolf with New Yiddish Rep. Menachem is the author of two plays, a children's book, and three novels, in addition to this memoir. He lives in New York City with his partner, Rena Berkowicz Borow. His three adult children, Josh, Alex, and Oriana, are all artists who share their unique and diverse talents around the world.